THE STRICKEN DEER

William Cowper

from the drawing by W. Harvey after
L. Abbott in the National Portrait Gallery

LORD DAVID CECIL

THE STRICKEN DEER

or

THE LIFE OF COWPER

CONSTABLE & COMPANY LTD
LONDON W C 2

LONDON
PUBLISHED BY
Constable and Company Ltd
10-12 Orange Street WC 2

INDIA
Longmans Green and Company Ltd
BOMBAY   CALCUTTA   MADRAS

CANADA
Longmans Green and Company Ltd
TORONTO

First published	. .	1929
Reprinted	. .	1930
Second Edition .	. .	1930
" Crown Constable " Edition		1933
Reprinted .	. .	1938
New Edition .	. .	1943
Reprinted	. .	1944
Reprinted	. .	1946
Reprinted	. .	1947

Printed in Great Britain by
Lowe and Brydone Printers Limited, London, N.W.10

To
I . P.

PREFATORY NOTE

COWPER has already been the subject of many books. But these, when they have not been primarily studies of his literary genius—like those of Mr. Goldwyn Smith and Mr. Hugh Fausset—have been definitive and documented biographies—like those of Hayley, Southey, and Mr. Thomas Wright. My purpose is rather, in the light of all the information gathered for us in these more elaborate works and elsewhere, to tell straightforwardly the story of this extraordinary man, with such analysis of his character and those of his friends and his period as may seem necessary to make it clear. We are able during large portions of his life to do this in the most intimate detail. From the mass of poems, letters and reminiscences that have come down to us we can reconstruct, not only the outward ordering of his life down to the way he spent each hour, and every article of furniture in his room, but also the trend and fluctuation of his solitary thought. Only twice, during his early manhood and in the period of his second madness, are we conscious of a want of sufficient information. But since history is only interesting as long as it is strictly true, I have not attempted to supply this want except by a few very tentative conjectures. If, therefore, my picture grows at moments hazy, its central figure indistinct, I ask pardon of my readers, and solicit their indulgence.

CONTENTS

THE STRICKEN DEER

A PROLOGUE

PAST periods, like foreign countries, become the fashion. Just as people like one sort of hat because it suits the type of beauty they admire, so people are attracted to a particular place or period because it suits their prevailing mood. Mankind, in its restless search for some ideal and fairy country which satisfies a fancy, dissatisfied with that in which it lives, will identify it with the civilization of some other time or people which appears to possess the qualities it most values, and to lack those which it most dislikes. The ancient world, Corinthian capitals, and Latin inscriptions were the fashion in the Italian renaissance; the celestial empire of China, porcelain, and short moral fables about people with Oriental names were the fashion in the eighteenth century; the Middle Ages, Gothic tracery, and the *Morte D'Arthur* were the fashion in the days of the Pre-Raphaelites. The mode of a bygone age flourishes again; a curious exotic, blooming in the warmth of the admiration of a later day long after its parent tree is withered and dissolved back into earth.

But the later day does not confine itself to admiration. It begins to imitate modes and styles and to adapt them to its own circumstances. The renaissance despots built classical temples and wrote classical poems and planted classical groves; the powdered dilettanti of 1775 bought English -chinoiserie vases

B

and French chinoiserie hangings and Chippendale chinoiserie chairs. The nineteenth century, thorough in everything, was thoroughly Gothic. Its connoisseurs made Gothic summer-houses, Gothic bathrooms, Gothic umbrella stands. They filled the house with stained-glass windows and even called their children by Gothic names—Blanche, Hubert, Edith.

But these imitations only serve to bring out in a stronger light the difference between the period they interpret and their interpretation of it. They re-create it in the image of their own desire; they intensify the elements that charm them; they modify those that offend against their conventions. And the result is a blend of the style they are imitating and their own, that, by its very indication of what they admired, is an exquisitely characteristic example of their own civilization.

There is nothing more typical of the English eighteenth century than an eighteenth-century chinoiserie chair, with all the flowering graces of Pekin, tamed into the delicate regularity of Bath. Nothing brings back the feel and atmosphere of the first French empire like an empire sofa, with its rigid sphinx heads and garlands, and bundles of fasces copied exactly from an ancient sarcophagus, in brass and mahogany, and upholstered in red ribbed silk. How Victorian are the Rowenas and Rebeccas of the paintings illustrating Scott's novels that covered the walls of the Royal Academy from 1825 to 1850, with their sloping shoulders and downcast eyes and jet-black hair *en bandeaux !* And the Arcadian shepherd of Elizabethan pastoral, dressed in a mantle of blue silk, his hair stuck with gilly-flowers, spouting conceits; and the scholastic-tongued sages of antiquity of Dante's *Inferno*; and the sultans that strut in so Parisian a minuet through the tragedies of Voltaire. How precisely, how intensely, they bring their age

before us by their every word and gesture! These
corporate creations, the spirit of one age expressed in
the dress of another, possess a fanciful charm of their
own; bouquets whose scent mingles many flowers,
music whose harmony is made by a peculiar combination of instruments. But they derive this charm
from the vivid way in which the unwonted dress reveals
the individuality of its wearer. The period appears
more clearly itself because it is vainly trying to look
like something else.

To-day the eighteenth century is the fashion; we
print eighteenth-century memoirs; we reprint eighteenth-century novels; we anthologize eighteenth-
century poems; we translate eighteenth-century
romances. On weekdays we perform eighteenth-
century ballad operas; on Sundays eighteenth-century
comedies. Our most up-to-date writers eulogize
Baroque and Rococo; our most Olympian critics
prefer Mozart's operas to Wagner's. And, like earlier
ages, we imitate as well as admire. Modern architects
design in a severely classical style, all pilaster and
pediment. Modern story-tellers emulate the gram-
matical nakedness of Defoe. But we are as much the
creatures of the time we live in as were the people of
other periods; and our interpretation of the eighteenth
century is no more like the reality than a renaissance
statue of Apollo is like a Greek statue of Apollo, or
the Houses of Parliament are like a Gothic cathedral.
People like the eighteenth century because they see
it as the Golden Age of the qualities they value; and
so they conceive it as possessing these qualities and no
others. They like its sensibility because they dislike
emotion, and it seems to express itself in emotions so
deliberate as hardly to deserve the name at all. They
profess to like pure form, whatever that may mean;
and the eighteenth century had a talent for form. So
they represent its music as all form and no matter, its

novels all form and no morals, and its religion all form
and no faith. Finally, they dislike the nineteenth
century, and they see the eighteenth century as its
opposite, and therefore their idea of it exaggerates
everything in which this opposition lies : its elegance,
it cynicism, its impropriety, its frankness of speech,
its foppishness of manner. The eighteenth century
of their imagination is a series of salons, where people
with snuff-boxes and a worldly-wise outlook make
mots in a mood of urbane scepticism born of an ex-
tensive experience of the brighter side of life in the
capitals of Europe.

It is the land of their dreams ; but it is not at all
like the England of the eighteenth century, the
teeming, clamouring, irregular, enthralling England
of the eighteenth century. In order to mould the
age they love nearer to their heart's desire, they have
successfully shattered it to bits. For one thing, their
idea is too homogeneous. Only countries of the
mind are so much of a piece. The past does not, any
more than the present, escape that incompleteness,
that inconsistency which is the essential characteristic
of life as we know it, as opposed to life as we should
like it to be. An historical period is not a water-tight
compartment, containing only what it has itself
created, sharing nothing with what has gone before
and what comes after. It is a tangle of movements
and forces, of various origin, sometimes intertwined
and sometimes running parallel, some beginning, some
in their prime, some in decay; streaked by anomalies
and freaks of nature ; coloured by physical conditions,
by national characteristics, by personalities; struck
across by unexpected, inexplicable stirrings of the
spirit of God or of man ; yet with every strand part of
what is past or what is to come : a great river ever fed
by new streams, its course continuous and abrupt,
chequered and unfaltering, now thundering over a

sudden cataract, now partially diverted into a back-
water, and carrying on its mysterious surface fragments
of wreckage, survivals of an earlier day, not yet dissolved into oblivion.

To describe any period, then, as all of a piece is as
inaccurate as to paint a picture of its streets with all the
houses of the same age and style.   Even if the eighteenth-century spirit as we imagine it was really prevalent in the eighteenth century, it would be as false
to imagine it as exclusively prevalent, as to imagine all
the furniture was made by Sheraton and all the decora-
tion done by Adam.   But it was very far from prevailing ; it is altogether too much made up of modish-
ness and mockery.   Of course, some of the typical
figures of the eighteenth century are modish and
mocking—Casanova, Voltaire, Lord Chesterfield. But
though unlike in other respects, they were alike in
outraging most of their contemporaries very much.
Casanova succeeded in shocking visitors to Venice
even more broadminded than those of our own day.
Lord Chesterfield was looked upon by the ordinary
man as having, in the words of Johnson, " The manners
of a dancing master and the morals of a whore."
While to imagine that Voltaire expressed the general
opinion of his time is as sensible as to imagine that
Jonah expressed the general opinion of Nineveh.
He represents a characteristic and important aspect
of eighteenth-century thought, a vivid thread in
its tangled skein, but anyone who thinks that it is
the only aspect, above all in England, has a conception
of the period that is wrong from start to finish.   For
how many-sided the eighteenth century was can be
seen by anyone who looks at the mass of novels,
plays, poems, sermons, memoirs, letters and speeches
that go to make up a library of the period.   If we
would find the true spirit of the eighteenth century
we must leave the eighteenth century of to-day, the

eighteenth century of the stage, of the book illustrator, even of the historian, and seek it in its own books.

For a happy moment let us shut the door on the modern world and retire in fancy to some Augustan library. The curtains are drawn, the fire is lit, outside the silence is broken only by the faint, crackling whisper of the winter frost. How the firelight gleams and flickers on the fluted mouldings of the bookcases, on the faded calf and tarnished gold of the serried rows of books : the slim duodecimo poems and plays ; the decent two-volumed octavo novels ; the portly quarto sermons, six volumes, eight volumes, ten volumes ; the unity of brown, broken now and again by a large tome of correspondence, green or plum or crimson, only given to the public in our own time. The whole eighteenth century is packed into these white or yellowing pages ; all its multifarious aspects, its types, its moods, its morals, self-revealed ; the indefinable, unforgettable perfume of the period breathing from every line of print. For the shortest, dullest letter really written in a past age can bring its atmosphere home to you as the most vivid historian of a later time can never do.

Here, through this long line of volumes, of correspondence, crystallized into a diamond immortality by the fragile brilliance of Horace Walpole's style, streams the life of that small dazzling Whig world that ruled England, with its habits and fashions and whims, its political secrets and its private scandals, its heroes, its buffoons and its beauties. It is the world of the nobleman who was educated till he was eleven at his ancestral home by a tutor who was also the chaplain ; who, after a severely classical four years at Eton, left England for the Grand Tour in his Berline ; who was speechless with shyness at Madame du Deffand's parties in Paris, who bought Guido Renis in Bologna ; who admired Frederick William I's Guards in Potsdam, ſtepping together like giant marionettes controlled by one hand; who came back to England; married the daughter of a nobleman as Whig as himself; sat for a pocket borough belonging to himself or a relation; attacked Walpole or maybe Carteret; played Loo; made rotund orations, ſtudded with Latin quotations; colleᶜted curious antiquities; laid out his gardens in accordance with the grandiloquent plans of Capability Brown; who spent half the year lounging in the windows of Brooks's and half among the oaks and elms of his country seat; who was painted in youth by Allan Ramsay, and in age by Romney; who was brought up to like Pope, but grew to prefer Ossian; who patronized Dr. Johnson; who talked and wrote voluminous letters and composed compliments in verse; who laughed at the royal family and drank too much port and died. It was a society at once narrow and cosmopolitan, as much at home in Paris as in London, but knowing few people in either. It knew every aspeᶜt of its world, but that world was small. It liked painting and politics, but painting meant Leonardo and Raphael, and nothing else, and politics meant the Whig cause and the balance of power, and nothing else. Even the classical learning from which it quoted so freely was more Roman than Greek, and more French than Roman: precise and rhetorical, a colleᶜtion of apothegms, full of patrician independence and uninsular patriotism. It was conventional, too; lukewarm in religion, but scrupulous about going to church; slack about morals, ſtriᶜt about the proprieties; often republican in theory, always ariſtocratic in praᶜtice.

But though it was outwardly so formal and so cosmopolitan, it was really very English, impulsive, copious, untidy, full of exceptions to the rule, of eccentric charaᶜters, excited by sudden guſts of enthusiasm, that make it as different from that

contemporary French society to which its conventions gave it an outward likeness as a portrait
by Gainsborough is unlike a pastel of Latour. No
Frenchman would have suddenly put up a ruined
castle in his garden, like Lord Holland, or had fully-
grown cedar trees planted by torchlight, like Lord
Chatham. It was, indeed, the most original, as it
was far and away the most amusing and attractive,
society England has ever known. For its unquestioning acceptance of the conventional structure of life
left its whole energy free to develop the individual.
It was because their world was so small that they could
touch so many sides of it, because they took the facts
of existence for granted that they could cultivate its
graces, because they never doubted they were born
to rule that they could say, with Pitt, " I believe I can
save the country, and no one else can."

But eighteenth-century England is not only its
aristocracy. Take down this volume of Fielding.
Here you may see the life of the middle classes, the
life that we see in Smollett and Gillray and *The Beggar's
Opera*, whose painter was Hogarth, not Reynolds,
whose engraver was not Bartolozzi, but Rowlandson ;
a life spent among tradespeople in the town and squires
in the country, the life of the road and the tavern ;
with its virtuous side lived in those decorous, irreligious,
classical churches with large-cushioned box pews and
a sounding-board over the pulpit ; and its vicious
among the pimps and pickpockets, the gambling hells
and disorderly houses behind Drury Lane. It was a
life sensible, coarse and moral ; in high spirits, but
with its feet planted firmly on the earth ; the life of the
plain man, in a decent brown-stuff suit and shoes with
steel buckles, who lived over his shop, and went to
Vauxhall on a holiday and sat under Seed or Jortin on
Sunday ; who gave money to an orphanage and took
his wife to see an execution. For its conception of

morality is that expressed in Hogarth's prints of the idle and industrious apprentice. The idle apprentice is hanged, the industrious apprentice becomes Lord Mayor. You might fall into an occasional lapse among the rosy, frankly-bosomed trollops and doxies of Covent Garden, but it was soon proved to you by a sober and unenthusiastic clergyman that respectability was the best policy.

It had its adventurous side, too, that adventurous side of life which filled eighteenth-century literature from the novels of Defoe onwards. Adventure was undertaken in a very matter-of-fact spirit, drawing its excitement from its incidents alone, and not from any romantic light shed on them by the temperament of its hero; the adventures of the young men who were pressed for sailors, or taken by pirates, like Captain Singleton; or who explored New Zealand with Captain Cook; or were shipped off as incorrigible rakes at eighteen years old, to make fortunes as Indian nabobs, like William Hickey. It is a whimsical contrast between the dying Mogul empire, still illumined by gleams of fantastic splendour, shadowed by omens, wrapped in all the immemorial and coloured mystery of the East, and its prosaic red-faced conquerors with an unappeasable thirst for good living, and without a nerve in their bodies.

But the eighteenth century was not altogether without nerves. Look at that fat collection of paper-bound three-volume novels, about fashionable life. They are the expression of that neurasthenia that at its worst produced the vapours and at its best *Clarissa Harlowe*; the condition of mind of the languid ladies, with waxen hands and small caps poised dizzily on a tall fan of hair, that droop at one so pensively out of the canvases of the Reverend William Peters. Their nerves affected not their imaginations, but their feelings. Natural sentiments—filial love, maternal love, conjugal love—swelled to such an extent under the tender and unrelaxed attention of their owners as to endanger their healths. If one is to believe the novelists who describe them, these ladies spent whole days writing letters, seated on elegant, uncomfortable chairs, except when they walked, muffled in swansdown, to the willow tree on which the loved one had carved their names. How absurd and morbid and unreal it reads to us! But from time to time the sentences melt into a delicate beauty for which in the works of the robust and healthy-minded we search in vain.

For beauty in eighteenth-century literature always comes as an expression of the feelings. Look at those long, unread, unreadable shelves of poetry. The descriptions of Nature by Thompson or Crabbe are exact, but they are untouched by the light that never was on land or sea, but which illuminates all great poetry. They would convey no pleasure to a reader who did not know the English scenery they were describing and therefore could not recognize how accurate the description was. Only when the heart of the poet is touched does his poem glow into real beauty, the sentiment gaining an added ring of pathos from the formal language in which it is expressed.

> " For who, to dumb forgetfulness a prey.
>   This pleasing anxious being e'er resign'd,
> Left the warm precincts of the cheerful day,
>   Nor cast one longing, lingering look behind ?
>
> On some fond breast the parting soul relies,
>   Some pious drops the closing eye requires,
> Ev'n from the tomb the voice of nature cries,
>   Ev'n in our ashes live their wonted fires."

Horace Walpole, Fielding, Hickey, Richardson, Gray, what differences of outlook do these names conjure up! I cannot think of a single quality common to them all, except a uniform unlikeness to the modern idea of the eighteenth century. And they do not exhaust the varieties of the eighteenth-century scene. There are the astrologers and magicians, Cagliostro and Mesmer, whose practices quiver with a lurid light round the French monarchy in its decay. The Jacobites, shabby, silly, romantic; the miners of Cornwall, howling and foaming at the mouth under the eloquence of the Methodists; the bishops, whose dioceses were in Wales and whose residences were in London, and who edited, with dignity, the more scabrous classical authors.

But there is another strain in the skein of the period, that cannot be so briefly dismissed. I mean that literary intelligentsia which derived from Addison and reached its zenith in the Club; that centred round Burke and Garrick and Goldsmith and Miss Burney, but which could extend to include Gibbon on the one hand and Mrs. Barbauld on the other; the circle whose greatest figure is Dr. Johnson, and whose spirit, lingering on into a new century, flowered once more, a late autumnal blooming, in the chaste talent of Jane Austen.

If eighteenth-century England must have typical representatives, these are the typical representatives of the English eighteenth century. The essential characteristic of their point of view was a disbelief in extremes. They were gregarious but not giddy, stay-at-home but not solitary, often devout but never mystical; if urban in their tastes, not modish, if rural, without any transcendental sentiment about nature; plain-spoken but not salacious, domestic without sentimentality. They disliked the paradoxical, the ecstatic, because they thought them false. What was the value of an idea, however entertaining or original, if its conclusions could not be carried out in ordinary life, or of an emotion, however intoxicating, that could not stand the wear and tear of prosaic every-day? But they were not cynical. Indeed, their distrust of the extreme arose from their deep belief in the moral purpose of existence, and their consequent distrust of any fancy or feeling that might distract them from this purpose. You lived in order to be good; theories and feelings were valuable in so far as they helped you in this, and no further. They despised all speculation that was not practicable, all emotion that was not durable. With a robust and rational capacity for enjoying themselves, they thought self-pity and self-depreciation neither sensible nor healthy. But they looked at life with open eyes, and they were too honest and too clear-sighted to expect very much from it.

The shelf of their works is long indeed, and the best books of their time are on it. They wrote the best biography, the best history, the best political pamphlets, and they rocked the cradle of the domestic novel. And they gave the literary tone to other writers whose lives were lived far from their company and according to ideas not theirs. Of these not the least distinguished was William Cowper, the poet, whose story is the subject of this book.

His poems are not much read now. Bound in solid leather and adorned with the sober magnificence of gilt lettering, they rest upon the upper shelves of old-fashioned libraries, unread from year's end to year's end, their backs growing drab, drained of hue and lustre by the strong, destroying sunlight. They are become merely furniture, less valued because less noticeable than the globes and grandfather clocks and greying mezzotints that crowd the room around them. When, on tiptoe, one drags a volume from its place and opens it, pouf—the page is clouded for a moment by the shaking out of the dust that has accumulated for so long there. And the words seem dusty and faded as the paper on which they are printed. Pedantic epigram, antiquated compliment, pompous, didactic apostrophe, follow one another, as lifeless as the half-obliterated signs on an ancient and undeciphered papyrus. It seems impossible to believe that this was ever the genuine expression, however formal, of a living person's mind. And then suddenly one's attention is caught by a chance word; the page stirs to life; a bit of the English countryside appears before one's mental eye as vividly and exactly as though one really saw it; or an ephemeral trifle, a copy of verses addressed to Miss M. or Mr. D., laughs out of the page with the pleasant colloquial intimacy of a voice heard over the teacups in the next room. And now and again, as if from the strings of a tarnished, disused harp stumbled against in one's rambles round the library, there rises from the old book a strain of music, simple, plangent, and of a piercing pathos, that fairly clutches at the heart.

> " To me the waves that ceaseless broke
>   Upon the dangerous coast
> Hoarsely and ominously spoke
>   Of all my treasure lost.
>
> Your sea of troubles you have past
>   And found the peaceful shore,
> I tempest-tossed and wrecked at last
>   Come home to port no more."

Here is no Byronic pessimism, rhetorical, exaggerated, the expression of a posture or at best a passing mood. Through these quiet verses trembles the true voice of despair.

And the contrast between them and the wooden versification in which they are embedded is not more striking than it is between them and the poems of Nature or of home in which, alone of all his other work, Cowper rises to real poetry. These are the parallels in verse of *Cranford* and *Our Village* in prose. He paints with simple pathos and gentle humour the home life of country gentlemen and doctors and clergymen in the late eighteenth and early nineteenth centuries; peaceful, cosy, friendly, civilized, full of small excitements, and family jokes, and innocent enjoyments; knitting and sketching and playing on the pianoforte and reading aloud and cribbage and a little harmless gossip; easily shocked, easily amused; enacted in studies and drawing-rooms furnished with Heppelwhite chairs, the walls hung with silhouettes and samplers, and the tightly-shut windows with curtains of striped chintz.

> " Now stir the fire, and close the shutters fast,
> Let fall the curtains, wheel the sofa round,
> And while the bubbling and loud hissing urn
> Throws up a steamy column, and the cups
> That cheer but not inebriate, wait on each,
> So let us welcome peaceful evening in."

And his Nature poetry describes the same life out-doors. It is authentic English landscape; not the wild, naked landscape of the North, but the tamed country of the Home Counties, coated with human associations. And Cowper's mood is tamed too; amused, contemplative, passive; observant of every-thing, carried away by nothing. He might know more about plants and trees than the ladies and gentlemen of his acquaintance, but that is because they are in his line, as hunting or painting on silk might be in theirs.

> " Ye fallen avenues ! once more I mourn
> Your fate unmerited, once more rejoice
> That yet a remnant of your race survives.
> How airy and how light the graceful arch,
> Yet awful as the consecrated roof
> Re-echoing pious anthems ! While beneath
> The chequered earth seems restless as the flood
> Brushed by the wind, so sportive is the light
> Shot through the boughs, it dances as they dance
> Shadow and sunshine intermingling quick,
> And darkening and enlightening, as the leaves
> Play wanton, every moment, every spot."

What is there in common between the last two quotations and the overpowering grief, without alleviation
and without hope, of the first ?   What sort of man was
he that could write all three ?   What sort of life that
could embrace three such different moods ?   We look
at his portrait, and the same anomaly strikes us.   The
face is a plain, everyday sort of face, with ruddy,
weather-beaten cheeks, and a wide, gentle mouth.
The set of the lips, precise yet kindly, shows refinement,
but it is an old-maidish kind of refinement; and the
impression of old-maidishness is added to by the
poet's curious head-gear—a sort of homely English
version of a turban, finished off on top with a neat
white bow.

But out of this face glance a pair of eyes which
change its whole expression ; startled, speaking eyes,
fixed on something outside the picture which we cannot
see, in fear, in horror, in frenzy ; luminous, dilated
orbs ; the eyes of an artist, of a seer, can it be of a
madman ?

This duality is the central fact of Cowper's life.
We search the little heap of dingy volumes, the few
faded bundles of correspondence, that are all that
remain to us of the endless, thrilling panorama of
his earthly existence ; all the evidence, conscious or
unconscious, that we can gather from his own entranc-
ing letters, the pompous panegyrics of his friends, the
chance words of his acquaintance, the long-winded
exhortations of his spiritual directors.   And there
emerges a drama whose action is as simple, as strange,
and as terrible, as that of a classical tragedy.   It took
place in a small circle in the soberest and most peaceful section of the sober, peaceful, professional class of
the day, its humdrum cheerfulness much further
removed from tragedy than the glittering whirl of
fashionable society or the harsh and unremitting
struggles of the very poor.   And Cowper himself, in

his virtues and limitations, is the very epitome of his
environment : scrupulous, timid, a little provincial,
weak on the logical side ; but candid, constant,
cultivated, humorous, skilled in the small tactfulness,
the minor charities of domestic life. He felt more
intensely and expressed himself with greater brilliance
than the people round him ; but what he felt was what
they felt ; and his superior sensitiveness and brilliance
only helped him to express it more exactly.

But he was under a curse. From his earliest years
there loomed over him, born in disease, nurtured in
fanaticism, the frightful spectre of religious madness.
And his life resolved itself into a struggle, fought to
the death, between the daylit serenity of his natural
circumstances and the powers of darkness hidden in
his heart. For a time it seemed that they would be
defeated. Yet even when the light shone most
brightly on his face, the shadow lurked behind his back ;
around the sunny, grassy meadows crouched the black
armies of horror and despair. At a moment's weakness
they would advance ; inch by inch they gained ground ;
till, with a last scream of anguish, his tortured spirit
sank, overwhelmed.

CHAPTER I

FROM the first the atmosphere in which Cowper passed his life was domestic. He was born in the country; but the country was the country of Hertfordshire, even in those days the least sequestered of all the districts in England not confessedly urban. The small green Hertfordshire landscape, with its flattish fields and leafy coppices and well-kept canals, with here and there the blue smoke of a chimney, rising from one of the placid red-brick cottages with which the country is speckled, was the first view of the world that he saw from the sash-windows of his father's rectory of Great Berkhamsted. And his life in that sleepy, well-to-do little town was as comfortable and quiet as the scenery surrounding it. The Cowpers were a large, respectable family, connected, though distantly, with an earl, and boasting among their most recent members a Speaker of the House of Commons. And on his mother's side William was connected with the Donnes, a family honourably known all over Norfolk, who traced their pedigree back as far as the great Dean Donne of St. Paul's. It is a whimsical thought that this eccentric sixteenth-century divine, alone of Cowper's family, could have truly understood and expressed the pity and terror of his spiritual tragedy.

On both sides his relations were numerous, though legitimate; and much of Cowper's memories of his early years was concerned with visits to and from little

Donnes and Cowpers—racing round the garden with them, picking currants in the orchard, giggling in the parlour. But he was a shy child; his affections were concentrated on what he was most used to; and the dominating fact of his early life was his mother. His father, a prosperous Anglican clergyman, innocent of mysticism, did not play much part in his existence. Few children's fathers are intimate with them till they are ten years old at least; and intimacy to Cowper implied that caressing confidence, those small endearments, which are peculiarly maternal. His father was always the papa of Anne and Jane Taylor's poems; whom one was fond of as one was fond of one's old home, but who, like one's old home, formed part of the background of life, and took his walks and wrote his sermons and, if he was Mr. Cowper, composed ballads, with the unnoticed regularity of the seasons.

He felt a more personal interest in his brother. But the deepest affection of which his heart was capable was poured out on that mother from whom he had inherited his eyes and his mouth and his temperament. It is a great mistake to think that people's characters alter as they grow older; though different circumstances may bring different sides of them into prominence. Cowper the child was like Cowper the man : a defeatist, hating decisions, frightened of the unknown ; the creature, not the creator, of his destiny; liking someone or something on which to lean. But he had a genius for affection, and would devote himself to anyone he loved with all the strength of a nature humble, steadfast, exquisitely tender, and nearly selfless. His mother satisfied all his needs ; he worshipped her, and she sheltered him from the onslaught of an existence he was not coarse or self-confident enough to face by himself. It was she who showed him how to prick out a paper pattern of pinks, violets and jessamine from the figured brocade of her gown ;

who came to say good-night to him in bed; who, when he was old enough to do lessons, wrapped him up in his red cap and velvet cloak and sent him off to learn his book at the dame's school down the street; who waited smiling with "a biscuit or confectionery plum" for him on his return; who soothed his brows with lavender water when he had a headache. And it was from her homely piety he learnt the elements of that faith which was to bring him the few fleeting moments of ecstasy he was ever to know.

For these first six years of his life were the only unshadowed ones. As time went on his mother's figure shone forth in his memory as the beneficent and omnipotent goddess of that golden age when he was absolutely happy. Forty-seven years later he writes: "I can truly say that not a week passes, perhaps I might with equal veracity say a day, in which I do not think of her." And when, a grey-headed man of fifty-nine, scarred with agony and achievement, he was given her picture, he was in a tremor; passionately kissed it; and hung it at the end of his bed, that it might be the first thing on which his eye alighted when he woke.

But when he was six the evil fate that was to pursue him through life struck its first blow. His mother died. He watched from his nursery window the funeral cavalcade trail off; and as he turned away in tears, his nurse, to comfort him, told him his mother was coming back to-morrow. But to-morrow came, and another, and another, and she never came back. The first of his life's illusions was shattered.

It was tragic, for no one was less qualified than Cowper to live the independent life of an orphan. The support round which his shy, clinging nature had wound itself had been suddenly taken away; the old idyllic life at "pastoral" Berkhamsted was over for ever when its centre was gone. But a worse blow was to follow. His father, uncertain what to do with

him at home, sent him to school at the small town of
Market Street, about seven miles from Berkhamsted.
Going away to school for the first time is as purely
painful an experience as there is in most men's lives.
It is like a rehearsal of one's execution. Strung up
by two or three weeks' agonized and helpless anticipation, relentlessly, inevitably, the day arrives when one
is plunged into a world probably hostile and certainly
unknown, without a single link to bind one to the world
of one's experience. But such a fate, cruel in any case,
was for Cowper especially cruel. By temperament he
fastened himself with a peculiarly tenacious hold to the
people and places to which he was accustomed, and
now, when he was already tottering under the loss of a
mother around whom his whole world revolved, his
last roots were cut from beneath him, and he was
deposited, bruised and bleeding, in a place where there
was not a face, not a tree, not a smell, he had ever
known before.

And it was a place of torment. Boys have never
been humane; nor did the robust axioms that governed
eighteenth-century education believe in protecting
people from the natural discipline administered to
them by their contemporaries. Cowper, shrinking,
lonely, six years old, was quite incapable of standing up
for himself. With the consequence that within a
short time of his arrival he had become a mere
quivering jelly of fear. He was so abjectly terrified
of his chief tormentor, an overgrown lout of fifteen,
that he only recognized him by his buckled shoes;
he had never dared to lift his eyes to his face. Such
a situation could not go on for long even in those days;
his tormentor was expelled. But Cowper's nervous
system was ruined for life.

Such sufferings alone would be quite enough to
account for it. But obscure hints reach us of a more
sombre cause for Cowper's youthful sufferings. It is

alleged that he suffered from an intimate deformity, and from early years the thought of it preyed on his mind. The whole subject is mysterious. In later life his emotional experience was normal and developed perfectly spontaneously. On the other hand, he never was a passionate man; and there are certain facts in his later life for which such a deformity would offer a convincing explanation. If he was deformed there is no doubt that he must have learnt about it early, possibly from the deriding lips of his tormentors. The effect on him would inevitably have been disastrous. Boys dislike above all things to be different from other people: nor was Cowper of an age to estimate coolly the relative importance of his abnormality.

At any rate, from whatever cause, he left Market Street with the rooted feeling that he was different from other people, different from no fault of his own, but differing for the worse. It was morbid of him, because no one had more in common with his fellow men, and for the rest of his life he was unusually attractive to every type, age and sex. But there remained buried in the hidden foundations of his mind the idea that he was under a dark and shameful curse; that other people could not help him, for he was not as they were; that he started life with the dice loaded against him, and come what might, in the end he would lose the game. He was despondent by nature, and his first experience of the world had proved to him that his despondency was justified.

But his strange sufferings were visited by consolations not less remote from the ordinary child's experience. One day he was huddling on a bench in the deserted classroom, free for one short moment from that terrible pair of feet—cruel, purposeful feet; heard on the stairs, in his bedroom, in the garden, now creeping, now scampering, now climbing, but always in pursuit of him; awful, headless feet, who haunted him in his dreams, who might even now be stealing up behind him to trample on his raw and shuddering spirit. His dazed mind wandered back to that happy home life, so distant that it seemed like a story told long ago and now forgotten. He saw in his mind's eye his mother, and himself sitting beside her while she read to him. Suddenly there flashed into his mind a fragment of the Bible, heard often in those days, but now fraught with a new and tremendous significance: " I fear nothing that man can do unto me." His whole being was filled with a strange spiritual exaltation, far more intense than the happiness of his early childhood; for that arose only from the absence of sorrow, and this vanquished sorrow in her extremest citadel. The forlorn child, hiding away from his bullying school-fellows, turned and faced his fate with the unearthly serenity of the mystic and the martyr. What did it matter what man could do to him? His soul was inviolate, at one with itself, at one with the Divine Spirit from which it sprang. It was only for a moment—and then he was back in the schoolroom, miserable, homesick, in fear, above all, of those terrible feet. But that moment had made as deep an impression on him as the sufferings that preceded it. He never forgot what he had felt. In the brief prologue of his first school-time, the two protagonists of his mental tragedy, the demon of his despair and the angel of his consolation, had both made their appearance on the stage.

Having made their bow, they retired; and the scene changes to comedy. For the next fourteen years his life returned to its ordinary, comfortable, daylight key. Buried in the recesses of his memory, the incident of his first school was to all appearance forgotten. In the light of his common day, nightmare and vision soon grew equally dream-like, the recollection of a life vague, painful, and utterly unconnected with present normal exiStence.   Children look forward, not back ; their spirits are so resilient that whatever inward bruises their nervous syStems have sustained are hidden, and they seem perfectly well again.   The obscene, crawling beaSts had sunk to sleep in the furtheSt corners of Cowper's spirit.   Later on they might beStir themselves and come forward and pounce.   But for the present all was soothing and unshadowed, at the house of Mr. Disney, the oculiSt, where Cowper was sent to be cured of some specks on his eyes.   Mrs. Disney was an oculiSt too ;   no one seemed certain which one went to consult.   But they were both very amiable people, though they did not have family prayers.   And the days passed in an easy round of treatment, walks, and a few mild lessons.   There were holidays too :   rambles alone, or trotting by his father through the woods and commons round BerkhamSted, already heavy with sentimental associations for him ; and visits to his Donne cousins in Norfolk, where he made the Still, autumnal garden ring with his and Harriet's shouts, and chattered to CaStres, and rocked tiny Rose on his knee and, when the curtains were drawn and the candles lit, recited Gay's fable of The Hare with Many Friends, in a high, treble voice, to the assembled company.

The years rolled by ;   his eyes got better ;   and he was sent to WeStminSter.   He muSt have seen the gate of his second school chilled with apprehension, remembering his experience at his firSt.   But if he did, he was agreeably surprised.   The easy flow of his days was not interrupted.   WeStminSter was as pleasant as BerkhamSted or the house of Mr. Disney. All around him surged and roared the palpitating, many-coloured London of 1741.   Nightly the torch-lit coaches joStled one another on the way to Masquerade and Rout ;   weekly the crowds swarmed to Tyburn to see a woman hanged for Stealing a yard of silk; Fielding, his aquiline nose bent over the paper, finished *Joseph Andrews*; Peg Woffington took the town by storm in the peruke and satin breeches of Sir Harry Wildair; Horace Walpole, just back from France, arranged objects of *virtù* in his house in Arlington Street; while every night, only a few hundred yards from where Cowper worked, old Sir Robert, tottering to his fall after his long ascendancy of twenty years, defended himself with dogged shrewdness against the fiery eloquence of the Boys and the Patriots. But the even tenor of Westminster existence was little disturbed by the thundering tide of life that ebbed and flowed around it. Governments might rise and fall, men commit crimes and be hanged for them, waistcoats get longer or shorter, but the boys and masters of Westminster pursued with an undeviating regularity the curriculum prescribed for them in the days of Queen Elizabeth. Like the pool in the middle of a cyclone, the school seemed all the calmer for the swirling rush surrounding it on every side. Every morning the deep bell sounded, the boys toiled or skimmed through their Latin prose, prayed in Westminster Abbey, played knuckle-taw if they were small, or cricket if they were bigger, under the green or fading plane trees.

The little world had its incidents, too. Young Lord Higham Ferrers and his friends kept the school alive by their pranks. Everyone talked of how he had visited the school dressed as a lady of title and was carried up the great hall in a sedan-chair, followed by the giggling boys, and preceded by the obsequiously bowing head master; or of how the little Duke of Richmond had set "Vinny" Bourne, the classical master's wig alight in order to have the pleasure of boxing his ears to put the flames out. Or Cowper himself did a good copy of Latin verses that were passed round, to the admiration of the masters, and

rewarded with a silver groat. He liked school very
well; he was by nature a scholar. To the end of his
life his genius was not creative except under the stress
of intense emotion. He had not a sufficiently strong
imagination. But though he could not weave, he could
embroider. He had an agreeable individual fancy and
a capacity for painstaking and exact work; given a
subject, he could make a very pretty thing of it. This
was just what was wanted for success in the scholarship
of his day. Cowper's verses followed the best models,
and yet were adorned by that touch of originality which
marked them as his own. His classical style was
formed by kind, untidy, talented "Vinny" Bourne,
of whom he grew very fond. At Westminster
Cowper tasted the sweets of friendship for the first
time. The boys were a distinguished lot. Looking
down the packed lines of the assembled school, beside
the humorous, gentle countenance of Cowper one's
eye would have lighted on the faces of Colman, Elijah
Impey and the pale cheek and lofty brow of Warren
Hastings. The impression made by the great before
their greatness is known is a fascinating study. Did
Hastings move among his school-fellows stamped with
the solemn seal of one whose destiny it was to direct
the fate of millions under an alien sun? Was Cowper
himself marked by his closest friends as possessing a
mysterious, individual something which, had they
known it, implied that power of expression which
alone can communicate with future generations and
achieve for its owner a printed immortality? Idle
speculations! Down what obscure vistas do they lead
us! Far from Cowper laughing with Legge and
Lloyd and dear Russell and the rest of his friends.
How he loved them! What fun he had with them,
playing cricket—he was good at cricket—or arguing
about the right way to translate Homer or, on his
leave-out days, examining the glittering weapons on

the walls of the Tower or staring at the lunatics at Bedlam! " I was not altogether insensible of the misery of these poor captives," he wrote, " but the madness of them had such a humorous air, and displayed itself in so many whimsical freaks, that it was impossible not to be entertained ; at the same time that I was angry with myself for being so." Poor Cowper ! he was not always to laugh so easily at madness. Sometimes they would go further afield and spend a day in the country, so close to London then ; and return home tired and hungry, their mouths stained with the blackberries and " sloes austere " which were all they had had to eat during the day. Though he liked Westminster, Cowper was a countryman by taste and education. He had lived the happiest days of his life there, and he was happiest there still.

He had his solitary pleasures, too. He loved animals : they provided a channel for his flow of natural tenderness. He bought a mouse. However, it ate its children, and he got rid of it in disgust. Later, he took to writing verses, mostly little occasional pieces for his friends on " A Lady's Shoe Lost at Bath," or some such subject. But when he was in a more serious mood his mind returned irresistibly to the woods and lanes he loved, and whose leafy silence afforded such balm to his sensitive spirit.

All this tended to make him more cheerful. Children have very little humour, even if their lives are happy ; and Cowper's, as we have seen, was only partially that. Nor does humour flourish in solitude. One must take oneself seriously alone. But in the social warmth of his friends' company his spirit expanded and flowered into a delicious self-deprecating irony which lights up the few scraps of his writing that survive from this part of his life, and which, except at his very gloomiest, was to shimmer round every sentence he wrote.

But he was not at peace. For he was continually worried by small fears. Sometimes they were of something concrete: that he was going to get into trouble at school. In consequence he grew as skilful as most public-school boys at telling a ready and convincing lie. But generally his fears were more subjective. When he was eleven he was possessed by the idea that he had got consumption. He was too shy to ask anyone about it, so that for years the horrible idea lingered in his thoughts, and would suddenly cross his mind when he was sitting, talking or writing, and strike a chill to his heart. But worse than the fear of illness was the fear of death. One evening he was picking his way among the grave-stones of St. Margaret's on his way home to bed. A blanket of darkness enveloped the world. It was a moonless, starless night. The great buildings that crowded him in on every side might have been a hundred miles away for all he could see of them. The only sound that broke the stillness was the recurring crunch of the sexton's spade digging a grave. Suddenly Cowper felt his leg struck by a round object; he bent down to examine it by the light of the dark lantern he carried in his hand. The light shone on the eyeless sockets, the smooth, repulsive contours of a human skull. With a sickening stab of fear he realized the transitoriness of human life. What good was it to avoid other dangers when here was a danger that could never be avoided? Every minute, every day, every year that one lived, was only a year, a day, a minute nearer this. Friends, books, what were they? Insubstantial masks conjured up by man to hide this bald, grinning horror that was the only reality. Distract oneself as one might, forget it if one could, this was what one came to in the end. The joys of life turned to ashes in his mouth, and he rushed shuddering home. His horror was followed by a strange reaction. With exhilaration he felt that whatever happened to other people, he, William Cowper, was fated never to die. But this feeling did not last. The terror of death was added to the other terrors of existence.

The truth was that at the bottom he had no confidence in life. By nature nervous and despondent, only an untroubled upbringing and the undivided personal attention of someone he loved and trusted could have persuaded him into anything like optimism. He needed the support of a solid foundation of realized happiness before he could meet the world with any confidence. But at the very outset of his life he had received two violent shocks. The first, the loss of his mother, by removing the corner-stone of his childish existence removed also his belief in the stability of human happiness, and taught him to feel that one must not trust in the continuance of the most assured source of protection. The second, the torments he suffered at his first school, convinced him that life was even crueller than he had feared, and that he was the specially selected object of its cruelty. As time passed he ceased to think of his youthful sufferings; at times even forgot them. But he had lost his nerve. Underneath the ebb and flow of his daily thoughts there was always the half-conscious feeling that life was trying to hurt him and it was no use relying on any earthly defence, however strong it might seem. It was not just that he could not stand a row. If he had not a real cause for fear he invented one; and as fast as he freed himself from that, he fell a prey to another. For they frightened him not in themselves, but as the changing manifestations of a constant distrust of life.

For such ills religion was the only real remedy. The work and play of ordinary mundane existence might distract him from his hidden fears, but they could not remove them; for they moved on a different

plane. In the light of common day his terrors would
have looked shadowy indeed, but it was of their nature
that they never saw such a light. He might feel
perfectly at ease when he was running about the school
yard; but when the lights were extinguished and he
was alone in bed the nameless horrors would return,
the more frightful for their short oblivion. But religion
did not only drive them to their lairs; it rounded them
up and cleared them out. Alone it met them on their
own ground; armed Cowper with a spiritual sword
to combat the enemies of the spirit; prescribed a
celestial antidote to the poisonous fear of dishonour,
disease and death. The ultimate source of all happiness was the soul; and over the soul they had no power.
He had felt this that morning in Market Street; and
now and again, notably during the time he was being
prepared for confirmation, he felt it still. For a
moment it seemed to be of no consequence if he did
lose his name or his health or his life. The only
treasure worth having was laid up in heaven, and that
was his for ever.

Unluckily his anxious mind, searching suspiciously
for the thorn beneath every rose, soon began to detect
as much cause for alarm in the question of his spiritual
as of his material salvation. He felt that his moments
of religious comfort were vouchsafed to him in order
to win him to the Christian life, by showing him a
glimpse of the heaven it was in his power to attain to.
But it is not easy to live a life of austere devotion if
you are a growing boy, enjoying yourself at a public
school; and Cowper's life followed much the same
course as it would have done if he had had no religion
at all. The result was that the whole subject grew
as disquieting to him as the fear it was its function
to dispel. He felt he would never be able to live up to
his beliefs. Would Heaven then withdraw its comforts in this world? Very likely. And in the next,

worse punishment might follow. Uneasily he diverted his mind from the subject.

However, it is foolish to emphasize the importance of these youthful worries. Cowper's nervous system was never so deranged as to render his views abnormal and deluded, not to be treated as those of a reasonable man. Life is precarious, tragic, surrounded by dangers; and if delicate and highly strung people are peculiarly conscious of this, it is because they alone are fully alive to their true situation; and are not, like the healthy, the dupes of their own good digestions. Youth, unacquainted with the world, dazzled by the enchanting prospect before it, is proverbially unaware of the possibility of failure and death; and Cowper's only abnormality is his premature delivery from the illusions of youth. Indeed, his nervous troubles were little more than the crises every imaginative boy goes through between the ages of twelve and twenty. And they occupied a very small part of his time. For one agitated night, he passed thirty in comfortable sleep; and from the worst fear he could be distracted by any ephemeral pleasure. On the whole he was very happy. The only formidable fact in his mental condition was that his happiness was founded on nothing stronger than the natural energy and spirits of boyhood; so that, if later he was attacked by a serious trouble, he had no settled confidence in the probability of ultimate happiness, with which to withstand its assault; which, coupled with his early acquired sense of the danger of human existence, might, in a temperament like his, lead to a catastrophe.

The years passed. Walpole was succeeded by Pelham; Ranelagh began to supplant Vauxhall as a centre of fashion; and Cowper left Westminster. He went to live with Mr. Chapman, a solicitor of Ely Place, Holborn, to learn law. But the colouring of his life did not alter very much. He was a young man, and not a

boy: he used to drink port with his friends, dressed
in small clothes in the evening by way of recreation,
instead of eating blackberries with them, dressed in
jackets in the afternoon; and he worked when he
liked. But the friends themselves and the subjects
they talked about were the same as at Westminster.
Cowper was not the sort of character that sows wild
oats. Apart from his natural sobriety, his mind continued absorbed by the subjects which had occupied
most of its attention at school. He was a scholar;
and that is to say that his school work was the beginning
of the work he did when he grew up, not a preparation for it. He estimated a man's ability by his
scholastic attainments. Nothing else seemed to him
so worth doing. Law bored him extremely; and he
spent most of the time he was supposed to be working
at it in writing Latin verses. For the rest he argued
and laughed with Colman and Thornton and Russell
about Homer and Horace just as he had done at
Westminster. Only now one had delicious conversations that could go on as long as one liked and where
one liked, without being called away to go to bed or
to apply one's mind to some dreary subject in which
one took no interest. He did not only talk about
scholarship. Politics stirred him deeply. He had
all the full-blooded eighteenth-century belief in the
superiority of England to every foreign country in
every respect. And beyond this, he just liked talking
about the world around him. In this, too, he was of his
period. The men of the eighteenth century always
aspired to be men of the world, restricted in its dimensions though that world might be. It was not then
the mark of a distinguished man to devote himself
exclusively to one interest, and count the world well
lost. Men of fashion knew about literature; artists
discussed politics. For, as everybody accepted the
general lines on which society was constructed, they

would have thought a man eccentric who rejected any activity that lay within them. But Cowper would have been interested in the world around him wherever he had lived. He was a born friend; always more interested in the man he was talking to than in the subject he was talking about; vigilant to follow his friend's mood, careless where it led him. And his interest therefore naturally played round such of his experience as he and his friends shared together. He was quick to notice all he saw in their company: the types and oddities of London; the fops and the pedants; the feeble young man who was dominated by his mother; the spoilt child who told tales of the servants; or, when he had gone on a visit to the country, the decaying village churches, whose cracked bells had ceased to ring; the worldly farmers' wives who came to church to show off their fine silk clothes. He began to make new friends. There was a young man called Thurlow also working with Mr. Chapman. He was much better at law than Cowper, but very merry and communicative. Easy-going Mr. Chapman did not bother them much; and they used to sit for hours, two excited boys in the decorous dress of 1752, discussing books and people and how best to dispose of money in charity; and going off into fits of laughter and then growing very serious again, while the evening sky darkened to night behind the worn traceries of St. Etheldreda's, Ely Place, and the bending trees in its churchyard.

But other friendships began to dwindle to a small place in his thoughts compared with that which grew up between him and his uncle's family in Southampton Row. Cowper made and liked men friends: he was so gregarious and so affectionate that he made a friend of an animal if he could not find a human being. But his natural *milieu* was a domestic circle. It gave him what he really cared for in converse with his fellow creatures : intimacy, the delicious sweetness of mutually enjoyed pleasures, an interest shared with someone else, a sorrow sympathized with by someone else, a joke laughed at with someone else. And it gave these to him enhanced by a thousand small graces that the most affectionate man friend could never provide. Cowper was always happy with women. They liked his warm heart, his charming interest in little things, his good sense, his delicate, unremitting care for the feelings of the individual ; while they alone were soft-hearted and refined enough never to jar on his sensitive taste. But he did not like meeting them at parties. He was shy, and liked knowing people well, if he knew them at all. Nothing else fitted in with all his wants so well as family life ; and it was doubly attractive to him as he had never had it except in that remote, sunlit past when he was happy with his mother. He grew to love all the little incidents and institutions of that cheerful, respectable Southampton Row household : the little parties, courteous and informal, for a few friends ; the little excursions to the country for a few weeks ; the tea-drinkings and wool-windings and readings aloud and nicknames ; the family jokes lasting for weeks that he bandied with his cousins. They were the magnet that drew him to the house. He was fond of his Uncle Ashley, a little man so like a mushroom in his big white hat with its yellow lining. But he was not Harriet or Theodora. Harriet was the beauty of the family ; a very Georgian beauty, dark-haired, with a blooming complexion, arched eyebrows and a decided mouth. When Cowper went to Ranelagh with her, all the young men turned to look at her. She had the ways of a beauty, too : little caprices and coquetries ; the desire to please ; the confidence that she could do so. And she was clever, vivacious, and well-read, with a fund of high spirits and high-spirited humour. Not that she was unconven-

D

tional. No, her ideas were those of the sensible, respectable society in which she lived, though perhaps she expressed them with more enthusiasm and force. She believed in living a decent, reasonable life, not without the pleasures that a decent, reasonable man allows himself. She approved of a decent, reasonable church; took a decent, though less reasonable interest in the royal family. These are the ideas that emerge from her well-written, underlined, entertaining letters. Cowper was very fond of her. How they used to laugh together! How well they understood each other! " So much as I love you," he wrote to her once, " I wonder how the deuce it has happened I was never in love with you." It was not really such a wonder as he said. One cannot be in love with two people at once; and he was in love with her sister Theodora.

Compared with her sister's vivid and definite, her personality seems curiously undefined. Her poignant figure glows through Cowper's story with a lambent light of its own; but a tender mist of love floats round it, blurring its outlines. Our rare glimpses of her detect her in some beautiful attitude of regret or tenderness; but we cannot distinguish her features. Through the haze her eyes shine out like stars; yet we fail to discern their shape and colour. Perhaps love inevitably thus cloaks its object. How many of all the love poems that fill the libraries of the world convey to their readers the impression of a living individual? What human being, indeed, can possess such transcendent qualities as to single them out and set them above all others? She is not loved for what she is, but because for one moment she incarnates to her lover the essential spirit of beauty, not found on earth, and partakes of its mystery. The end of that mystery is the end of love.

It may be that this is why we learn so little of Theodora from Cowper's poems and letters. And alas, time has silenced her own voice. We have none of her letters. Her one reported remark is facetious, but cryptic. Her father asked her what she would do if she married Cowper. " Wash all day," she replied, " and ride on the great dog all night." From what we can gather, she must have been vivacious, like her sister, enjoying a joke and an argument, able to treat Cowper with the orthodox caprice of a mistress. And, more than this, she felt for him a deep and touching sentiment. She loved him better than he loved her. To him she was attractive largely as the expression of that gay, secure domesticity which he desired. When in later life he gave up all idea of this, he never seems to have thought of her again. But she did not so easily forget him. She never married; secretly she followed all the events of his career: helped to support him, though he never knew it; and—pathetic illusion—as an old woman mistook a slight love poem appearing anonymously in the newspaper for one of Cowper's own, and rejoiced to think that his mind was still constant to that boy-and-girl romance that had ended nearly forty years before. However, all that was a long way away. For the moment Cowper gradually spent more and more of his time in Southampton Row, till at last he only slept at Mr. Chapman's. All through the hot July days, and through those of winter when the windows were never opened he used to sit with the sisters, and sometimes Thurlow, " giggling and making giggle." He was gawky and ill-dressed at first, but Theodora took him in hand, and improved his clothes and taught him how to come into a room, and how to talk and how to walk and how to dance, till, as he said, " No dancing bear was so genteel or half so *dégagé*."

Whatever his real feeling, he certainly enjoyed being in love with her; quarrelling with her and making it up; writing poems and letters to her; thinking of her.

When he went to stay with his cousins, the Donnes, in Norfolk, and they drove him about in a whiskum snivel, he thought of Theodora. When he went out shooting, the coveys flew over his head unnoticed; he thought of Theodora. He used to sit with a book on his knees for hours reading some pages again and again, and knowing no more about it at the end than at the beginning; he was thinking of Theodora. " Let her say," he wrote,

> " Let her say why so fixed and so steady my look
> Without ever regarding the person who spoke,
> Still affecting to laugh without hearing the joke;
>
> Or why when with pleasure her praises I hear,
> That sweetest of melodies sure to my ear,
> I attend and at once inattentive appear."

Meanwhile his time with Mr. Chapman came to an end. In 1752 he went into residence at the Middle Temple. And now within a few months a depression began to overcast his spirit. It was partly due to his age. The poison had always been there. But it had been counteracted by the routine of school life and the irresponsibility of youth. He forgot every worry as quickly as he could; and he had so much to do that he forgot them very soon. But adolescence breaks up the whole fabric of habit built up in childhood. Restlessly one reviews every element of past experience. One must understand; one must, if possible, assign each its proper place in the order of life. Even at twenty-one one tries to co-ordinate the different aspects of existence. One can no longer forget a real trouble under the spell of a momentary pleasure; especially if, like Cowper, one is by nature introspective and dejected. The melancholy induced by temperament, increased by early experience, latent throughout boyhood, bestirred itself and came into the forefront of his thoughts.

Any natural tendency to depression was increased by his manner of life. The Temple was a melancholy place. It was gay enough on a summer evening, when the fig trees were in leaf and the leading Counsel were taking the air, in ruffles and cocked hats, by the side of the Thames, gleaming in the level rays of the setting sun; or in Dr. Johnson's chambers over the way, where the pithy, brilliant talk flowed on till the candles flickered yellow in the pallid dawn. But to Cowper, who was not a leading Counsel, and did not know Dr. Johnson, the Temple meant solitude in a dusty set of chambers up a flight of dustier stairs.

Nor was he, as at school, distracted and occupied by the routine of daily work. In the Temple there was no routine, and very little work. He was without briefs; and such work as he chose to do he could do when he liked and how he liked. None of this would have mattered if he could have cared for his profession, if he could have looked on his present inertia as the inevitable prelude to an absorbing career. But he had only become a lawyer because his father had wanted him to; he disliked the subject and showed no talent for it whatsoever. He used to sit through the long days, with nothing to do but to brood over his future. How dark it must have seemed! Cursed from birth, pursued by misfortune in childhood, he had now taken up a profession which he hated, and in which he could not but fail. Yet there was no other that he liked better; and he was too poor to do nothing at all. Where was he to look for encouragement? To love? The amiable sentiment he felt for Theodora was not serious or passionate enough to take him out of himself. Was it not rather another cause of trouble? Physique and poverty alike might prevent him from marrying her. Nor could the thought of his friends much console him. What did the most intimate friend know of the viewless maladies of the soul?

And how could he heal them if he did know of them? The very classics lost their power to appeal to Cowper. He began to hate himself for the value he had set on these stony, pagan pages. As the months dragged on his depression deepened to anguish. With extravagant self-deprecation he cursed his weakness and incompetence. But his old sense that fate was his enemy made him hopeless of curing himself of them. In the lonely silence of his chambers he cried aloud in his misery. At last he turned to religion. It had helped him once, it might help him again. But religion he approached shaken by all the terrors of a conscience that felt he had neglected it. As he nerved himself to face a righteous God, his poor, pitiful little sins, his petty schoolboy lies, the Sundays he had not gone to church, assumed in his mind the proportions of great crimes. But God was always merciful; He cared for the poor in spirit, the failures, those for whom the world was too hard. Perhaps He would listen to him if he were sorry for his great sinfulness. He flung himself upon his knees; but his spirit was too numb to pray. Like Christina Rossetti, he longed for a heart of flesh instead of a heart of stone. He could not feel; he could only suffer.

One day he picked up a book of George Herbert's. The language was "rude and Gothick." Yet the spirit of fresh, untroubled piety that arose from the pages stole into his heart, and breathed there the first whispers of that spiritual consolation that more direct methods had been unable to entice. He was still in torture; but these simple verses, like a cold compress on an aching wound, brought momentary alleviation, and taught him to hope once more. From them he learnt of a world innocent and secure, where the light of faith shone steadily, unshaken by storms; where, across the little fields, the bells called clearly to church beneath a serene sky. Herbert taught him that the

state of mind he longed to attain was attainable by a
human being. Under his influence he grew more
composed; his heart warmed and softened; he felt
he could pray once more. For twelve months he lived
in the Temple alone, fleeing the world; still convinced
that he was fated to misery, but deriving a little comfort
from a self-appointed régime of devotion; praying,
writing prayers, reading Herbert.

It was an odd life for a young man of twenty-one. A
great deal too odd it seemed to one of his relations who
came to see how he was. With a misunderstanding of
the situation typical of the anxious relative, he attributed
all the trouble to Herbert, and urged Cowper to put
the book away. " It encourages all that is worst in
your condition," he said. In reality it had so far
improved Cowper's condition that he was able to leave
the Temple to go on a visit to Southampton with a Mr.
Thomas Hesketh, who was engaged to his cousin
Harriet. Cowper's disgust with life did not disappear
at once. But insensibly it grew more bearable. For
one thing, he could not feel so gloomy in the country.
His mind was unable to concentrate on its own woe, as
it could in the stuffy solitudes of the Temple, if he was
out all day rambling on the cliffs or lounging on the
hard sands. He could not lie awake all night in restless self-torment if he went to bed filled with that
delicious aching lassitude that comes from a day spent
in the open air. And his companions were most
tonic in their influence. Mr. Hesketh used to take
" meo considine," as he called Cowper, bathing and
sailing. Cowper liked the bathing better than the
sailing. He wore sailor's trousers and tried to enter
into the spirit of the thing; but he felt cramped.
Still, even this distracted his mind from more ethereal
woes. With Harriet, who joined them, Cowper used
to walk and read and incessantly to talk. His spirits
began to rise. The life which he now led, the pleasant

prosaic summer holiday, full of small events and fundamental peace, provided a sort of counter-attack to his mental terrors. How could he feel that he was the lonely victim of an awful fate when he was animatedly discussing the most agreeable " scheme " for passing the next day with Harriet and Mr. Hesketh ? And as the ordinary daylight of the mental atmosphere surrounded him, his fears began to appear the insubstantial figments of a diseased brain. One day after he had been in Hampshire for a few weeks a decisive change came. It was a beautiful cloudless day, and he had walked out to a hill overlooking the sea. Suddenly, silently, as at the bidding of a divine gesture, the clouds that had hung over his mind for so long that they had come to seem an inevitable condition of existence rolled away, and the sun shone out in a clear sky. Sitting there, his cheek caressed by the salt breeze, and far below him the shimmering sea, he was overcome with an indescribable sense of peace. Awful as the period of its dominion had been, his melancholy had not lasted for ever. It was not invincible, it could not ultimately stand between him and happiness. How could he ever thank the God who had not left him comfortless ? A gush of intense emotion, in which exaltation, gratitude and an exquisite sense of relief mingled like instruments in an orchestra, welled up in his heart and filled his eyes with tears.

As the days went on his troubles dwindled to still smaller proportions in his mind. He felt that they had been too trivial to be dignified by the name of spiritual : they were the result of some physical weakness. Accentuated by his cloistered life in the Temple, they had been banished by a change of air and scene. If he could lead a more normal existence, see more people and have more occupation he could easily keep them from troubling him. His spirits rose higher every day. He laughed with Harriet till

his sides ached ; and after a few cheerful months drove
back to London, burnt the prayers he had written, and
sallied out to find his friends.

The fit was past. Once again, as at school, the
vitality of youth had routed the shadowy battalions
of his nervous fears. And he now hoped that by
resolutely averting his mind from such subjects he
could keep them at bay for ever. Sometimes when
he was alone in his chambers dark thoughts would
begin to steal back into his mind. Hurriedly he would
take up his pen and paper and begin a letter,

> " 'Tis not that I presume to rob
>   Thee of thy birthright, gentle Bob, . . .
> That I presume to address the muse ;
>   But to divert a fierce banditti
> (Sworn foes to everything that's witty),
>   That, with a black infernal train,
> Make cruel inroads on my brain,
>   And daily threaten to drive thence
> My little garrison of sense :
>   The fierce banditti that I mean
> Are gloomy thoughts led on by spleen."

That was what he must hold on to. His gloomy
thoughts had no rational foundation ; they were the
result of spleen.

For the moment this method of dealing with them
was successful enough. The dark mists that had
shrouded his spirit were dissipated. Already beside
the sunny realities of his holiday life they had shrunk
to a cloud no bigger than a man's hand. A varied
existence of work and play, with no time left for moping,
would surely make them vanish altogether. Perhaps
after a few busy, happy, normal years he would look
back on his troubles of 1751 as a trivial green sickness
of nerves, such as any young man might pass through
in the difficult first years of maturity. Perhaps——

CHAPTER II

September 2nd, 1762.

"Your letter has taken me just in the crisis; to-morrow I set off for Brighthelmstone, and there I stay till work brings all to town again. The world is a shabby fellow and uses us ill: but a few years hence there will be no difference between us and our fathers of the tenth generation upwards. I could be as splenetic as you, and with more reason . . . but my resolution is never to be melancholic while I have a £100 in the world to keep up my spirits. God knows how long that will be, but in the meantime Io Triumphe! If a great man struggling with misfortunes is a noble object, a little one who despises them is no contemptible one; and that is all the philosophy I have in the world at present. . . . Did you ever know a man who was guided in the general course of his actions by anything but his natural temper? And yet we blame each other's conduct as freely as if that temper was the most tractable beast in the world, and we had nothing to do but to twitch the rein to the right or the left. . . . This is a strange epistle, nor can I imagine how the devil I came to write it; but here it is, such as it is, and much good may you do with it. I have no estate, as it happens, so if it should fall into bad hands I shall be in no danger of a commission of lunacy. Adieu.

"Yours ever,

"WILLIAM COWPER."

The Cowper who sat writing these words to his friend Clotworthy Rowley was now thirty-one. With the passage of time his features had set: the mould of the big nose and the fine lips was now defined; little lines of laughter had drawn themselves at the corner of mouth and eyes. But otherwise he and his situation had altered little. He was still in the Temple, still without briefs, still as far from real peace of mind as before. Indeed, Clotworthy Rowley, or anyone else who cared to read between the lines of this letter of September, could see that it was written by a man who, for all his boasted stoicism, was profoundly discouraged about life. Of course he was never likely to shake himself free from a constitutional depression by simply refusing to think about it; for that method left the roots of his melancholy untouched. He was still afraid of it. Occupy himself as he might, he could not rid himself of the unspoken conviction that he was diverting his mind from a dark tangle of horrible shadows, which he must not think of lest it should make him mad. And his fears were still mysterious fears. He had never had the courage to turn them out and examine them in the light of day: so he had never been able to reconstruct his scheme of existence to include and control them. They remained anomalous to it, a nameless blackness whose origin he had not traced and whose powers he could not gauge. As long as they kept quiet he was happy enough; but if they became active he understood them too little and feared them too much to do anything but succumb. Yet they would only keep quiet as long as his life was untroubled. For as he had made no rational attempt to discover their true strength, his only weapon against them was to maintain a cheerful vigour— vigour in the light of which mental terrors appeared trivial and without substance. To a temperament like Cowper's such a mood was only possible as

long as his horizon was unclouded. But the per-
spective of his past life down which he gazed as
he leant back in his armchair in the Temple room
was a grey one, undisturbed by any shattering grief,
but unillumined by any lasting joy—an image of
failure, of vacuity, of the sad, futile fleetingness of
human life.

In 1756 he lost his father, and with him the last link
that bound him to his happy childhood, to his mother
and the green meadows of Berkhamsted. He went
down to the funeral. " Then, and not till then," he
wrote, " I felt for the first time that I and my native
place were disunited for ever. I sighed a long adieu
to fields and woods from which I once thought I should
never be parted, and was never so sensible of their
beauties as when I left them all behind me to return
no more." He had lost Theodora. The long court-
ship had dragged on two years, three years, four years,
and at the end her father, for reasons of health or of
money, had said that it could not be. Perhaps they
had never expected it would come to anything. But
it had been a delicious dream while it lasted. Now the
dream was broken, and it seemed to Cowper that he
must forever climb life's rough path alone. He had
loved her, and she had adored him; but their
stars were contrary; and they must part. And with
Theodora went the chief charm of that sunny life in
Southampton Row which had proved itself so sturdy a
bulwark against his melancholy. He turned more
and more to his men friends. Within a year Russell,
closest of all since Westminster days, was accidentally
drowned. This third blow struck Cowper hard.
Friendship without intimacy meant nothing to him;
and it seemed as if fate was determined to deprive
him of all those with whom he was intimate. He
became moody and silent, and unable to talk in
company.

" Doomed as I am in solitude," he wrote to Harriet Hesketh, " To waste

> The present moment and regret the past
> Deprived of every joy I value most,
> My friend torn from me and my mistress lost:
> Call not this gloom I wear, this anxious mien,
> The dull effect of humour or of spleen.
> Still, still I mourn with each returning day
> Him snatched by fate in early youth away
> And her through tedious years of doubt and pain
> Fixed in her choice and faithful—but in vain."

That was five years ago now, and time had a little dulled the edge of his grief. But he had never altogether recovered his spirits ; and lately a more mundane trouble had begun to disturb him. Cowper had never been rich ; now he was becoming poorer. And poverty, though it may not be so desolating at any given moment as the loss of friends, is more persistently worrying to the nerves. It shuts one in on every side. If Cowper felt downcast he could not go abroad or keep open house at home. He was not rich enough. But the difficulties imposed by having little money now were nothing compared to those raised by having less in the future. He was not luxurious, and, like all timid people, he could easily learn to put up with any sort of life if he felt it to be safe and certain. But he was proportionately more upset by not knowing what was going to happen to him. He must find some way of increasing his income. But what ? He had been a failure as a lawyer. He loathed it, and had never tried to work at it properly. Perhaps if he made an effort now—but at the thought a sort of impotence seized him. The more important he felt it to be that he should work, the less he seemed able to do it. He had followed the idle bendings of his inclination so long, had become such a slave to chance desire, that he could not make himself work regularly—especially if it was at something he disliked. Indeed, though he did not realize it, lack of regular work was one of the subtlest causes of his depression.

If you are working hard all day at a given task you cannot become the victim of your own moods. You are just part of a machine; and if you are to perform your function properly you must attend to it, and not to your own mental condition. This forcible diversion from your own thoughts saves you from succumbing to them : it clamps you to reality. But if, like Cowper, you have no regular work, you judge the value of all you do or see by what you feel about it. Nothing has any objective value, outside the emotional response it rouses in you. And as the same emotional response can never be aroused for long by the same stimulus, nothing seems to have a constant, solid value on which you can rely. Life flits by you without purpose or arrangement : like a series of airy pictures, that must not be looked at too closely lest they should fade.

And without regular occupation the will, too, ceases to function. You lose the habit of making yourself do something at a definite time, with the consequence that when an occasion arises when it is necessary to act at once, the spring of action is rusty and will not move. Cowper simply was not able to work at law. But he felt he was getting too old for anything else. And this reflection merged in a more general and a more fundamental melancholy, born of the flight of youth. Youth cannot take a consistently pessimistic view of its lot; for it thinks of its mode of existence, not as real life, but as the preparation for it. So that, however much it may deplore the present, it is hopeful about the future, which must be different, and will probably be pleasanter. But with maturity hope begins to flag. One has grown up and settled to a profession and made one's friends, and the course one's life will wend is clear before one. If one is still weighed down by the burdens of youth, it seems likely that one will carry them to the grave. Cowper was now thirty-one; he had been ten years a member of his profession. And he had as much experience as falls to many men in their whole lifetime. He had lived in a great capital, he had made many friends, he was a scholar, he had loved. But he had found no lasting source of happiness, and the lack of confidence that had tormented him in youth was as strong at thirty-one as at twenty-one.

Nor could he hope to throw it off as he had hoped then. When he had come back to London in 1754, in high feather at recovering from his first fit of despair, he had thrown himself into a thousand activities: written poems, pamphlets, political ballads; founded a dining club, the " Nonsense Club "; contributed to a magazine, the *Connoisseur*. How his heart had swelled when Wolfe took Quebec! How it had beaten with admiration and excitement when he first read Sir Charles Grandison! But now his interest in books, in social life, in political events seemed nothing but a vain attempt to fill a life essentially futile and void. They moved him when they were new and he was young; but in the clear, sunless light of advancing age he began to see how little real hold they had on him. His youth was over, and he had done nothing. He began to wonder if he ever would. One evening, drinking tea with Thurlow, now a successful lawyer, he suddenly exclaimed, " Thurlow, I'm nobody, and I shall always be nobody, and you will be Lord Chancellor." He loathed himself for his ineffectiveness. And yet he could not feel he was really to blame. He had tried to do what he thought right as hard as most men he knew. But Fate had been against him. It was a thought that struck a responsive chord in the deepest fibres of his nature. His old distrust of destiny revived with a doubled and compelling force. It had never been wholly latent. At twenty-one, in the first rosy dawn of his love for Theodora, he could write to her

> " Fated to ills beyond redress,
>   We must endure our woe ;
>   The days allowed us to possess
>   'Tis madness to forego."

And his experience since then had confirmed his gloomiest forebodings. One by one the objects on which he had set his affections had borne sad witness to the nature of their mortality. His mother was dead, Russell was dead, his home was sold, Theodora lost to him for ever, and youth itself was passing. Nor were his present prospects brighter. He was poor, and seemed likely to become poorer ; he had failed in his profession ; yet he felt incapable of making an effort at that or anything else. Fate had dogged his footsteps with disaster. Fate had created him powerless to drive it away.

He should, as in 1752, have sought consolation in his religion. But, unluckily, religion had become nothing but an added sort of discomfort to him. As at school, he felt that he did not live up to it sufficiently to be rewarded for it. If Christian doctrine was true, then in order to be saved one ought to dedicate oneself to the Christian life. But he lived a life which, though not vicious, was solely concerned with the ambitions and pleasures of the world. Nor did he feel equal to changing it now. In spite of his theoretical acceptance of orthodox Christianity, it had not since 1752 been able to raise the feeblest spark of response in his emotions. He made the worst of both worlds. He passionately wished religion to be true, as only by its help could he extricate himself from the ruthless mechanism of nature. But if it was true, then his neglect of its precepts was in a fair way to lead him to eternal perdition. Noisily and persistently, almost as if he wished to persuade himself that he was as sure of them as he said he was, he would assert his beliefs amid companions infected with the scepticism fashionable among intellectual young men of the period. One evening when he had defended the austere tenets of the Church till late into the night over the guttering candles and the wine-stained cloth, the man he was addressing said with a note of asperity, " Well, if what you say is true, you are damned by your own showing." At these words an access of self-loathing swept over him. What a contemptible creature he was! Unable to do right, able only to talk about it, and to render his views ridiculous by his inability to act on them. God Himself had called him, yet he could not tear himself away from pleasures he did not really enjoy to follow the call.

As he ruthlessly scanned his life, his self-disgust attached itself not to spiritual shortcomings alone; it merged into a general revulsion from his whole moral character. Had he been a professing hedonist he would not have been so unhappy. His life, though confined, was peaceful: he could enjoy the passing hour, and wander at his will. Indeed, his nerves were too fragile to stand a career of strenuous well-doing. But the Puritan ideas among which he had grown up, and to which, it must be admitted, he had taken only too readily, taught him that no moment of one's existence is justified unless it furthers a moral purpose. His moral ideals were too high for his nervous system; with the consequence that he lived in a state of war with his own nature, disapproving of it as it was, but was without power or inclination to turn it into what he thought it ought to be.

If he could only have faith, if he could be actively convinced of the truth of the Gospel, he felt he might be able to change his life. But at the thought of making any effort to induce faith, his distrust of destiny

E

crept in and blighted his spiritual, as it had blighted his material hopes. Perhaps he was doomed not to believe. Fate was against him in this world : would not Fate be against him in the next ? He brushed the idea aside, but it had made religion a painful subject to him. Like his past and his future and his own character, it was one of those things he must try not to think about.

It is over religion, above all, that people nowadays so often fail to understand a past age. Their historical imagination fails them. They cannot, as it were, fit the religious pieces into the rest of the evidence about an historical character so as to make up a convincing human being. Cowper's religious ideas seem to them incongruous both with the period he lived in and with the other sides of his own personality. His letters, were they not so well written, might be written to-day. They reveal a character as educated, as sensitive, and as complex as our own. We do not feel, as we do when we open a mediæval, or even a Renaissance book, that we have left the ordinary daylight of modern life for another atmosphere, alien, crude and mysterious. Yet suddenly Cowper will make a remark revealing that in some respects his ideas are those of the Middle Ages, literal, limited, anthropomorphic. He sees nothing improbable in prophetic dreams and special providences ; he believes he is deliberately pursued by a conscious and malevolent fate.

But human beings were quite as consistent then, as they are now. It is just in their attitude towards such subjects that the difference between them and us lies. Their view of the physical world was still that held in the Middle Ages. They believed in a fixed order of the universe. Theists and atheists alike thought that the world and everything in it was originally created exactly the same as it is now, except in so far as the conscious reason of man has impelled him to alter it.

If this were generally assumed, their very rationalism would lead them to think that such a complex scheme of things must be the deliberate creation of a conscious Will. And if every individual man is the result of an act of conscious Will, it seems likely that that Will will continue to follow and control his destiny.

But since the eighteenth century the developments of natural science have completely altered that conception of the nature of the universe which, vague and unquestioned, underlies the ideas of the average person. The earth is conceived of as a minute atom, among millions of other atoms, evolving from no one knows what, in a manner no one knows how, and in a direction no one knows whither; while man himself, sadly fallen from his former dignity, is become merely an animal, like other animals, a late, haphazard, and ephemeral development of some automatic principle of life unknown. The consequence is that religious ideas are now confined to religion. His reason working on his usual assumptions about life no longer leads a man to search for a religious explanation of any phenomenon he does not understand. But it did in the eighteenth century. The visitation of God seemed to him the most probable explanation of an epidemic, as defective sanitation might seem the most probable explanation to us. A hundred and fifty years ago even those who rejected Christianity believed in a first cause. Voltaire himself would have been surprised at some of the views held by an orthodox clergyman of the Church of England in 1929. Cowper's conviction of God's personal interest in him, and his fears of immediate damnation if he disregarded it, may have been morbid, but they were not unreasonable. And they were perfectly consistent with the conception of the Cosmos held by everyone of his day.

With the failure of religion the last solid ground between him and disillusionment split and subsided.

Whichever way he looked he saw no stable fact or idea to which he could pin his hopes or on which he could build his life. Love, youth, friendship, the things of the mind, the things of the body, they all passed. Nothing was constant but his disillusionment and the dim fears that for ever prowled in the background of his consciousness. For experience that had destroyed his belief in the reality of everything else had left these untouched. Indeed, it had laid him more open to their attack. He could no longer restore his inner life to its true proportion in the scheme of things by comparing it to the world outside. For in his present mood he could no more use the world outside as a standard by which to measure the reality of his inner experience than he could use a cloud as a standard to measure the size of a building. He believed in the actuality of nothing but himself, the secret drama of his own soul; and about that nothing could seem incredible.

He was not acutely miserable, but he was without a moment of genuine happiness. Sometimes for a short time, as he sat at his open window and watched the branches feathery against the sky and listened to the water splashing and gurgling from the pumps in the court below, he could fancy he was in the country, and be for a little soothed. But when he turned back into his dingy room, the dreary realities of life would sweep back into his mind again, all the more painful for his moment of forgetfulness. He used to try to comfort himself with trite maxims : " Never despair," " The best way to meet misfortune is to scorn it." But he did not believe them : and he knew he did not. Was he not painfully aware that the only strong feeling left in him was superstitious fear of the future ? The army of his thoughts kept a semblance of marching order. But their morale was gone. At any shock they would become a rout.

Such, as far as we can judge, were the main facts of his mental condition at thirty-one. And they must be kept in mind if we are to have any understanding of the terrible, the momentous events that followed. Cowper had reached the turning-point of his life. In a short ten months his personality was to undergo a change only less catastrophic than death. The nervous, scholarly barrister of the Temple was to die in a lurid agony of despair and madness, and be born anew in another place, stripped of worldly possessions and worldly interests, but strong, single-minded and sustained by inspiration from an unseen world. This is the fact, the astounding, terrific fact. But the process of its accomplishment is mysterious. Tracing a man's history through the records time and chance have left to us is like reading a novel from which important pages have been torn out at random. Characters appear in the front of the stage; clearly they are to play some significant part in the story; but the next pages are missing, and when we take up the tale again these characters have left it for ever. A few years pass blank and unmentioned. Suddenly a brilliant light is turned on to the scene. We see the chief persons at a crucial moment in their lives : every detail of their every day is revealed with the graphic meticulousness of truth. But before we have realized the full purport of the drama the light is withdrawn as suddenly as it appeared, and we see no more. In vain we scan the imperfect records left to us in an effort to understand the real origin of Cowper's catastrophe : the slim volume of confessions he wrote when he recovered ; a few chance references in later letters; a handful of gossip collected from contemporaries by his first biographers. But though some episodes are lit up in vivid detail, though the mystery is chequered by many gleams, clues to revelation, we never see the event in the round, are never certain that we have had a full view of all its features. We must guess, draw our conclusions, put two and two together, if our portrait of Cowper is to have that completeness which is as necessary to history as to other arts. But it is a difficult task : much of the evidence makes the event not less, but more mysterious. The ostensible causes seem so much too slight to have produced so great a catastrophe. It is here that a realization of Cowper's nervous condition helps us. This condition was already such as to make some catastrophe inevitable. As we have seen, any shock would be enough to upset him altogether; and it was impossible that he should live an ordinary life in an ordinary world without experiencing some sort of shock some time. His inner life was now his only standard of reality, so the most severe shock would be one that stirred up his inner fears. And thus it might well be given by some event that will appear trivial to the outside observer.

It was, in fact, given by an effort to relieve the most pressing of his cares. By the convenient system of Government appointment prevalent in the eighteenth century, his cousin, Major Cowper, had the right to present to the post of Clerkships of the House of Lords and to those of Reading Clerk and Clerk of Committees to the House of Commons; and he had always promised to offer one or more of them to Cowper. This promise had been Cowper's one hope of improving his financial position, and he had often laughingly lamented the long life of their present occupants, and said how he wished they would die. Now at last one of them did; while soon after, the other two resigned. And one February morning his cousin arrived in Cowper's chambers, offered him both the Clerkship of Committees and the Reading Clerkship, the two most lucrative of all the posts within his presentation. It was the end of Cowper's financial troubles; and it should have awakened a glow of happiness in his heart. But, strangely, it did not. He returned to his rooms filled with a sense of anti-climax, of doubt, even of depression. A thousand difficulties began to trouble his mind. What would be expected of him in his new occupation? Would he be equal to it? Did he deserve it? And here his conscience, inflamed by years of introspection, began to worry him. He remembered that he had wished for the poor Clerk's death in order that he might take his place: and now he had died, and he was going to. He felt that he was no better than a murderer. No good could come of an advantage gained in such circumstances. He longed to ask his cousin for the House of Lords Clerkship instead of the other two, even though it was worth less. But this idea brought its attendant anxiety. If he took the less lucrative post, people might accuse his cousin of keeping the others back in order to sell them to the highest bidder: he would be injuring his own benefactor. In spite of this, after some weeks of painful indecision he made up his mind to ask him. But though Major Cowper lived just over the way, Cowper did not go to see him, but wrote him a long letter explaining what he wanted. It was granted. And for a moment Cowper felt relieved, even hopeful. It was not for long. The anxiety he had experienced was far too unreasonable to be stilled by the mere removal of its occasion. The conscience that made itself guilty of the Clerk's death, the state of mind that led him to compose an elaborate letter to a relation living next door, were not likely to leave their possessor long at rest. After the first sensation of relief had worn off Cowper began to grow as anxious about his new post as he had been about his old.

And, unlucky day, circumstances now arose which gave him a legitimate cause for anxiety. The Clerk-ship of the House of Lords had especially attracted Cowper, as he could take it up without passing a public

test or in any way exhibiting his shrinking figure before
the eyes of strangers. But in the summer of 1763
he was horror-struck to hear rumours that a party
hostile to his family connection was forming against
them, and was ready to go to any length to get the
Cowper nominee rejected. The rumour proved true,
and the intrigues of this mysterious party succeeded in
persuading whatever authority decided such things to
decree that the candidates for the Clerkship must pass
a public examination. Picture Cowper's horror. He
had always been agonizingly shy in public, and now if
he was to retrieve his fallen fortunes and be a credit to
his benefactor he must stand up and submit to a *viva
voce* examination by the whole House of Lords:
a House of Lords many of whose members would be
trying to trip him up in favour of another candidate.
All the chords of his nervous system, already stretched
to breaking-point during the last few years, were set
trembling and vibrating. His fatalism convinced him
he would fail; his inability to work stopped him from
acquiring the information required to prevent him
failing; his horror of the unknown conjured up a
thousand new obstacles which the opposing party might
put in his way; while the fear of persecution, latent
in him since Market Street, filled him with panic at
the very fact of opposition. He had little reason to
feel it. He would have to prove utterly ignorant before
his cousin's choice could be quashed, and it would be
quite easy for any man of sense to learn what was
required in five months. But Cowper was no longer
a man of sense. He could not sleep, he could not
think, he could not work. The journal books in
which he was to be examined were thrown open to
him, and every day he went down to the office to read
them. The clerks there were in his opponents'
interest, and did nothing to help him; but he was far
too agitated to have profited by their help had they

been willing to offer it.   His pulse beating in his ears, his head heavy like lead, he read and re-read the same page without understanding a word of it.   Every morning when he arrived at the office he said he " had all the sensations of a criminal arriving at the foot of the scaffold."   And every morning that passed was a morning nearer the examination.

At last, after three months, remembering his experience of 1752, he decided to try a change of scene, and went to Margate for August and September.   For the time being it certainly did do him good.   He was practised at putting aside unpleasant thoughts by now, if he was helped by any sort of distraction.   As he lay on the sand, watching the irregular line of wave break sparkling, and recede, and break again, as far as eye could reach, his troubled spirit sank into a kind of tranquillity.   A mist rose up between him and London. With a heart nominally at peace he lounged on the beach, and walked amid the false Gothic ruins, lancet window and chantry chapel open to the sky, which Lord Holland had erected in the dells of Sandgate Park : absurd castle of Udolpho, where perhaps Charles Fox, a swarthy boy of fifteen, was rambling at the same time—Charles Fox reckless and high-hearted ; Cowper expectant only of despair.

But his outward agitation alone was stilled : the trouble that caused it was still as formidable to him as before.   Though he could put them behind him as long as he was occupied, his sleep was disturbed by bad dreams.   And when he woke in the morning and his vitality was low, and there was nothing to come between him and his fears, he was in anguish.   " I looked forward to the approaching winter," he says, " and regretted the flight of every moment which brought it nearer ; like a man borne away by a rapid torrent into a stormy sea where he sees no possibility of returning and where he sees he cannot submit."

How little good Margate had done him became clear the moment he got back to London. When he returned to his work at the House of Lords Office all his old agitation came back, rendered worse by the consciousness that he had tried the only remedy he knew of, and that it had been found wanting. He was in a trap. If he went through with his ordeal he must be publicly humiliated; if he gave it up he would injure a benefactor to whom he owed every gratitude. And a failure in loyalty and affection was especially hateful to him. He felt he would never be able to go through the examination; and yet how decently could he get out of it? Alone in the maddening silence of his chambers, his mind turned round upon itself like a squirrel in a cage.

From henceforward the story is clouded by the smoke, distorted by the lurid light of madness. Horrible hints reach us as to the nature of the fears that tormented him. In the hurricane that was sweeping over him the depths of his personality was stirred up and obscene monsters that had slept there for years came to the surface. He believed, it is said, that his enemies had discovered his secret deformity and were threatening to expose it. It is an unlikely story. How could it help them? Why should such a deformity prevent a man being made Clerk of the House of Lords? On the other hand, there may well have been a more intimate reason for such a catastrophe as overtook him than the mere fear of making an exhibition of himself. And if it is true he was deformed it is possible that, already suffering from some kind of persecution mania, he now associated it with the shameful secret which had done so much to infect him with his fundamental distrust of life.

In his despair he cut himself off from his friends. Aloud in his solitary chambers he cursed the hour of his birth. If he was weak, he was no worse than many

other men.   He had tried to be good.   What had he
done to deserve this frightful crucifixion ?   To ease
his pain he began taking drugs.   But they only
numbed, they did not remove it.   And such comfort
as they gave was neutralized by the awful awakening,
when he looked out wretchedly into the dawn, livid
over the Temple roofs, and realized that the relief of
the night before had been an illusion.

Once more he turned to prayer.   But it was as the
last resort of an anguished soul, not as the result of
any religious impulse.   And the spirit which had
been rendered incapable of prayer by the youthful
melancholy of 1754 was now far beyond concentration on any world but its own.   He soon gave up the
attempt.

Physical and spiritual remedies had both failed him.
And every day the thought of his examination grew
more intolerable.   He would never be able to face it,
never, never.   He would go mad first.   And he only
hoped madness would come as soon as possible.   But
day followed day, each more swiftly than the last ;
and he remained horribly sane, his mind working with
exquisite clearness ;   his sensibilities sharpened to the
finest point ;   his eyes fixed, open and fascinated, upon
the doom that was advancing on him.   God was even
going to refuse him the terrible mercy of madness :
he must drink his bitter cup.   But he could not, he
would not.   And now the idea of suicide began to steal
into his thoughts.   Death, which had thrown a faint,
persistent shadow over his whole outlook on existence
ever since he had first realized it in St. Margaret's
churchyard twenty years before, now appeared infinitely
desirable, a cool dark pool of refuge where he might
rest in peace his bruised and burning spirit.   The
God of his faith had indeed forbidden a man to kill
himself.   But Cowper's faith had been too much a
thing of words, the result rather of a will to believe than

of a genuine conviction, to influence his actions in such a crisis. Maybe there was no God. If there was, no hell to which He could consign him could be worse than his present life. But what did he know of God ? Perhaps He did not condemn suicide. The great men of antiquity, the idols of that classical scholarship by which all Cowper's young ideas had been moulded, had all praised, and some of them committed, it. Why, his own father had not thought it wrong. He remembered well a curious occasion about eighteen years before when his father asked him his opinion on the subject. He had ardently declared against it, but his father had looked at him with a strange expression, and had not applauded what he said. The real reason for this had been that an old friend of Mr. Cowper's had just killed himself, and he did not wish to speak harshly of him. But young Cowper had not known this; and the incident stuck in his mind, and now exercised a powerful effect on his judgment. For he had become so obsessed by one idea that he saw the rest of existence only in relation to it, and its incidents only as arguments for and against self-murder. The slightest fact or the lightest word was to him an indication of that fate predestined for him in heaven, and against which it was useless for him to struggle.

One evening, at a coffee-house, a gentleman entered into conversation with him and, strangely enough, the conversation turned on suicide. Stranger still, the gentleman, a respectable elderly man, advocated it. Another day, at the little chop-house near the Temple where Cowper took most of his meals, a stranger began to talk to him, and again argued strongly in favour of suicide. It seemed as if he were being directly pointed to it by some higher power. It could not be by the God of his childhood. But Cowper's very atheism was superstitious. He was so religious by temperament that if he forswore a Christian Providence, it was only to direct his life in accordance with the dictates of some dark amoral totem of his imagination.

These two conversations finally decided him; and one dark evening he went into a chemist's, and in a voice as natural and unconcerned as he was able to muster, asked for laudanum. The chemist looked at him curiously, appeared to hesitate for a moment, and then gave him what he wanted. But there was a week before his examination, and he shrank from taking it at once. For seven long days, alone in his chambers, he waited and waited, his fingers pressed to the cold laudanum bottle in his pocket, hoping that something would happen to stop the examination. But of course it did not. Two days, three days, four days, five days passed; and now before the day after to-morrow he must choose between death and humiliation. At eight o'clock he woke, threw on his clothes, and dragged himself to Richard's coffee-house to get some breakfast. He picked up a newspaper. The first thing on which his eyes rested was a letter advocating suicide. This last touch was too much for his already tottering self-control. It seemed to him that the author must have known of his case and was writing about it. Crying out, " Your cruelty shall be gratified, you shall have your revenge," he rushed from the room. He meant to go to the deserted fields that lay round London in order to put an end to himself in some ditch. But before he had gone far his mind began to waver. There was no necessity for him to die. He could sell what he had in the funds in a few hours and take a boat for France, there become a Roman Catholic and, cutting himself absolutely off from England, pass the rest of his life in the cloistered peace of a monastery. He hurried back to his chambers to pack; but he had hardly got back when his mind underwent a reaction. His thoughts fell back into their former proportion and he felt that only death could assure him of peace. It could only be cowardice that had stopped him before, that cowardice which was perhaps the most hateful and contemptible of all the weaknesses that had dogged him throughout his mortal life. He must kill himself at once. But again a wave of indecision swept over him. Where should he do it ? He was sure to be interrupted in his chambers. He made up his mind to take a coach to Tower Wharf and do it there. But when he arrived, the first object he saw was a porter seated waiting on a pile of goods, as if sent there to prevent him. He got back into the coach and told the driver to go back to the Temple. " I drew up the shutters," he writes, " once more had recourse to the laudanum and did determine to drink it off directly, but God had otherwise ordained. A conflict that shook me to pieces suddenly took place, not properly trembling, but a convulsive agitation which deprived me in a manner of the use of my limbs, and my mind was as much shaken as my body. Distracted between the desire of death and the dread of it, twenty times I had the phial to my mouth and as often received an irresistible check, and even at the time it seemed to me that an invisible hand swayed the bottle downwards. I well remember that I took notice of this circumstance with some surprise, though it effected no change in my purpose. Panting for breath and in a horrible agony, I flung myself back into the corner of the coach. A few drops of laudanum, which had touched my lips, besides the fumes of it, began to have a stupefying effect on me. Regretting the loss of so fair an opportunity, yet utterly unable to avail myself of it, I determined not to live; and already half dead with anguish, returned to the Temple. Instantly I repaired to my room, and having shut both the inner and the outer doors, prepared myself for the last scene of the tragedy. I poured the laudanum into a small basin, set it on a chair by the bedside, half undressed myself, and lay

down between the blankets, shuddering with horror
at what I was about to perpetrate——I reproached myself
bitterly with rank cowardice at having suffered the
pain of death to influence me as it had done, but still
something seemed to over-rule me and to say ' Think
what you are doing, consider and live.' At length,
however, with the most confirmed resolution, I
reached forth my hand towards the basin, when the
fingers of both hands were as closely contracted as if
bound with a cord, and became entirely useless. Still,
indeed, I could have made shift with both hands, dead
and lifeless as they were, to have raised the basin to
my mouth, for my arms were not at all affected, but this
new difficulty struck me with wonder; it had the air
of a divine interposition. I lay down in bed to muse
upon it, and while thus employed heard the key turn
in the outer door, and my laundress's husband came in.
By this time the use of my fingers was restored to me.
I started up hastily, dressed myself, hid the basin, and
affecting as composed an air as I could, walked out
into the dining-room. In a few minutes I was left
alone. The man had just shut the door behind him
when a total alteration in my sentiments took place.
The horror of the crime was immediately exhibited to
me in so strong a light that, being seized with a kind
of furious indignation, I snatched up the basin, poured
away the laudanum into a phial of foul water, and not
content with that, flung the phial out of the window.
. . . The sense of the enormity of the crime which I
had just experienced soon entirely left me."

Day dawned, chill November day ; and now there
was only one more night between Cowper and his
examination. He still meant to kill himself, for there
seemed no other way of escape. But the mental
torture which he had undergone the previous night had
left him for the moment without the power of doing
anything. His mind dazed, his nerves numb, he passed

the day in a stupor of misery. Automatically he got up, dressed himself, took his meals, went out, came in again. The sun rose, reached its zenith, declined, set: there were only twelve hours left. "That evening a most intimate friend called upon me, and felicitated me upon a happy resolution which he heard I had taken, to stand the brunt and keep the office. I knew not whence this intelligence arose, but did not contradict it. We conversed a while with a real cheerfulness on his part and an affected one on my own; and when he left me I said in my heart, ' I shall see thee no more.' I went to bed as I thought to take my last sleep in this world. I slept as usual, and woke about three o'clock. Immediately I arose and, by the help of a rush-light, found my penknife, took it into bed with me, and lay with it for some hours, directly pointed against my heart. Twice or thrice I placed it upright under my left breast, leaning all my weight upon it: but the point was broken off and would not penetrate. In this manner the time passed till the day began to break. I heard the clock strike seven, and instantly it occurred to me there was no time to be lost: the chambers would soon be opened, and my friend would call upon me to take me with him to Westminster. Now is the time, thought I, no more dallying with love of life. I arose and as I thought bolted the inner door of my chambers. I was mistaken. My touch deceived me, and I left it as I found it. Not one hesitating thought now remained, and I fell greedily to the execution of my purpose. My garter was made of a broad scarlet binding, with a sliding buckle being sewn together at the ends: by the help of the buckle I made a noose and fixed it about my neck, straining it so tight that I hardly left a passage for my breath, or for the blood to circulate. At each corner of the bed was placed a wreath of carved work, fastened by an iron pin. The other part of the garter which made a loop I slipped over one of these and hung by it some seconds, drawing up my feet under me that they might not touch the floor; but the iron bent, the carved work slipped off and the garter with it. I then fastened it round the frame of the tester, winding it round and tying it in a strong knot; the frame broke short and let me down again. The third effort was more likely to succeed. I set the door open, which reached within a foot of the ceiling, and by the help of a chair I could command the top of it, and the loop being large enough to admit a large angle of the door, was easily fixed so as not to slip off again. I pushed away the chair with my feet and hung my full length. While I hung there I distinctly heard a voice say three times, ' 'Tis over.' Though I am sure of the fact, it did not alarm me. I hung so long that I lost all sense, all consciousness of existence. When I came to myself again I thought I was in Hell: the sound of my own dreadful groans was all that I heard, and a feeling like that of flashes was just beginning to seize upon my body. In a few seconds I found myself fall over with my face to the floor." In a minute or two he rose, stumbled across the room and flung himself on the bed. He did not try to kill himself again.

Indeed, his attempt had not been very successful. It was worthy of notice that either his decision weakened just when it should have been put into effect, or when at last he was forced to take action he was unable to carry it through. In later years he put this sequence of failure down to the hand of God, Who had always intervened, as he thought, to save him from committing a mortal sin. But at the bottom his horror of death was as strong as ever, and except in moments of intensest agony, when anything seemed preferable to what he was going through, he never can really have meant to do it. There was no reason why he should not have killed himself in his chambers.

F

But his whole being revolted from the act, and he unconsciously invented some excuse so as not to have to do it. And at the last, when he finally decided on death, his hand faltered. To return to the story. The laundress had heard him fall, and now came in to see if he had been seized with a sudden fit. " I sent her to a friend, to whom I had related the whole affair, and despatched unto my kinsman at the coffee-house. As soon as the latter arrived, I pointed to the broken garter which lay in the middle of the room ; and apprized him also of the attempt I had been making. His words were, ' My dear Mr. Cowper, you terrify me. To be sure you can't hold the office at this rate. Where is the deputation ? ' I gave him the key of the drawers where it was deposited. He took it away with him, and thus ended all my connection with the Parliament house."

The fear which had tormented him since July was removed. But it had provided the single shock needed to overturn the tottering structure of his nervous system. And once it was overturned the harm was done. He was deranged ; and the removal of any extraneous cause for his mania only forced him to search for another in himself. It was not difficult to find one. As often happens after a great strain, he was seized with a violent revulsion from the act he had tried to perform. His superstitious terror, his consciousness of sin, the fear of God's wrath which had tormented him since Westminster, overwhelmed him as never before when he thought of the crime he had so nearly succeeded in committing. And the horror he felt was even more unbearable than his horror at the prospect of examination from the House of Lords. That had only made him feel that he was predestined to unhappiness in this world ; this shut him off from hope in the next as well. With every advantage of upbringing, and no real provocation, he had deliberately tried to

commit the heinous sin of self-murder, the sort of sin
he had read about in the lives of great criminals and
shuddered at when a child. Damnation, probable
before, was now certain. He was the deserving object
of God's righteous wrath, a reprobate from whom any
decent man would shrink in disgust.

He began to fancy they did. Roaming wild-eyed
about the streets, he would sometimes come across an
acquaintance, and it seemed to his suspicious eye that
he was avoiding him; or, if not, he read covert
allusions to his sin into every sentence he spoke. And
as he turned his back surely did he not hear him
break into a peal of mocking laughter. Nor was it only
his acquaintance whom he suspected. As he listened
to the ragged ballad-singers who filled the streets with
their strident shouting, he began to imagine that they,
too, were speaking of him, that his sin was the chief
among the tales of sordid crime they were crying for
sale. The whole world knew about him, the whole
world was against him, the whole world mocked him.
And he deserved every bit he got.

Sometimes he tried to distract himself by reading.
But even the voices of the dead accused him. He
opened Tillotson's Sermons, to find a reference to the
barren fig-tree. As he read it seemed to him that the
parable must have been written about him. In his
thirty-three years what had he produced but leaves—
showy, rustling leaves of good intention, but never the
fruit of works? And how had he been cursed?
Another day he picked up a volume of Beaumont and
Fletcher's plays that was lying on the window-sill.
His eyes wandered over the page and was caught by
the line:

"The justice of the gods is in it."

Surely words so applicable to his own case could not
be there by chance. No; God had damned him, and

God was announcing it to him through every one of His created works.

Brooding day after day on his past existence, gradually its purport became clear to him. Like the rest of mankind, he had been offered the choice between good and evil, between the world and God. From childhood he had chosen the world. But God, in His particular mercy, had made one last effort. He had plunged him in a melancholy when he was twenty-one, had turned his thoughts to religion, and filled him with the divine grace. After this supreme favour Cowper had, with open eyes, returned to wallowing in his mire. Now he was reaping his punishment. For the last ten years he had been increasingly anxious about his spiritual condition ; but had beaten down his fears. At last, bereft of false consolation, he saw himself as he was. His last ray of hope was dispelled by a dream. He thought he was standing in the nave of Westminster Abbey. From within the choir came the sound of the organ, and the ethereal voices of the choir-boys uplifted in a hymn. He walked up in order to join in the service. When he reached the door of the choir the iron gates were clanged in his face : and he awoke. Such a dream could only be a message of his damnation. He must drag on his life, more unbearable than physical torture, till death should consign him to an eternity compared with which all pains of present existence would seem pleasurable. Spasms of terror ran through him, so acute that sometimes he could not stand, but staggered about the room like a drunken man ; for a moment he could see nothing but darkness, and then, as it were, whorls and tongues of leaping flame.

Seated at that writing-table where in other days he had penned urbane articles for the papers, playful letters to Harriet, with trembling hand he now poured out in a strange Sapphic metre the torrent of his anguish.

" Hatred and vengeance, my eternal portion
Scarce can endure delay of execution,
Wait with impatient readiness to seize my
        Soul in a moment.

Damned below Judas ; more abhorred than he was,
Who for a few pence sold his holy Master !
Twice betrayed, Jesus me, the last delinquent,
        Deems the profanest.

Man disavows, and Deity disowns me,
Hell might afford my miseries a shelter ;
Therefore Hell keeps her ever-hungry mouths all
        Bolted against me.

Hard lot ! encompass'd with a thousand dangers ;
Weary, faint, trembling with a thousand terrors,
I'm call'd, if vanquish'd, to receive a sentence
        Worse than Abiram's.

Him the vindictive rod of angry justice
Sent quick and howling to the centre headlong ;
I, fed with judgement, in a fleshy tomb, am
        Buried above ground."

The monotonous round of his melancholy was broken into by his brother, now a Don at Cambridge, whom he had written to just after he had given up the idea of suicide. John Cowper had a family likeness to his brother. He was scholarly and good-natured and fanciful. But he was saner and sleepier, and his nerves, though not strong, were less strained. Perhaps this was owing to his profession. Anxiety is foreign to the academic life. Picture the horror of this placid Don when confronted with a brother, white-faced and wild-eyed, who before he had time to speak ushered him with twitching hands into a chair, and assured him with a flood of incoherent and unconvincing detail that he was damned. He settled in London for the time being and devoted himself to trying to cure his brother. Hour after hour he reasoned with him. It was no use arguing with a madman. Reasoning supposes a common basis of argument, and the central feature of such a madness as Cowper's is that the victim imagines that he is in a different condition from anyone else, so that no analogy from ordinary life will be true of his own. Every day his agony of mind increased. One day he found himself saying, " Evil, be thou my good." He wondered if it was his soul involuntarily declaring its true nature. He began to set himself traps to find the way it was tending. He got out of bed one night and tried to pray; but the words did not come. He tried to say the Creed to himself; but a fog seemed to descend upon his memory, and he could not get beyond the first clause. This last experience was too much for his self-control. His brother opened the door to find him stretched on the floor howling with terror. " Brother," he gasped, " think of eternity; then think what it is to be damned." John Cowper was at his wits' end as to how to reassure him. The voice of his decorous academic religion could never make itself heard amid his brother's ravings. Perhaps his cousin, Martin Madan, a member of the new Evangelical party, would do better. He distrusted what he had heard of his religion; but he felt he ought to try everything. Martin Madan arrived, seated himself at Cowper's bedside, and in a melodious voice, vibrant with an unquestioning faith, assured Cowper of his certain salvation, if he would repent. Cowper was too dazed to understand his words exactly; but the fire behind them stirred, for the first time, a movement of hope within him. " Ah," he sighed, " if I could only be sure ! "

A seed had fallen which was to bear fruit later. But for the moment his soul was too petrified with suffering to let it sink in. After Madan's visit he

relapsed into his former gloom.   Events now moved
swiftly to their climax.   " Then did the pains of Hell
get hold of me.   A numbness seized the extremities of
my body, my hands and feet became cold and ſtiff.   A
cold sweat ſtood upon my forehead.   My heart seemed
at every pulse to beat its laſt.   No convicted criminal
ever feared death more, or was more assured of dying.
When I traversed the apartment in the moſt horrible
dismay of soul, expecting every moment that the earth
would open and swallow me, my conscience scaring me,
the Avenger of Blood pursuing me, and the City of
Refuge out of reach and out of sight, a ſtrange and
horrible darkness fell upon me.   If it were possible
that a heavy blow could light on the brain without
touching the skull, such was the sensation I felt.   I
clapped my hand to my forehead and cried aloud with
the pain it gave me.   At every ſtroke my thought and
expressions became more wild and incoherent ; all that
remained clear was the sense of sin and the expectation
of punishment."   His wish of ten months back was
terribly fulfilled.   He was a gibbering, raving maniac.

The next five months passed in an incoherent agony,
firſt in London, and then in Dr. Cotton's Home for
Madmen at St. Alban's.   Harriet Hesketh came to see
him before he left the Temple ;   but he turned his
face away.   He was far paſt her homely miniſtrations
now.   Nor could the jolting journey through the lanes
of Herefordshire rouse him.   His whole mind was
dominated by the thought of his damnation : he
believed that God at any moment might ſtrike him
dead.   And, faced with such a prospect, the episodes
of outward life passed remote and unnoticed as the
noise of a diſtant ſtreet to a man working in an upper
room.   Day after day he lay upon his bed at Dr.
Cotton's, bound, for fear he should kill himself, with
the words " I am damned " repeating themselves in
his head like the insiſtent tap of a drum.   Suddenly

their full implication would flash upon him. He felt the flames licking his feet, he heard the wails of those who would be his companions for eternity. And then, the spasm past, he would fall back into a stupor, broken only by the incessant reiteration of his damnation.

The powers of Darkness had beaten him. The fragile, intricate cocoon of taste and habit that he had so vigilantly spun around himself was stripped off; Cowper, the scholar and the friend, with his intimacy and urbanity and self-restraint, was gone; and in his stead was only a poor shivering creature bereft even of reason, forcibly fed, forcibly detained, whimpering and cowering from the bogies of his imagination. But it was not the end. For there is in the human spirit an upward thrust of vitality that can only be defeated by death. Torn up by the roots, trodden underfoot, cast upon the dust-heap, the soul will yet, after a little time, again revive, and stretch its tendrils upwards, and put forth leaves to the sunlight. Cowper's spirit, so fragile, so tenacious, so bruised, so resilient, once more began to climb from the abyss into which it had fallen. But it was led by other lights than those which had played round the happiness of his earlier years. The homely serenity of normal every day had failed him : the story of his life had changed from a Trollopean comedy of domestic manners to the soul tragedy of a Dostoieffsky. And he was to rise from hell borne on the sublime ecstasies of an Alyosha Karamazof.

In the quiet of the country the fury of his despair died down, and he began to look on his future with a certain resignation. With a curious revulsion from his former self-upbraiding, he wished at moments that he had committed more sins, since, anyway, he was going to be punished everlastingly. However, his damnation did not seem likely to be immediate, so he felt that he had better make the best of what time he had left on earth. The course of his life became more normal. He began to eat and drink with appetite and to laugh at kind old Doctor Cotton's jokes. Winter softened to spring, spring glowed into summer, and in July his brother came to see how he was. At first he was disappointed. William eyed him with dejection. After an awkward pause John asked how he felt; but he only replied, " As much better as despair can make me." For the last time John burst out in protest; urged, argued, insisted that it was all a delusion. At these words William felt the heavy load that had weighed down his mind so long stir in its place. Could his brother's words be true? Was it conceivably, marvellously possible that he should yet live to look back on all that he had gone through as an unsubstantial nightmare? His returning vitality leapt out to meet the thought. " Oh," he cried, and as he spoke his breath caught in a sob of emotion, " oh, if this be a delusion, then am I the happiest of men!" And he burst into tears.

But though his brother's visit had unsealed the fountain of his hope, there was as yet no channel through which the stream might flow. He felt ready for happiness, but he had no intellectual conviction with which to justify such a feeling. As he paced the sunlit garden he trembled with expectancy; whether of joy or sorrow he could scarcely tell. But every moment, and with a growing persistence, something whispered in his heart that there was mercy for him. His spirits were further raised by a dream. He thought that a child about four years old came dancing up to his bedside, radiant and beautiful as an angel from heaven; and that at the sight of it an indescribable sense of peace and freshness stole into his heart. He awoke, but the memory of the dream had spilt a perfume of happiness over his thoughts, that lingered there all day. Like his fall, his recovery imaged itself in dreams: flowers of an imagination blossoming in sleep, or intimations from another world, who can tell?

A few days later, walking in the garden, he came upon a Bible lying on a bench. He opened it at the twelfth chapter of St. John's Gospel, and read the account of the raising of Lazarus. The beauty and pathos of the story moved him profoundly. Could there be any bottom to the depths of a compassion that was able to vanquish death itself? Might it not extend even to him? Within a few hours he received his answer.

" Having risen with somewhat of a more cheerful feeling, I repaired to my room, where breakfast waited for me. While I sat at table I found the cloud of horror which had so long hung over me was every moment passing away. I flung myself into a chair near the window, and seeing a Bible there, ventured once more to apply to it for comfort and instruction. The first verse I saw was the 25th of the III Romans, ' Whom God hath set forth to be a propitiation through faith in his blood, to declare his righteousness for the remission of sins that are passed through the forbearance of God.' Immediately I received strength to believe it, and the full beams of the Sun's righteousness shone upon me. I saw the sufficiency of the Atonement he had made, my pardon sealed in his blood, and all the fulness and completeness of his justification. In a moment I believed and received the Gospel. Whatever my friend Madan had said to me long before revived in all its clearness the demonstration of the spirit and with power. Unless the Almighty arms had been under me I think I should have died of gratitude and joy. My eyes filled with tears, and my voice choked with transport, and I could only look up to heaven in silent fear, overwhelmed with love and wonder."

The fears and pains of his troubled thirty years had

fallen off him like rags. Sin and sorrow and dis-
illusion, madness itself, were nothing and less than
nothing in the transcendent glory of his spiritual
reconciliation. But the supreme moments of religious
ecstasy, like the supreme moments of æsthetic experience, are not to be expressed in words. Dante
measured hell and purgatory, described their smallest
detail with a meticulous exactitude; but when he
reached the final circle of Paradise, and was face to face
with that Divine Spirit by Whose Will the whole
huge system lived and moved and had its being, he was
conscious only of a blinding light.

CHAPTER III

THE EVANGELICAL PHASE

THE Evangelical movement ſtands out in violent con-
traſt to the prevailing thought of its time—a black,
melodramatic silhouette againſt the precise, freshly-
hued colour print of eighteenth-century England.
Where the prevailing thought believed that religious
feeling should be disciplined by common sense or
refined by sensibility, it believed that only at its raweſt
and moſt violent was it sincere.   Where the prevailing
aim was to develop you on every side, the Evangelical
said that all aĉtivities not direĉtly conneĉted with
religion should be shunned.   Where the prevailing
theological opinion emphasized the moral aspeĉts of
religion, the Evangelical rejeĉted these as worthless
except in so far as they were signs of a healthy spiritual
condition.   For, excluded from other syſtems of
thought, there poured into the narrow channel of
Evangelicalism all the myſtical and transcendental
emotion of the period.

In its early decades, the Church, tired with two
centuries of religious ſtrife, had fallen into a polite
lethargy.   Its faults can be, and have been, exaggerated.   It was learned, rational and dignified.   It did
not, as in earlier times, occupy itself with persecution,
nor, as in modern times, with hyſterical bickering over
trivialities of form and ceremonial.   But it removed
religion from common life : it did not touch the heart,
nor gratify the longings of the soul to penetrate
beyond the veil of its mortality.   Mankind, however,

a stranger on the earth, bears these longings within him, an integral part of his nature; and if the religious system in which he is educated does not cater for them, he will change it for one that does. Unsatisfied by Bishop Berkeley on the one hand and Parson Adams on the other, the spiritually-minded person turned to Wesley and Whitefield. Their movement started about 1730. Most of its early work was done among the very poor, and took the form of revivalism, with its accompanying faults of theatrical emotionalism. The Church at first looked askance at it; and its first founders broke with the Church. But the fire of their spirit gradually permeated all the religious life of the time : it took firm hold of the middle classes, and penetrated up into the aristocracy. The more distressing eccentricities of the early movement were removed, and by the second half of the century Methodism, pruned, tamed and polished into Evangelicalism, was the animating force behind the most active, if not the most numerous, party in the Church of England.

Their religion was an exclusively emotional one. The movement really came from a sense that the good life is not merely the fulfilling of an ethical code; but the achievement of a state of mind, that is at its highest a state of religious ecstasy. And they therefore evolved a theological system according to which the achievement of this ecstasy was the only aim of religion. Mankind, they held, has by its own act become utterly depraved, incapable of a good action or even of a good intention. The laws of Divine justice demanded that it should be punished for its wickedness. But God, by an act of ineffable love, had Himself borne this punishment in the person of His Son, so that now the only thing necessary for a man to be saved was that he should fully realize this—should, in their phrase, "lay hold of his salvation" and be "converted."

And they identified this consciousness of conversion with the supreme moment of religious ecstasy. This consciousness was the sole test of religious life. If you had it, you were saved; but without it a life spent in good acts was of no avail. For any act must necessarily be that of a child of sin, and therefore evil. Such a view of life, logically pursued in practice, would lead man to do nothing but sit and wait for Heaven to convert him. But the Evangelicals were no more logical than other fatalists. And the end of all their teaching was that man must make it the object of every act and thought to attain conversion, to enter into that small band whom the Divine love has snatched from the eternal misery which they deserve.

It is not hard to foresee how such a creed would apply itself in practice. Your whole energy is concentrated on achieving the state of grace, and maintaining yourself in it when you have got there. In so far as it helps you to do this, an activity is good, and should be encouraged; in so far as it does not, it is bad and must be avoided. For, as one of their leading divines put it, " A man only stays in the world to do the work of his Creator, as he might stay out in the rain to deliver an important message." The pleasures of the world are particularly to be shunned; for, by presenting you with the image of false good, they distract you from following the true. Nor were learning and reason much better. They were as much within the capacity of a child of wrath as of a child of grace; and encouraged man to forget his incompetence. To the afflictions of life, on the other hand, the Evangelicals had less objection. For these discouraged man from looking for happiness in this world. While death itself, the final disaster, was to them the highest blessing; for it took you out of the world altogether. Such worldly activities as he must take part in should be made as far as possible to serve some religious purpose, and so preserved from that taint of sin which is inherent in their nature. If you wrote a letter or paid a call or read a book, you should do so in such a manner as might lead other people to grace.

The form of this creed derived directly from sixteenth-century Calvinism. Indeed, the renunciation of the world under the impulse of religious experience is behind all ascetic religions. But such an impulse generally expresses itself in a corporate organization. The believers band themselves together to abandon the normal way of life in order the better to do the work commanded them by God. But the structure of society was too generally accepted in the early eighteenth century for people to contemplate any corporate break with it. So, in consequence, all this volume of lyrical emotion, this fear of hell, this shuddering horror of sin, this faith that would remove mountains, expressed itself not in a Thebaid or a Covenant or a Crusade, but in the ordinary affairs of conventional life. Instead of commanding their followers to forsake their family and their business, and to follow the Cross throughout the world, the Evangelical preachers had to assure them that family life and business, carried on in the right spirit, could be the life of the Cross.

In this incongruous contrast between its motive impulse and the mode of its expression lies the distinguishing characteristic of eighteenth-century Evangelicalism. In every class of society, in every walk of life, little centres grew up: domestic monasteries, homely outposts of salvation. In nearly every country village there was one family who had prayers morning and evening and went to church three times on Sunday; who read nothing but the Bible and the works of a few " experiential " divines, never wore bright colours, and modelled their conversation on the precepts of some preacher, Mr. Venn or Mr. Romaine, whom they had once " sat under "; who collected money for foreign missions and distributed tracts; who would hardly move out of the house on Sunday and would not dance or play cards on any day of the week at all. In regiment and on battleship, among the Hogarthian naval and military society of the day, the jolly, brutal Commodore Trunnions and Captain Plumes, with their carbuncled faces and brazen voices, their swearing and wenching and drinking, would suddenly appear a man, like one of Cromwell's Ironsides risen from the grave, who never swore or got drunk, who read prayers to his men, and who spent such time as he could spare from the stern performance of his duties in religious meditation. An uneducated serving-boy would be moved by the Spirit and, to the irritation of his employers, hold prayer-meetings for his fellow-servants, like Humphrey Clinker. A peer of the realm, like Lord Dartmouth, would withdraw from rout and racecourse and dedicate himself to the fulfilment of his more serious obligations under the guidance of a " faithful " chaplain. The mixture of religious and conventional life extended itself to the way in which the Evangelicals expressed themselves. In their hymns the mysterious doctrines of atonement and redemption are incongruously packed into the mild dactylic metres of eighteenth-century pastoral and set to the matter-of-fact melodies of eighteenth-century ballads. Their preachers, in well-brushed wig and Geneva gown, would discourse to a respectable London congregation on the wickedness of Sunday travel, in the bloodstained imagery originally used by some half-naked prophet to an Oriental tribe among the precipitous cliffs of a Syrian desert.

This combination of the religious and the conventional had its defects. For one thing it made practice often inconsistent with precept. The austere tenets of Calvinism had to be considerably modified

to suit eighteenth-century custom; the rude " Gothic "
canvas had to be cut down before it fitted the neat
Adams panel. The middle-class Evangelical could
not feel it wrong to make money, however little one
should enjoy it when it was made; and he would spend
Sunday in proclaiming the vanity of earthly riches, and
weekdays in amassing as much of them as he could.
Nor could he allow his conviction of man's equality
in sin to imperil the social order. If he and his wife
confessed their abject unworthiness to receive earthly
honours, they did it from a cushioned pew in the front
of the church, while the cook and the foot-boy repeated
the same sentiments from a convenient bench at the
back. These were not the only defects of Evangelicalism. Its repudiation of the world cut it off from the
whole sphere of æsthetic achievement. Other religions
have bequeathed us cathedrals; Methodism only
yellow-brick Little Bethels. Its doctrine of conversion
tended to arrogance. Those who considered themselves converted became too familiar with God, too
contemptuous of man. And its emphasis on the
emotional side of religion often led to false emotionalism; hot-house fruits of the spirit, unctuous soul-
confessions, luscious mechanical ecstasies.

And of course the Evangelicals were often highly
ridiculous. They had rejected reason, and reason
soon rejected them. The Rev. Alfred Hutchinson, a
respectable divine, carried his belief in verbal inspiration so far as to hold that Hebrew alone of human
languages had the syntax and grammar competent to
express the mind of God, and that all the possible
discoveries of physical science, mysteriously evaporated
in the process of translation, could be found in the
Bible if read in its original tongue. The Evangelicals
could discern a special providence in the most trivial
occasions. If a man fell into a puddle, it was because
God was chastening him; if he avoided falling in,

G

because God had given His angels special charge over him. Their language is as absurd as their thought. Elderly clerics write to young ladies to urge them not to use rouge, in a style which combines, but which does not unite, those of Jeremiah and the polite letter-writer. Middle-aged women paint their feelings on meeting a favourite preacher in the voluptuous imagery of the Song of Solomon. The world of *Tom Jones* is not most happily described in the language of the book of Job. Elijah among the teacups cannot fail to be a comic figure.

Yet in spite of its defects, its absurdities, one cannot refuse the Evangelicals one's admiration. For they imposed a moral order on life. Ignorance and fanaticism made it an imperfect order; but it was none the less an order. And to those who believed in it the happenings of daily life were no longer isolated and purposeless trifles, but integral parts of the great structure of existence—a structure which, with all its limitations, was centred around the profoundest elements of man's nature. It alone among the philosophies of its time took account of man's spiritual side, wove into the tapestry of his ordinary life his visions, his enthusiasms, his exaltations, faced and tried to explain the mystery of his existence, the omnipresence of evil, the inevitability of death. The merchant in the counting-house, the spinner in the factory, the old maid in the village, all felt themselves actors in the great drama of mankind's salvation. Revealed against this tremendous background, their lives assumed heroic proportions. What did the trivialities of mere outward circumstances matter? Their friends were exultations, agonies and love and man's unconquerable mind. And the compelling power of their faith was shown by their actions. It was they who purified the morals of English society, who founded modern philanthropy, who stopped the slave trade. Nor could any creed

less passionately exclusive have so effectively inspired
them.   You must look only to the Cross to be a
successful crusader.

Finally Evangelicalism—and in this also it was
unique among the philosophies of its day—could
satisfy the temperament of the artist.   For it alone set
a supreme value on that emotional exaltation in which
the greatest art is produced, it alone made the imagination the centre of its system, and not a mere decorative
appendage to it.   An attitude of civilized disillusionment is all very well in its way, but it is not conducive to
creative art.   Wesley could have understood Dante as
Voltaire or even Dr. Johnson could never have done.
The Evangelicals may have disliked poetry, but their
sublime conception of the universal plan is the most
imaginative poem of its day.

Surging and swirling, flowed on the vari-coloured
stream of eighteenth-century life.   People were born
and grew up ; made money or lost it ; were serious,
were frivolous ; yielded to a good impulse, yielded to
a bad one ; had moments of ecstasy and forgot them ;
made resolutions and failed to keep them ; married
and grew old and died—their life an incoherent tangle
of hopes and fears, desires and inhibitions, aspirations
and apathies ; heterogeneous, hand-to-mouth, without
order or sequence.   But through it moved a small
band of people for whom the whole multifarious complex was resolved into a single and majestic action—
that conflict which, as long as life lasts, the children of
light must wage with the Prince of the power of the
air.   They were sometimes feeble and sometimes
erring, for they were mortal ; but they never faltered
in their effort to measure their every word and act by
the highest standard they knew.   They did what they
thought right whatever trouble it got them into, and
whatever pleasure it deprived them of.   Indeed, the
ephemeral joys and sorrows of the world meant little

to them. On their brows lay the shadow of the wings of death, and in their ears chimed ever the bells of Paradise.

It was among this band of people that the next eight years of Cowper's life were passed. Their world was a very different one from that of his youth—mildly interested in everything, enthusiastically interested in nothing. But Cowper was a different man. At the outset of his life his nervous system had been infected with a deadly poison. He had tried to expel it by throwing himself into the life around him, trying to identify himself with its interests, its pleasures and its difficulties. The struggle had been long, but in the end he succumbed. After two years his natural vitality re-asserted itself and he recovered; but the interests of his old life had lost all value in his eyes. Society, family life, scholarship, public affairs—they had been weighed and found wanting. Indeed, they were inextricably mixed in his mind with failure and diaster. His returning energy rejected them and turned elsewhere to find a worthy object for existence—turned to religion. He had always had leanings that way. From childhood his fundamental conception of life had been a religious one. The very nervous diseases which had sent him mad had taken the form in his mind of a conviction of damnation; and his rare moments of religious emotion had been the only moments of his life when he was completely free from nervous terror. It is true he had sought consolation from religion without success; yet even when he had felt such consolation furthest from him he had never lost the conviction that it was the highest good, were it possible to achieve it. Now, after his crucifixion of the last ten months, it remained the only good of his early life that had not been spoilt. All other things on which he had set his heart had proved powerless to protect him against the onslaught of his secret enemy.

His spirit, filled to overflowing with the gratitude and delight of recovery, saw in religion, and in religion alone, the worthy object on which to pour itself out. And the returning tide of his health, the tremendous reaction of joy after the anguish of the last three years, all the vigour of his restored mind and body, gushed in one irresistible torrent down this single channel. Under its pressure his imaginative life rose to a pitch of intensity never touched before. At last the earthy curtains through which elusive gleams of Paradise had penetrated to him were torn down, and he stood forth in the full blaze of the mystic vision.

He must never lose it again : his whole life must be dedicated to its preservation. As people always do under the stress of strong religious impulse, he longed to incarnate his ecstasy, to find some tabulated pro-gramme of beliefs and duties, some rule and ritual of daily life in which it could have permanent, practical expression. He was a convert, but he needed a Church. It was this need that led him to the Evan-gelicals. He was not likely to be satisfied with the religion of his childhood. He wanted a new form in which to express a new emotion; and the only new religious form accessible at St. Albans in 1765 was Evangelicalism. It was peculiarly accessible to Cow-per, because Dr. Cotton was an Evangelical, and only too willing to encourage a tendency towards the truth in anyone else. But Cowper needed no encourage-ment. The Evangelical creed might well seem created to suit his particular case. It explained his difficulties so exactly, so perfectly enshrined his aspirations. He knew, none better, the inefficacy of works. For thirty years he had lived a moral and respectable life. Yet he had never known a moment's real peace of mind ; and when the powers of evil had attacked him, he had succumbed with hardly a show of

resistance. He realized man's inability to save his
own soul. Had not the Divine Grace shone forth on
him long after he had ceased to struggle against evil,
and was lying bereft even of reason ? He knew that
faith alone justified. The faith inspired by his moment
of vision had raised him to a level of spiritual exaltation,
that all the vigilant virtue of his youth had never
brought him within sight of. In the light of the
Evangelical creed, the wretched tangle of his life-
history fell into a simple beneficent order—the plan
by which an all-wise and all-loving God had reclaimed
a soul stubborn to seek its own destruction. He had
been born a child of wrath, incapable of a good thought
or a good deed, predestined to damnation. Once or
twice God had let fall a ray of His grace upon him, but,
seduced by the pleasures of the world, he had shut his
eyes. On the threshold therefore of his manhood
God had plunged him into a melancholia, had overwhelmed him with spiritual fears ; and then, as
suddenly, had removed them and filled him with
spiritual happiness. But again he had neglected His
message. Then indeed God, determined to save him
in his own despite, had turned to stronger measures.
Gradually He removed from his life all that might
distract Cowper's soul from the love of Him ; He
deprived him of his love, friends and family. But just
when Cowper, maddened by misfortune, was about to
decide his damnation by committing the frightful sin
of self-murder, God miraculously rescued him, showed
him to himself as the vile creature he really was, and
revealed the hell that was in store for him if he proceeded
in his evil doings. Finally, when he was still trembling
under this newly-found consciousness of sin, He turned
the full light of His grace upon him. He saw it and
was converted.

Seen from this angle, those evils for which he had
thought his life was singled out from the rest of man-

kind ceased to appear evil, or vanished altogether. If he was weak and contemptible, a puppet in the hands of a higher power, so was every other created being. And that higher power was no inexorable, malevolent deity, but a loving and omnipotent Father. Again, happiness was no longer a transitory and precarious condition. His present happiness arose from the fact that he had at last " laid hold of his salvation," and the state of his salvation was of its nature eternal. He was in the hands of God, and no torments could touch him ever any more.

Nor did the ascetic side of Evangelicalism put him off. The pleasures of the world held no attraction for him ; and the very idea that they might distract him from the right way was enough to make him give them up. But he had no fears that he would ever be so distracted. He, nervous, apprehensive William Cowper, whose whole existence had been dominated by the desire to avoid real or imagined danger, could now turn and look at life and see only good. No wonder he wished to consecrate his whole life to the God who had so wonderfully blessed him. The span of man's existence seemed all too short to express his joy and gratitude. His ordinary mental condition for months on end was a pitch of ecstasy such as most men experience once or twice in their lives for a single moment. He seemed to live his life to a sound of celestial music, to get up and go to bed, to work and eat and sleep, to the accompaniment of an unseen orchestra of flutes and shawms and violins. Summer bloomed in his heart as it bloomed in the garden outside. · Up in the trees the birds were singing, and in his thoughts too the birds of happiness sang and soared and clapped their wings of silver and gold. Every word he spoke, every letter he wrote, was breathless with ecstasy. Lyrically, incoherently, garrulously, he proclaimed and re-proclaimed the glory of his redemption. The quiet Hertfordshire garden used to ring with his rhapsodies.   They could not command an adequate audience —it was confined generally to Sam, the kind, solid servant who had nursed him through his illness, the cobbler's boy Dick Colman, an open-mouthed urchin of seven years old, and Dr. Cotton himself. Poor Dr. Cotton! He sometimes wondered if Cowper saved was much saner than Cowper damned. He was certainly quite as great a strain to talk to. However, Dr. Cotton was an Evangelical, and accustomed to such ordeals, and he strove to calm his patient by giving him a book to read called *Meditations among the Tombs*.

So passed a year.   In May 1765 Cowper was ready to leave St. Albans.   But where was he to go ? His friends lived mostly in London, but London he held in horror—it was connected indissolubly with his miserable past. It was there he had fallen away in 1753; and there he had passed through his most frightful agony. He wanted to shut the door on his past altogether and settle in some secluded spot where, undisturbed by painful memories and unseduced by worldly pleasures, he could devote himself to religious contemplation.   It was exactly the same impulse as makes people go into monasteries. But Cowper's religion provided no monasteries. However, an unofficial hermitage in some country place would do as well.   He had always turned for happiness to the country, to rural sights and sounds and silence; and such a change would most effectively cut him off from his old life.

In nothing has English life changed more since 1765 than in the relative positions of town and country. Before the day of trains and motors and newspapers and wireless, country people lived in a different world from townspeople, a world that did not centre round London at all. They got up at a different time, dined at a different time, did not try to follow town fashions. They only heard such news of London as could be gleaned from a fortnight-old *St. James's Gazette* lent them by the squire. Their very speech was different. Old comedy is full of loutish country squires, Sir Wilful Witwould and Sir Tunbelly Clumsy, who arrive in town to find themselves the butts of the wits for their queer clothes and queerer accents and their ignorance of the outstanding events of the day. And country districts were as remote from each other as from London. To go to live in a different part of the country was like going to live abroad to-day. You had to learn to order your life according to new customs, to call common objects by new names. Nor could you hold much communication with the place you had left when it was distant two or three days' journey in a creaking, stuffy coach over a road like a cart-track, and it cost five shillings to send a letter. Near relations lived within twenty miles of each other without meeting for ten years. Cowper's decision to live in the country meant that he was only likely to see the friends of his youth once or twice again before he died. It was a fitting symbol that he had begun life anew.

His relations, however, did not want him to go beyond all reach of help. In the end it was decided that he should settle, for the time being at any rate, somewhere near Cambridge, so that his brother could keep an eye on him. The nearest place in which his brother could find the cheap, quiet lodgings required was Huntingdon. It was over fifteen miles from Cambridge—too far for John Cowper to see William very often—but to William in his present conditio solitude meant only more time to be alone with God.

> " Far from the world, O Lord, I flee," he sang,
> " From strife and tumult far ;
> From scenes where Satan wages still
> His most successful war.

> The calm retreat, the silent shade,
>   With prayer and praise agree;
> And seem, by Thy sweet bounty made,
>   For those who follow Thee.
>
> There if Thy Spirit touch the soul,
>   And grace her mean abode,
> O with what peace, and joy, and love,
>   She communes with her God!
>
> There like the nightingale she pours
>   Her solitary lays;
> Nor asks a witness of her song,
>   Nor thirsts for human praise."

The lodgings were engaged, and on June 17, 1765, he started for Cambridge, where he was to spend a night on the way. He could not forbear a tremor as he got into the coach. For two years he had been virtually out of the world; and now, at his first encounter with it, his natural timidity swept irresistibly over him. Perhaps someone would blaspheme against the God whom he served: and then, fearful thought, it would be his duty to reprove them. Fortunately the coach travelled all the way from St. Albans to Cambridge without a single oath passing anyone's lips. He sat up late that night with his brother, pouring forth the story of his conversion, and exhorting him, in a trembling voice, to follow his example. John Cowper felt embarrassed. His religion was a mild, cultured affair with leanings towards Unitarianism; and he, like Dr. Cotton, thought Cowper's apocalyptic rejoicings only less insane than his apocalyptic despair. On the other hand, he did not wish to hurt his feelings by speaking against something which had made his brother so happy. He made a few tentative objections, and finally tried to close the discussion by saying that he was sure that at bottom they meant the same thing. William Cowper did not think so at all. He had been talking for hours in order to prove exactly the reverse.

He relapsed into a disappointed silence, only comforting himself with the hope that for some good purpose his brother's conversion was being delayed till a later time. Four days later he left Cambridge and drove over to Huntingdon. At first he could not restrain a slight feeling of depression. It was all very well to praise solitude at Dr. Cotton's, with kind faces and kind voices within call whenever he should need them; but sitting in his poky little lodgings in a completely strange town he could not help feeling rather lonely. There was not a soul he could talk to within miles. And he was so shy of making new friends. However, the fire of his faith was not so easily extinguished. "I walked forth toward the close of day," he wrote, " in this melancholy frame of mind, and having wandered about a mile from the town, I found my heart at length so powerfully drawn towards the Lord that, having gained a retired and secret nook in the corner of a field, I kneeled down under a bank and poured forth my complaints before Him. It pleased my Saviour to hear me in that this my depression was taken off and I was enabled to trust in Him." On the following day he was confirmed in this quickening of the spirit. It was Sunday; and for the first time since his illness he went to church. The dignified ceremonial, the stately English of the prayers, the music, the building, above all the unaccustomed sense of corporate worship, profoundly stirred a spirit ever open to aesthetic impression. The lesson was the beautiful story of the Prodigal Son. To Cowper it seemed a parable of his own life; as he listened to it his soul was again filled with some of the ecstasy of the moment of conversion. He could hardly restrain his tears; his heart leapt out in love to the people round him; especially, as he naïvely puts it, to those in whom he observed " an air of sober attention." He gazed at a gentleman singing psalms in

his pew, blessed him in his heart and blessed him
again. How foolish had been his despondency!
Had it not always been the triumphant boaſt of
his faith that it could uphold and console him in any
circumſtances? And had not this, his firſt solitary
adventure into the world, proved this boaſt abundantly
juſtified?

However, as the weeks passed he found he did not
have to rely solely on spiritual compensation for his
loneliness. Life at Huntingdon possessed more
mundane sources of comfort. For one thing there
were the pleasures of Nature. He did not, indeed,
admire the country : nothing could be further from the
bosky groves and smiling glades which were what the
eighteenth century meant by beautiful scenery than
the fens, that ſtrange no man's land between earth and
sea, but more like the sea, as it ſtretched, level and bare,
into the diſtance, with here and there a church ſticking
up from it like a ship, and over all the vaſt, varying
sky ; now gleaming blue, now hidden by driving rain,
now troubled with moving masses of cloud ; by night
swarming with ſtars, tragic in the red light of the
setting sun. Cowper told Lady Hesketh it was
merely " flat and insipid." He could not feel in it
that sense of space and wind and lonely freedom which
it shares with other flat landscape, Holland and
Romney Marsh ; which blows so poignantly from the
canvases of those painters of Norwich who depiĉted
it forty years later. But any country was better than
no country ; and he enjoyed bathing in the River Ouse
and wandering along among the blue willows on its
banks. Not that he was always alone, either. He
made some acquaintances : two clergymen, Mr.
Hodson and Mr. Nicholson, who, if not Evangelical,
were at leaſt unworldly ; and Mr. Pemberton, the
woollen draper, who was so kind as to offer to lend him
St. James's Gazette. And once a week, mounted on

the back of a horse, he clattered off to Cambridge to
see John.

Still, it became clear that such a mode of existence
could only be temporary. From a purely practical
point of view Cowper was incapable of managing for
himself. Buying meat, for instance, was a terrible
problem. First he bought a leg of lamb, and that was
too much ; then a sheep's heart, and that was too little ;
then he fell back on liver, but that soon began to pall.
" I never knew how to pity poor housekeepers before,"
he writes pathetically, " but now I cease to wonder at
that politic cast which their occupation usually gives
to their countenance ; for it really is a matter full of
perplexity." You have to eat even if you are saved.
And the worst of the whole affair was that within four
months he had spent a year's income.

But over and above all this, he felt the mental strain.
Nothing is more wearing than living alone. The
ordinary mould of social habit and custom by which
life is directed and regulated in any corporate form of
existence is removed. You go out when you like, and
work when you like, and go to bed when you like. All
the thousand trifling acts of daily life become the
subjects of decision ; and making a decision is the most
tiring thing in the world. It was especially tiring
to someone like Cowper, who all his life had liked
something to lean on. His very dislike of meeting
strangers arose in great part from the fact that such
meetings involved his taking the social initiative. The
only mode of life that exactly suited him, the only mode
of life that had ever exactly suited him, was family life ;
it provided the quiet social circle he liked, and in it all
the practical side of life was managed for him. But it
was hard to get what he wanted. The obvious way to
get family life is to marry and have a family of your
own ; but Cowper in his present state of mind had no
thoughts of marriage. It would have to be someone

else's family, and, if he was to be really happy, one that would sympathize with his religious views. What he needed was a family of pleasant, cultivated Evangelicals who would be willing to take a strange young man just out of an asylum and with hardly any money to live with them indefinitely. It seemed an unlikely thing to find; but for once in his life Cowper was lucky. He found it at Huntingdon.

One September morning as he was taking the air under the trees after church, he was accosted by a young man, who said that his name was Unwin, and that he had often wanted to speak to Cowper before, but that he had felt too shy, as he had heard that he avoided new acquaintances. Cowper liked the look of him. He had a bright, open, friendly countenance and a forthcoming manner; and Cowper asked him to tea. The meal confirmed his good impression. His new friend was everything he liked best—intelligent, full of youthful spirits, simple, unassuming, and, best of all, a strong Evangelical. Within a short time he had told Cowper all about himself—how his father was a clergyman, and how he was going to be a clergyman too; that he was working at Cambridge, but was living in Huntingdon with his father, mother and sister. On his departure Cowper flung himself on his knees, to ask a blessing on this friendship from the God to whom he had vowed to consecrate all his activities.

Next day he returned Unwin's call, and found the rest of the family as delightful as himself. On arriving he found himself in the little parlour with the daughter. He had never seen her before; but she began conversation in such a friendly, quiet way that soon he felt quite at his ease. The father was a scholarly old parson, " as simple as Parson Adams "; while the mother, much younger than her husband—in fact only eight or nine years older than Cowper—struck him as having " uncommon understanding, and more polite

than a duchess." He enjoyed his visit immensely.
He sincerely hoped he would see more of the Unwins.
He did not know that his connection with them would
only be severed by death.

The Unwins were as pleased with Cowper as he
with them. They had originally moved from Grimston
and come to live in Huntingdon because Mrs. Unwin
wanted better company than the sequestered position of
Grimston afforded. Huntingdon had not proved very
fruitful of good company. The people there were
either stupid or too worldly in their interests for the
Evangelical Unwins; and these soon found themselves as much alone as they had been at Grimston.
Imagine their delight on meeting a young man, clever,
educated, with the most charming manners, and even
more Evangelical than themselves. With such goodwill on both sides the acquaintance could not fail to
ripen quickly into friendship. The Unwins asked
him to come whenever he liked. He was shy at first;
but they were so friendly, and he was so solitary, that
they did not have much difficulty in winning him over.
And soon he spent the best part of every day with
them. " Go when I will," he writes, " I find a house
filled with peace and cordiality in all its parts. I am
sure to hear no scandal, but such discourse as we are all
better for. You remember Rousseau's description of
an English morning—such are the mornings I spend
with these good people. The evenings differ from
them in nothing except that they are still more snug and
quieter. Now I know them, I wonder I liked Huntingdon so well, and am apt to think I should find any place
disagreeable which had not an Unwin belonging to it."

For life at the Unwins' satisfied his desires as no
other could have done. It combined the two things
which in his chequered thirty-three years really won
his affection—family life and the Evangelical faith.
From the very first meeting, the Unwins had looked on

him as a relation, and had not, in the manner of their time, treated all his visits as ceremonious occasions, but admitted him to share in their ordinary occupations and conversations as if he were a brother. And he enjoyed with them all the intimacy, the companionship, the cosy fireside fun, the sense of communal cousinly work and play that he had hankered after ever since his mother's death, and that he had tasted for a little with his uncle's family in Southampton Row. But here was Southampton Row purified from all taint of the world, and sanctified by that faith which since St. Alban's had been the lodestar of his life. Life at the Unwins' was dedicated to religion. All their employments, their conversations, their reading, their music were religious. Cowper felt he had forsaken the world to follow the Lord, and now the Lord had rewarded him by giving him back all that had made the world attractive. The roomy, red-brick house, with its rambling garden with the pear tree in it, seemed a sort of earthly paradise to him, in which Mrs. Unwin sat enthroned—the patron saint.

Gradually, as the weeks went by, she began to stand out from the others. All that he loved in the Unwin household tended to identify itself with her. As the weeks went by her name appeared in his correspondence with growing frequency. Suddenly at the end of a letter to Joseph Hill about something quite different, he would add as a postscript : " And I know no one as like Mrs. Unwin as my Aunt Madan—I do not mean in person, but in character." And again, to Lady Hesketh : " I met Mrs. Unwin in the street and went home with her. She and I walked together nearly two hours in the garden, and I had a conversation which did me more good than I should have received from an audience with the first prince in Europe. That woman is a blessing to me, and I feel every time I see her as being the better for her company." The rest of the family began to recede into the background. Old Mr. Unwin, indeed, was rather out of the Evangelical picture. He belonged to a less zealous type of eighteenth-century clergyman. Polite and scholarly, he doubted the divinity of Christ, and was incurably idle in the performance of his duties. Grimston was not a large parish, but he seems to have christened, married or buried hardly anyone in it. At Huntingdon his duties were even lighter; but there he never performed them at all. His unfortunate parishioners censured him frequently, and even threatened to expel him; in vain. As he began to know him better, Cowper could not reconcile his conscience with whole-hearted approval of Mr. Unwin. Miss Unwin, too, ceased to occupy much of Cowper's attention after their first interview. He noticed that she was bashful and unwilling to speak when her mother was there. Perhaps she alone of the family did not altogether like the new visitor. For charming, ardent William Unwin, Cowper's affection showed no signs of waning. But he was only twenty-one, and he was not a woman. Cowper's most intimate friends were always women; for they alone could give that particular moral support of interest and sympathy which he most wanted in a friend. As a child he had leaned on his mother; as a youth on his cousins; and now, as a mature man, worn with suffering and ecstasy, he turned to Mrs. Unwin.

She was peculiarly fitted to bear the weight. Like the life of which she was the centre, she gave him all he had loved in his old existence, with additional qualities it could not provide. Beside Harriet and Theodora she would, it is true, have seemed a little provincial. Her manners had a country stiffness. Her talk was sprinkled with the curious Biblical phraseology of Evangelicalism. " The Lord Jehovah will be alone exalted when the day of his deliverance comes," she writes of Cowper when he was not

H

well.   But she was not unsocial—had she not come to
Huntingdon for company ?—she had humour, though
of the kind that sees rather than makes jokes ; and she
was well read in a serious Evangelical sort of way.
Her distinguishing qualities, however, were to be found
not in her mind or in her manners, but in her character.

It was simple, its interest centring exclusively round
two objects—the religious and the personal.   And it
was strong, but with a feminine strength, instinctive,
passive, tenacious.   In religion she was a disciple, not
a leader ; and in the outward ordering of her personal
life she was chiefly concerned to carry out the wishes
of those she cared for.   But within her own sphere
she acted with the unhurried confidence of supreme
determination.   She never analyzed her feelings or
questioned her beliefs ; she thought some things right
and did them, and some things wrong and did not do
them.   If by chance she erred, she made no excuses
for herself, but wasted no time in useless self-upbraiding.
Her personal feelings were of a piece with the rest
of her—strong but not violent, deep but not overflowing.   She was not given to outbursts of emotional
feeling ; but when she did give her heart, it was
absolutely and for ever.   There was no sacrifice she
would not make for someone she loved.   Yet even in
regard to them she adhered rigidly to her simple code of
right and wrong.   She would not allow her affection
to blind her to their faults ; nor would she tell them she
approved of them when she did not, for fear of hurting
their feelings.   She was at one with herself ; and from
this her personality drew a calm force which differentiated it from that of the ordinary pious domestic woman.
Even now, from the dingy, ill-drawn engraving which
is all the portrait we have of her, her eyes gaze out
beneath her clear forehead with a serene, direct,
sensible expression that soothes us, as it soothed Cowper
long ago.

It was no wonder he liked her. For she supplied all the qualities he lacked. He did not mind if she was limited, unsubtle, without ideas of her own. He wanted not guidance, but support; and support was just what she was fitted to give. Strength and sanity and repose were the qualities he always liked in a friend; but he generally found them only in people who thought his religion queer. She believed all the same things as he believed, but with a contented, equable confidence quite beyond his compass. He was certain that whatever doubts and terrors, " flaws and starts, impostors to true fear," he might feel, however much his mood might vary between unreasonable exaltation and unreasonable despair, she would always be the same —firm and safe and sure; that when he came into her room trembling from some qualm of conscience, some horrid vision of the night, she would turn untroubled eyes upon him, lay aside her work, and in quiet tones and unexaggerated terms affirm those consoling truths he was longing to hear. And he would be reassured.

Their intimacy increased all the quicker on account of its peculiar circumstances. Mrs. Unwin's position as the centre of a grown-up family had presented her to Cowper in a maternal light. It was part of her attraction to one who, ever since he was six years old, had felt the need of a mother so keenly. And of course it removed any embarrassment he might naturally have felt at becoming so intimate with a strange woman. But, in fact, she was almost the same age as himself; so that he enjoyed in her company all the understanding and sense of sympathetic equality that one only gets from a contemporary. She was, in fact, Theodora and Harriet and his mother all in one. He supplied her needs as she supplied his. She was still a comparatively young woman, but her husband was old and her children were grown up. Her life was empty: it lacked object, interest, occupation. And she had no one to guide her in that Evangelical faith which was beginning to play such a large part in her life. In Cowper she found someone who needed her and who could act as her spiritual director. And the drab, provincial society in which she had hitherto lived laid her peculiarly open to the charm he always had for women.

After he had known the Unwins three months, he went to live with them. Ever since he had met them, his dislike of living alone had returned with a redoubled strength. How could he persuade himself he enjoyed it when he had the pleasures of family life every day before his eyes? One day it crossed his mind that the Unwins might take him in as a lodger. He tried to put the idea out of his thoughts. He felt it the work of the flesh trying to mould his life according to its selfish desires; and was it not his creed to purge himself of all selfish desire, and accept whatever fate God might choose for him? But he could not silence his longings; and try as he might he thought of little else for three days. By the end of the third he had succeeded in fixing his outward attention, at least, on something else. But as he was sitting meditating in his room the words " The Lord of Hosts will do this " came unawares into his mind, and began to run in his head like a tune ; reiterating themselves, as it seemed, louder and louder and more and more urgently, till at last he began to think that someone was whispering them in his ear. They must be a sign from Heaven ; but a sign of what? He turned involuntarily for an explanation to the thought that had never ceased to dominate his subconscious mind. Could it be that God wanted him to live with the Unwins? It should be, it must be so! Joyfully snatching at the idea, he rushed off to see them. They accepted the proposal, and within a few days he had moved in.

He had found his monastery. Here at length was

that calm retreat, that silent shade, in which he could
consecrate his existence to keeping pure and bright the
ethereal flame of spiritual ecstasy that was all that made
life worth living to him. Cowper's life with the
Unwins is the complete example of the Evangelical
ideal, of the holy home, in the world, but not of it —
the religious life lived in conjunction with the customs
and comforts of the ordinary eighteenth-century
middle-class family. It is a perfect period piece, rising
before one's inner eye, as one reads of it, like a series
of faded mezzotints after Morland—The Pious Family
in Four Plates : Morning, Noon, Afternoon, Evening
—their titles engraved beneath them in slim copper-
plate, in which gentlemen in huge cravats and ladies in
voluminous skirts of white muslin read the Bible, and
relieve the poor, and take part in family worship, with
an expression of discreet benevolence on their small
faces. Cowper's day was mapped out in accordance
with a strict scheme of Evangelical devotion. On
waking he spent a little time in prayer. Breakfast was
between eight and nine, and afterwards the family
assembled in the parlour, where Cowper or young
Unwin read aloud the Scriptures or the sermons of some
faithful preacher, while the ladies listened with heads
bent and needles flashing over their work. By a
quarter to eleven it was time to get ready for church,
which lasted till twelve. After that came a break.
Dinner was at three, and till then you could do what you
liked. On wet days Cowper used to sit up in his room
reading or writing letters. But he preferred to be out,
riding or walking, or, best of all, gardening. He had
never had a garden before, but there was something
in the occupation at once so innocent and so civilized,
so rural and so domesticated, that was in harmony with
his whole nature. And the steady manual work was
now especially soothing to his weak nerves and strong
body. He spent hours digging and planting and

weeding in the old tangled garden, where the air was sweet with the scent of jessamine, and where the lime trees stood up leafy beyond the wall. At three o'clock came dinner; then a little conversation in the garden till tea, an hour later. And after tea, except in mid-winter, when it had to be taken earlier, came a walk. This walk was the central point of the day. Cowper generally went with Mrs. Unwin; they walked four miles at least, and talked all the time. Can we not picture them, moving very slowly—for it was impossible to move quickly in their clothes—Mrs. Unwin dressed neatly, but a little behind the fashion, her hair parted smoothly beneath her little cap, and Cowper's lanky figure inclined towards her in an attitude of old-fashioned courtesy; while far around stretched the fens, drowsy green in the summer sun, or a sheet of steel-coloured water when the winter floods were out? After the walk they spent the time in serious talk and reading till supper; or, sometimes gathered together in that quiet sitting-room, with the night shut out by curtains, the little band of believers would lift up their voices in a hymn of praise to the Author of their conversion; while the simple strain echoed itself in the frail, precise tones of the harpsichord played by Mrs. Unwin as accompanist. Prayers for the household followed. And then they climbed the stairs to bed, their candles casting ludicrous leaping shadow shapes of themselves on banister and ceiling, so that Cowper pranked round Cowper up the stairs and even Mr. Unwin saw himself fantastic. One last prayer, and Cowper was in bed and asleep before the church clock chimed half-past ten.

So passed the day; and so passed every day that followed. Outside, the genteel society of Huntingdon dined and played cards and went to the races. But the Unwin household saw as little of all this as if they lived a hundred miles away. The rigid order of their

existence closed them in as with a high wall. For
them the passage of the year was marked not by the
mundane occasions which marked it for the rest of
England, but Moslem-like, by calls to prayer. They
paid as little heed to the serious, as to the frivolous
affairs of the world. In 1767 George the Third,
mistakenly anxious to direct the policy of the country
himself, dismissed Lord Rockingham's Government;
and Huntingdon, in company with the rest of England,
was the scene of one of those drinking, brawling,
bribing elections that live for us still on the canvasses of
Hogarth. How Cowper would have thrilled to it in
the old days! How he would have argued and shouted
and tossed his hat in the air! Now he hardly spared
the time to give it a passing contemptuous glance.
" Truly I wish it was over," he commented to Hill,
" for it occasions the most detestable scene of profligacy
and riot that can be conceived."

Corporate activity generates an ardour unattainable
alone; and the Evangelical zeal of the little household
grew with every day they spent together. Mrs.
Unwin's old acquaintance—decent, respectable people
who were not above liking their joke—complained
when they came to see her that she had lost all her
old sprightliness and was grown quite a Methodist.
As for Cowper, one would have thought it impossible
to become more religious than he was already; but he
did—at least more exclusively religious. Ever since
his conversion the world had lost its attraction for
him; but he had not altogether forgotten its existence.
Now, required as he was to concentrate on religious
ideas every hour of the day, he ceased to be able to
turn his mind to any other. Indeed, to do so was
against the principles of his faith. His very recreations
grew religious. When he talked it was to discuss some
theological point or to recount his religious experiences; when he read, his book was devotional. If he

wrote poetry it was a hymn; if prose it was a meditation
or the pious chronicle of his spiritual pilgrimage.   His
literary style was changing with the change in his ideas.
In his letters passages about secular life in the easy,
humorous, Addisonian style of his youth alternate
with others on religious topics written in the regular
Evangelical manner—surging, ejaculatory, riddled with
repetitions, stiff with Biblical phrases.   " If I were as
genteel as I am negligent I should be the most delightful creature in the universe," he would write in one
sentence, and then, a few lines later: " A thousand
worlds will vanish at the consummation of all things.
But the word of God stands fast, and they who trust in
Him shall not be confounded."

Every incident of his uneventful life he now
examined and judged from an Evangelical point of
view.   He began to apply a sort of moral microscope
to his actions.   In the April of 1767 young Unwin
went on a visit to Hertfordshire, and Cowper gave him
an introduction to a cousin, Mrs. Cowper.   It seemed
a harmless enough thing to do.   But his conscience
soon found something to deplore in it; and he felt he
ought to make a confession to his cousin.   " Though
my friend," he wrote to her, " before I was admitted
as an inmate here was satisfied that I was not a mere
vagabond, yet I could not resist the opportunity of
furnishing him with ocular demonstration of it, by
introducing him to one of my most splendid con-
nections; that when he hears me called ' that fellow
Cowper ' he may be able, upon unquestionable
evidence, to assert my gentlemanhood and relieve me
from the weight of that opprobrious appellation . . . you
will be more ready to excuse me than I am to excuse
myself.   But in good truth it was abominable pride
of heart and indignation and vanity."

This Mrs. Cowper was gradually usurping Lady
Hesketh's place in Cowper's correspondence.   He

had never known her well before; but she shared his religious views, and in his present state of mind he cared only to talk of religion. How could he speak of it freely to Lady Hesketh, who would not believe that he had ever been a great sinner, and who showed only too clearly that she considered his present condition dangerously "enthusiastic"? Indeed, for all her seeming virtue, was she not herself a child of wrath predestined to damnation? He hated to believe it, but believe it he must. "How lovely," he exclaimed wistfully, "must be the spirits of just men made perfect, since creatures so lovely in our eyes may yet have the wrath of God abiding on them." They both felt that an unbridgeable gulf had opened between them; and tacitly, without hard feeling on either side, their connection lapsed. He was no happier about Harriet's father than about Harriet. What was he to think of a man who, at the age of sixty-six, regardless of the pit of Tophet to which at any moment he might be consigned, published a volume of secular poems? And such poems, too! "That holy and blessed Name to which he bows his head on the Sabbath is treated with as little reverence as that of Mahomet. He has, indeed, packed and jumbled them together in a manner very shocking to a Christian reader." As far as he could see, except for Mrs. Cowper and the Madans, his whole family were likely to go to hell. He began even to have doubts about the fate of his father. Dr. Cowper, it is true, had never so far forgotten himself as to put the name of his Creator in an unseemly juxtaposition to that of Mahomet. Cowper himself admitted that he was "everything that was excellent and praiseworthy towards men." But if he were not in grace this would avail him nothing. And had he died in grace? Poor Cowper! He could not but feel that any doubts on such a subject were unfilial; but in the exalted atmosphere he now moved in he tended to lose his sense of natural obligations.

His relations thought that he had lost his sense of other obligations as well. Cowper had no more money of his own now than he had before he went mad ; and he was principally supported by a fund made up by his family. What was their irritation to learn that not only had he, by sheer mismanagement, exceeded his yearly income by £140, but that he had brought Dr. Cotton's servant—Sam Roberts—and Dick Colman, the cobbler's boy, from St. Alban's to live with him. His motive in doing this had been pure benevolence. He believed them to be on the high road to conversion, and wished to keep them with him lest they should be distracted by the temptations of the world. Unluckily he had no money to support them ; so that they had to be supported by his unconverted relatives. And to their unenlightened minds it merely looked as if he kept two servants at their expense. They were very angry, and one, Major Cowper, threatened to withdraw his subscription. Cowper explained and apologized profusely, and was so patently innocent of any wish to impose on anyone, that the storm blew over. The Unwins helped him to reduce his expenditure by letting him off half his rent, and he paid his debts by a small sacrifice of capital. But, try as he might, he never became a good manager. A faith that might remove mountains could not make him economical.

In spite of these small clouds, he was very happy at Huntingdon. His life was beautiful, with the beauty of the cloister, where, far from the aimless hurry of the world, and freed from the pains of expectation and disappointment, man passes his existence in a peaceful round of devotion to God. But it was the cloister without its chill, its unnatural renunciation of natural feelings. On the other hand, it managed to avoid the dowdy unloveliness of the Puritan home. It was more like the Anglican community of Little Gidding than anything else—that community where Crashaw wrote his poems and John Inglesant met Mary Colet. But its spirit differed from that of Little Gidding as the eighteenth century differs from the seventeenth, or the hymns of Charles Wesley from those of Henry Vaughan. It was less jewelled, less soaring, less sacramental, more friendly, easier, more intimate. There was a snatch of morning about it, a nursery freshness, an innocent, lavender-scented sweetness. The very Calvinism it professed so conscientiously had lost its sting. In that kindly atmosphere, superstition and narrowness assumed the character of quaint, almost lovable, foibles. It thought a great number of things wrong, but it did not exult in fierce delight over the probable fate of the sinner ; it shunned the vanities of the world, but approved a decent comeliness and order. Its monotony is enlivened by little courtesies, movements of impulsive kindness, flights of gentle humour. As Cowper said, " Such a life is consistent with the utmost enjoyment."

It was suddenly broken into. One day, about two years after he had gone to Huntingdon, old Mr. Unwin fell off his horse and cracked his skull. For four days the family hung over his bed striving to catch, in his delirious mutterings, some trace of that Evangelical faith that alone, in their view, could save him in the world he was about to enter ; on the fourth he died. Cowper's life was unavoidably changed. There was no question, indeed, of his separating from Mrs. Unwin. Each had become an indispensable condition of the other's existence. To him she was that rock of support and sympathy for which he had yearned ever since he was a child ; while she found in him at last a worthy object on which to pour forth the energy of her devoted, undemonstrative, possessive nature. The personal bond that united them was the closest either was ever to know. Was it a bond of love? Cowper, fearful of any idea that might interfere with their present perfect intimacy, clung to the view that the relation was filial. " Mrs. Unwin," he assured a correspondent with anxious emphasis, " looks on me completely as a son." But it is not natural to live in a filial relation to a woman only a few years older than yourself, to whom you are not related, and whom you had never seen till you were thirty-three. It could not last. Already Cowper was imperceptibly growing to feel on more equal terms with her. And with a few more years his feelings were to settle into a simple tenderness that had its roots in the very fibres of his being. It was a sentiment of exquisite beauty, vigilant, humble, selfless, and it shines through the mingled gleam and dark of his later years like a clear white flame. Nor was his relation with her without that sense of emotional adventure, that intimacy some-how closer for the very formalities through which it must be expressed, that can only come between persons of different sex. But it never had the distinctive character of passionate love—it lacked the doubts and ardours and jealousies that characterized even so lukewarm an affair as Cowper's youthful sentiment for Theodora. Passion, indeed, was alien to his nature ; his deepest feelings were all affections. It is foolish to suppose that a man must be passionately in love with every woman he singles out for intimacy, above all a man of the ethereal, hyper-civilized type of Cowper.

Her feelings were altogether more straightforward. At first, indeed, she cannot have thought herself in love, any more than Cowper did, or, with her principles and her strength of character, she would have felt forced to break with him. And to the end of her life she always alluded to " Mr. Cowper " with the decorous formality of an acquaintance. But for his sake she was to show herself prepared to risk the loss of her income, her family and her good name—prepared, in fact, for the loss of anything except Cowper. Him she would not even share with anyone else. Her nature was a simple one, not given to fine feelings or fine distinctions. It is unnecessary to try to believe that she was not in love with Cowper.

Mr. Unwin's death, then, did not break up the little household; but it decided its removal. Now that they were free to do so, both Cowper and Mrs. Unwin longed to gratify that dearest of all wishes of the Evangelical heart, to settle in a " faithful " neighbourhood near some " experiential " divine. From him they would learn how best to put their faith into practice; and, daily drinking at the fountain of his enthusiasm, they would grow strong to brush aside any doubt or despondency the Devil might whisper to their hearts.

But who was this prophet to be ? Where should they go ? Aldwinkle in Northamptonshire ? Rivaulx in Yorkshire ? Cowper earnestly canvassed the question with his more serious correspondents. Actually it was settled by the prophet himself. One day, not long after Mr. Unwin's death, there arrived at the house an Evangelical clergyman called Newton, who said that he had been recommended to call by a friend of Mrs. Unwin. He was an odd, unclerical-looking little man with a big nose. But he had a bright, compelling eye : and when he began to speak, it was with a force and an animation that fairly flung them off their feet. They had never met such a dynamic personality. Within a few minutes he had taken them completely under his wing, was advising them about their most intimate concerns. And before a week was out he had written offering them the alternative of three houses, if they would come and live in his parish of Olney in Buckinghamshire. They were not unwilling.

Mrs. Unwin had found Newton sympathetic over her husband's death; and Cowper was dazzled by the flaming certainty of his faith. But even if they had been unwilling, they would have been unable to stand up against such a whirlwind. The only difficulty was that all the possible houses in Olney seemed to be so far from the church. However, Newton brushed that aside. He knew of one, two, three houses nearer; and if none was available, he would always be ready to come and hold a service in their house, wherever it might be. He had taken a great fancy to them: they were just the type of people the place needed: they must come. And come they did. Within three months their belongings had been packed up and bundled across England, and unpacked again at Orchard Side, Olney. It was not an attractive house. Its tall façade of dingy brick, faced with dingier stone, and crowned by a row of false Gothic battlements, frowned down upon one "like a prison," thought Cowper, as he caught sight of it, at the end of the long Olney High Street. Its garden was only a narrow strip of about fifty feet by twenty, between two high walls. All its rooms looked north, and it abutted on Silver End, the worst district of the place, whose sordid jollities were a constant offence to Cowper's simple but fastidious taste. However, it was near the church, and it was near Newton. You had only to open the gate at the end of the garden, and cross a bit of orchard, and there you were, looking in at the white-painted sash windows at the back of the Vicarage, still spick and fresh as a doll's house, for it had been built for Newton by his patron, Lord Dartmouth, only three years before. For the rest, Cowper did not take much to Olney; and never did, though he lived there twenty years. If it was at all like it is now, one can understand it. It is a typical small country town, with a long, straggling High Street and an avenue down the middle of

it, a bow-windowed inn, and a roomy, Decorated
church. But it lacks the cheerful charm associated
with such places: its streets are stagnant, but not
peaceful. On the other hand, Cowper loved the
country around. To us it seems much of a piece with
the town: tame and trivial, a network of villages and
fields, neither flat nor hilly, devoid of distances. But
it reminded Cowper of Berkhamsted; it had the same
leafy hedgerows and thatched cottages half buried in
trees, the same atmosphere of green, domesticated
peace. And the landscape of Berkhamsted, the first
he had ever admired, was still the most beautiful in
the world to him. As he gazed pensively south, across
the sleepy Ouse towards Hertfordshire, the memory
of other days would flood his mind, a thousand forgotten
incidents would start before his eyes, and he would
feel at home.

Not that he had much time for such unprofitable
musings. His life was a very much more strenuous
affair now than it had been at Huntingdon. For it
was dominated by the extraordinary man who had
brought him there. In his later years the Reverend
John Newton published, for the edification of his fellow
Evangelicals, an account of his life, entitled *An
Authentic Narrative of some Interesting Particulars in the
Life of John Newton*. It is a fusty, forbidding little
book, and more than half of it is pious platitude; but
it enshrines within its stilted sentences one of the most
fantastic fairy tales that was ever the true story of a
human being.

John Newton was born in London in 1725, the son
of a shipmaster. Even as a child he showed himself
possessed of a superstitious, inflammable imagination,
and a boiling, dynamic energy, always restlessly searching for an object on which to expend itself. His
mother, an old-fashioned Puritan, wished him to
become a clergyman, and for the first few years of his

life his mind was forced to concentrate itself on religion.
From time to time he would be seized with a fit of
violent devotion. Once, at the age of fifteen, he was
so excited by Beattie's *Church History* that for three
months he would not eat any meat, and hardly opened -
his mouth, for fear of letting fall one of those idle words
for which he would have to give account on the Last
Day. However, his mother died. And with adolescence his virile nature began to react against the ideas
to which he had been brought up. He was incapable
of doing anything by halves; and he became a militant
atheist. His father had sent him to sea; he threw
himself with gusto into the rioting, buccaneering
life of the eighteenth-century sailor, and especially
took a fierce delight in blaspheming against the
God he had so lately scrupulously honoured. From
time to time, indeed, the convictions of his childhood would reassert themselves, and visit him in
mysterious stirrings of conscience. Once, for example,
he had a curious dream. It seemed to him that his
ship was riding at anchor for the night in the harbour
of Venice, where he had lately touched : the exquisite,
worthless Venice of Longhi and Goldoni, a strange
setting for the sombre fantasies of his Nordic imagination. It was his watch on deck, and as he stood gazing
across the inky waters of the lagoon to where, on the
lighted piazzetta, contessa and cisisbeo stepped masked
from their gondolas to revel at the Ridotto, a stranger
came up to him and gave him a ring, which he implored
him not to lose, as he valued his life. This stranger
was followed by another, who as eloquently adjured
him to throw the ring away. And he dropped it overboard. Immediately the spires of Venice were lit up
with a lurid glare ; behind them the Euganean hills
burst into flame ; and his tempter, turning on him
with an expression of triumph, told him that they were
lit for his destruction. But at this moment a third

stranger appeared.   As he stepped on board the flames
died away ; and he drew the ring from the water, but
would not give it back to Newton, saying, with a
solemn emphasis, that he should have it at some future
time.   Shuddering with terror he awoke.   The dream
seemed to him a parable of his own spiritual life : the
ring his salvation, the second stranger the power of evil.
He could not get the dream out of his head.

However, it could not for long divert his mind from
following its natural course.   Already, indeed, it was
dominated by a very different theme.   His turbulent
spirit found it hard to settle to any job, and about a year
before he had got a new appointment on a ship bound
for Jamaica.   A few days before it sailed he went to
pay a visit of courtesy on some people called Catlett,
to whom his father had given him an introduction.
He had hardly been in the house an hour before he
had fallen in love with Miss Catlett—a girl of fourteen.
His love was of a piece with his religion and his
infidelity—a flaming, tearing, devouring passion that
burned itself into the very marrow of his being.   For
the moment time ceased to exist.   His ship was due
to sail in a few days ; and he let it sail, while he sat day
after day with his eyes fixed, as in a trance, on the object
of his adoration.   And when at last he did go to sea,
it was only to dream of Miss Catlett, and work with
frenzied energy in order to make enough money to
marry her.   But now a succession of disasters began to
overtake him.   Recklessly lounging on Harwich Dock
in his sailor's check shirt, he was caught by the press-
gang.   His vitality enabled him to support his new
condition with tolerable ease and cheerfulness.   He
soon became a midshipman, and he met a fellow-
officer who supplied him with many useful new arguments against the existence of God.   But when his
ship was ordered to New Guinea and he was faced with
the prospect of not seeing Miss Catlett for five years,

I

he deserted. He was caught, brought back in irons, and, in accordance with the savage penal code of the day, publicly stripped, flogged and degraded to the position of a common seaman. His rage knew no bounds. It was agony to one of his nature to obey when he had once commanded, and he felt he had lost his love for ever. He used to lie for hours, as the ship made its way through the calm tropical waters, brooding on his wrongs, till he was half mad. Sometimes he would decide to kill himself, sometimes the captain who had misused him, sometimes both. But always before he acted the figure of his love, all the lovelier by contrast with his present circumstances, would start before him; his heart would be flooded with a softer emotion; and he would stay his hand.

At last, after weary months, he arrived at Madeira, where he got exchanged on to another ship. His new captain was kind to him. But Newton was now so desperate that he became quite unmanageable, insubordinate to superiors, and given up to every vice. When they reached the Platane Islands on the west coast of Africa, he left the ship and took service with a planter. One would have thought it impossible that he should go through anything much worse than he had already. But he did. His master had a black mistress, who took a violent dislike to Newton. For two years he was treated more harshly than the meanest native slave, under-clothed and under-fed and overworked. An attack of tropical fever, during which he lay untended on the floor without even water to drink, was the final blow. He became like an animal, dumb and resigned, incapable of thought or emotion, or anything but a blind lust to satisfy the wants of nature. Only, now and again, memories of his early education would stumble into his numbed brain. He had somehow managed to keep a tattered geometry in his pocket through all his adventures, and he would steal out by night, half-naked skeleton as he was, and with its help laboriously trace arcs and triangles on the sand in the brilliant light of the African moon. After a year he got away, and became foreman for another planter in the neighbouring islands of the Bananoes. Here his life was supportable save for an occasional pang of regret for Miss Catlett. Such letters as he had written home had brought no reply. And he had given up all hope of getting back. He began more and more to live like the natives, gradually acquiring their habits and superstitions, so that he dared not allow himself to sleep once the moon was above the fronded palm trees. However, after two years and a half, a ship arrived from England with a letter from his father asking him to come home. His first instinct was to refuse. But the thought that he might see Miss Catlett again, though he now had little hope of marrying her, caused him to change his mind.

Newton was now very different from the stormy boy who had sailed from Torbay five years before. His conversation was still reckless and bitter and profane; so much so, indeed, that the horrified captain of the ship on which he travelled home began to fear it would bring a judgment on the ship. But the suffering Newton had undergone had left him with a disgust for the world. Its prizes no longer inspired his ambition, nor its pleasures his desires. Had he not followed the call of his passions wherever they had led him? And what had he got from them but bitterness and misery? But he could not resign himself to inactivity. His dynamic energy still boiled within him, seeking an outlet. He could not find it in worldly ambition or worldly enjoyment. Was there nothing more stable, more satisfying? Insensibly his mind began to revert for guidance to the beliefs implanted in it in infancy. A moment of danger brought it to the point of decision. Soon after the ship had left Newfoundland a violent storm got up, and within a few hours the upper timbers of the ship were torn away, and it was flooded with water. Provisions, cargo, and some men were lost, and during two days everybody worked at the pumps. For a time they seemed to be doing no good. With a thrill of fear Newton realized he was probably going to die. " If this will not do," he exclaimed unthinkingly, " the Lord have mercy on us." The true significance of his words suddenly came home to him. He thought, " If He really exists there will be very little mercy for me." In that moment of terrible crisis the whole of his past life moved in vivid review before him, and it struck him with overwhelming force that of all the objects that had in turn commanded his allegiance, now, at the point of death, only the religion of his childhood retained any value in his eyes. It alone had not proved worthless or unattainable : all his sorrows might be dated from the time that he deserted it. He resolved if he were saved to devote the rest of his life to it. He was saved, and for the last few days of the voyage began to put his resolution into practice. He could not, indeed, feel a lively faith in Christianity ; but he was convinced that such a faith alone had the slightest chance of giving him permanent happiness. And he hoped that, by consistently living in accordance with Christian precept, he might obtain it.

He arrived in England to find his father away on a voyage. But he had made arrangements with a ship-owner friend of his to offer Newton a job first as mate, and then as captain, on a line of ships trading in slaves ; so that his future was assured. More pleasing still, he found Miss Catlett still unmarried and still constant. And after his second voyage they were married. In the excitement induced by all these events he tended to forget his pious resolutions, though he still meant to keep them. But on one of his expeditions he saw a young man, an infidel just as he had been, dying in

terrible circumstances, friendless in Africa. The fear
of death and the terrors of his conscience revived again.
A dangerous illness at sea a few months after this finally
awakened him from his inertia; and from this time on
he entered on a life of rigid study and devotion. Every
moment of his day was devoted to some useful employment, and such time as he could spare from his profession
and his religion he occupied in teaching himself
Latin from a pocket Horace. It must have been a
curious scene—the ship moving with sails and rigging
aslant against the stars, among the mysterious islands
of that equatorial ocean, while the human cargo packed
together in the hold sweltered below, and above, the
captain paced the deck murmuring to himself the
compact urbanities of Horace.

He persevered in this life for five or six years, but
without achieving real satisfaction. The fact was
that eighteenth-century orthodoxy did not appeal to
his imagination, and so could not become that soul-
absorbing passion that to his temperament was a
necessary condition of happiness. His present religion
regulated his life and saved him from the worst sufferings into which he had been led by his infidelity. But
what he wanted was a doctrine that would demand the
absolute surrender of every energy of his mind and
body. One evening in 1754 when his ship was at
anchor in the port of St. Christopher he came across a
Captain Clunie, who told him about Evangelicalism.
Before the evening was out Newton had given himself
up to this new creed as he had to his love for Miss
Catlett. Here was the religion he wanted—a creed
that spoke to the heart, that commanded the undivided
allegiance of the whole personality, that fired the
imagination and gave scope to the desire for action.
It was the turning-point of his life. He had found
what he had been looking for ever since he was ten
years old. For the remaining forty years of his life

every thought, feeling and action was dedicated, without a faltering, to the faith of his choice. His life on board ship took on the ascetic rigour of a Trappist monastery. Every moment he was not working or sleeping he spent in prayer or reading the Bible, or instructing his crew in religion. His Latin studies were laid aside as useless frivolities. If he had female slaves on board he ate no meat, for fear it might strengthen his flesh to lust after them. After a time he made up his mind to give up his profession; not, oddly enough, because he thought slavery wrong, but because it was too interesting: it made him think too much about secular subjects. For five years he was a tide surveyor at Liverpool, where he continued his religious studies, and where he managed to get to know Whitefield and Wesley and other Evangelical leaders. Then in 1758 he decided to take orders. But here was a difficulty. He was not at all the sort of man who appealed to a Georgian bishop. Not only was he enthusiastic, and not quite a gentleman, but it was rumoured that he thought a Nonconformist had as good a chance of heaven as a member of the Established Church of England. Every bishop he asked refused to ordain him. Irritated at the rebuffs he received, Newton had thoughts of becoming a Congregationalist minister. But Lord Dartmouth, the good angel of Evangelicalism, stepped in, procured his ordination, and himself presented him to the living of Olney. Conversion had given Newton incentive, ordination gave him scope. All that virile vitality that had carried him triumphant through so many changes of fortune, that had enabled him to endure slavery, defeat sickness, and defy the Navy of England, now poured itself with irresistible force into the avocations of an Evangelical minister. He preached, taught, visited, held prayer meetings; he wrote hymns and pamphlets; even began a history of the whole world since the Creation, from the Evangelical point of view, in order to combat the subversive interpretations of Gibbon and Hume. But his most characteristic activity was his religious letters. All over England, with people of every sort—soldiers, politicians, schoolmasters, young ladies—Newton kept up a voluminous correspondence, in which he advised them about every detail of their moral and spiritual lives. His advice was always long and generally impassioned; and when, as sometimes happened, it was given unasked, it was not well received. But on the converted it made a tremendous impression. And by the time he met Cowper, Olney was already one of the centres of the Evangelical world.

His character is sufficiently shown forth by his story. He was primarily a man of action. If he thought he should do a thing he did it; and he often did it without thinking about it at all. Nor did thought mean anything to him except in so far as it told him how to act. He was incapable of speculation or self-analysis. Reason was to him a weapon which he used, not very effectively, to confute his opponents. His own acts and opinion were directed not by reason, but by unanalyzed instinct. He became an atheist because his instinct reacted against religion, and when instinct demanded religion again he threw his atheism overboard without even bothering to find replies to those arguments he had thought so formidable when his instinct had been on their side.

Yet he was not at all stupid. No one whose brain was not a strong instrument could have taught himself Latin on a ship with nothing to help him but a copy of Horace, and anything he took up, whether navigating or preaching or writing, he did well. But over and above all this, he had imagination. It is this quality that differentiates his narrative from those truthful fictions of Defoe which it so much resembles in its outward incidents—adventures, escapes, and sudden vicissitudes. No one could be less like the business-like heroes of Defoe, with their matter-of-fact love affairs, their unshakeable nerve, and the British common sense with which they confronted the most unlikely situations, than this passionate, superstitious creature who was guided in the most momentous decisions by omens and prophetic dreams; who trembled before the baleful influence of the African moon; and was upheld through the blackest misfortunes, and prevented from committing appalling crimes, by the memory of a girl of sixteen whom he was convinced he would never see again. He was extraordinarily sensitive to the influence of Nature; he found in later life that only from country solitudes could his soul soar easily to heights of spiritual ecstasy. His letters, too, crude and absurd as they are, are full of flights of naïve fancy, touches of beauty, humour and intimacy, only possible to a man of imagination.

Nor was this out of keeping with his whole character. The imagination is a thing of instinct rather than of reason, and often men of action have more of it than men of thought. Hobbes had less imagination than Cromwell, Luther more than Erasmus. Newton, indeed, had more in common with these heroes of the Reformation than with his own contemporaries. Like theirs, his character was heroic and unsymmetrical, freaked with a Gothic quaintness, misted with a Gothic sublimity. He had their faults, too. He was narrow and uncouth; he was not moulded of fine clay. He could hardly have survived such a life if he had been; and in so far as he was not like Luther, he was the eighteenth-century sailor he looked, clumsy, careless and insensitive. His kindness was generally tactless, and his piety sometimes profane.

But all these qualities, good and bad, remarkable

or commonplace, were subservient to the single one of fanaticism. His whole life was a succession of slaveries to successive single ideas. Now he was convinced that his own particular brand of religion was the best thing for anyone, anywhere, in any circumstances. His every word, whether serious or cheerful, trivial or important, whether it was connected with people or politics or gardening, was made to refer to religion. His very jokes were Evangelical. This exclusive devotion was bound up with the strongest sides of his character—his will, his passion, his imagination, his faith. He would have given his life for his beliefs, without a thought. But exclusiveness is also responsible for his defects. He carried out the precepts of his creed so literally as to be at times both indecent and ridiculous. " Good news indeed," he remarked, with conscientious joviality, on hearing of his favourite niece's translation to another world. It might sound heartless, but it was Evangelical, and therefore must be right. Again, whatever could not be by any means forced into connection with his religion must necessarily be of the devil. " If there is any practice in the land sinful," he exclaimed, " then attendance at the theatre is so." And all he could see in the graceful symbolism of Venice's *Marriage to the Sea* was " a lying, antiquated Popish Bull."

It is difficult to talk long about one subject without becoming boring. And Newton often did. He would have given his life to save your soul; but nothing could persuade him not to thrust his views down your throat. He tended to become arrogant. There was only one God, and John Newton was His prophet. So that though he was always repeating that he was sinful, he never admitted he was wrong. It was impossible to argue with him. If anyone asked Newton to explain a contradiction in his argument, he merely looked at him with the dreadful, glassy good-nature of the fanatic, forgave him for his error, and went on with his exhortation.

With such a man as his spiritual director, it was not odd that Cowper had little time to himself. Newton had made Olney a whirlwind of Evangelical activity. When he was not preaching—and he was sometimes in the pulpit for six hours a day—he was visiting the sick, or giving Bible lessons to the children, or holding a joint service with the Dissenters, or leading an extempore prayer meeting in the Great House, a large, empty barrack of a place, opposite the Vicarage. Into the midst of this whirlwind Cowper was caught up. He had to leave his monastery and come forth into the world, a preaching missionary friar. No more of those placid walks after tea with Mrs. Unwin. Dinner was at one and tea at four, and after that sermon or lecture till bed. Cowper did not object to the change in his life. His spirit was irresistibly drawn to Newton's buoyant vitality, as it had been to the calm certainty of Mrs. Unwin. He spent eight hours of every day in Newton's company; prayed with him; with him attended the bedside of the sick and dying; rode and walked by his side through the lanes, when he went to preach at a neighbouring village. Newton gave him some work of his own to do, too. He visited the poor and he taught in Sunday School.

Such work was easy to him. His kindly nature had always gone out to children; and he had a simple and diffident sympathy which made all the people he visited love him. It was a very different thing when Newton asked him to lead in prayer. His conversion had not cured him of that morbid horror of making a public exhibition of himself which had occasioned his first madness. When he first went to Huntingdon he had thought of becoming a clergyman, and then given it up because he could not face the publicity it would entail. And when, after Mr. Unwin's death, he had

been asked to lead the day's prayer for the family
and their two servants, he had almost broken down.
" I was so troubled at the apprehension of it," he
wrote, " and so dreadfully concerned at the conflict I
sustained on this occasion that my health was not a
little affected thereby." But this new task was far
harder. In front of a number of people whom he did
not know and who might not be in sympathy with him
at all, he was required to lay bare all that was most
sacred and most painful in his existence, and to speak
as he was used only to speak in his bedroom alone.
His whole being recoiled from the thought. However, Newton would not listen to such morbid hesita-
tions for a moment. And, indeed, Cowper himself
thought it only another sign of his uncontrollable
weakness and vanity. Was he, just because it embarrassed him to do so, to withhold from others, less
fortunate than himself, the encouragement they might
gain from the glorious testimony of his conversion ?
With set face he nerved himself to the task. For four
or five hours before service began he would sit shaking
with nerves. Then, in that barrack-like room, with
the lines of decent cottage people composed in respectful attention before him, and the summer dusk falling
on the fields outside, he would begin to speak. The
first sentences came toneless and halting ; but he
gathered strength as he went on. And soon he had
forgotten his fears, forgotten his audience, forgotten
everything, save that he was trying, wretched, helpless
creature as he was, to convey something of his gratitude
to the compassionate Saviour who raised him from the
depths of hell, to tell Him how exclusively, how
desperately, he put his trust in Him. The worn
sensitive features grew tense with an unearthly
enthusiasm, an uncontrollable emotion began to throb
in the quiet, educated voice. It seemed to the people
sitting round as if they were listening unseen to some

inconceivably holy, inconceivably intimate conversation, as if Cowper really saw his Lord in the room with him, and saw no one else. And they were moved as they had never been moved by the glib emotionalism of the professional Evangelical preacher. " I have heard many men preach," said an old villager years later, " but I have never heard anyone preach like Mr. Cowper."

Outside his religious activities his days pursued the same unvaried course they had at Huntingdon. It was a sensational event, for instance, when he and Mrs. Unwin had to cross the street to spend a few weeks at " The Bull " because one of their servants was ill with smallpox. One cannot well imagine a sleepier little country inn than " The Bull " ; but to Olney it represented the very epitome of worldly rush and frivolity. " What can you both do at the Bull," wrote Newton, " surrounded with noise and nonsense every night ? But," he adds with pious jocularity, " may the Lord preserve and comfort you in the midst of bulls and bears." Life was also varied by the stream of Evangelical men and visitors who were always coming and going at the Vicarage. Mr. Venn came, and Mr. Berridge, and Lord Dartmouth ; and on one occasion, formidable thought, thirteen Baptist ministers at once. Cowper's heart leapt up when he saw them all seated round Newton's dining-room table. " It was a comfortable sight," he exclaims, " to see thirteen Gospel ministers together." On another evening he sat watching the candlelight playing on the austere countenance and glittering regimentals of Captain Scott, " the pious captain," who had come over to spend the night with Newton in order to avoid the races at Northampton.

But most of the glimpses of Cowper's life which we get at this period reveal him occupied in the recurring avocations of every week, picking his way to early

service by the light of a lantern in the chill murk of a
November morning, while Mrs. Unwin clattered on
pattens at his side ; or at Evensong, in the Augustan
gallery lately fitted on to the Perpendicular columns of
the church in order to accommodate more worshippers,
listening to Newton praying with ardour for " my
maid Molly, who is troubled on the point of election."
Newton's servants were not the only ones whose
spiritual condition gave cause for anxiety. Cowper
and Mrs. Unwin had a great deal of trouble in that
way. When they had first arrived at Olney their
household had consisted of a man and a maid, both, as
they thought, in a happy state of grace. But the maid
early began to show signs of backsliding, and before
long behaved in such a dreadful manner that they
began to doubt whether she had ever really been converted at all. She left in a hurry. Her successor was
respectable, but grossly incompetent, and after Mrs.
Unwin had given her some " pious advice " she went
too. Finally they fell back on a young woman from
Olney, who, though religious, suffered from very poor
health. Cowper could only hope that " as the Lord
had designed her to the work He would give her
strength equal to it."

So passed 1767, 1768, 1769. But though the
outward circumstances of his life were so calm,
Cowper's mind was once again the scene of a terrible
crisis. Gradually, relentlessly, with gathering speed
and momentum, that faith which had signalized his
first recovery from madness, and upon which he had
rested the whole structure of his subsequent life, was
slipping away from him. The spell was breaking ;
the bridge was ceasing to bear ; the single flame of his
life's happiness was flickering to extinction. Indeed,
it was a wonder that it lingered so long. For the
method by which he attempted to keep it alive was
radically defective : his ideal of religious life was

a practical impossibility. Mortality is the first law of man's existence on this planet. Nor is his ecstasy exempt from its tragic jurisdiction. A breath of the Divine Spirit induced by love or art or prayer, suddenly it blows upon him; for a brief space of time he is swept up and borne along by the wind of its going; then he flags and falls back exhausted. It is beyond the power of his earth-bound spirit to sustain such an ethereal intensity of emotion for more than a moment: and such moments visit the most inspired of mankind only once or twice in a lifetime. Any system of life, therefore, which aims at constantly maintaining them must necessarily fail. But most of all one like Cowper's, which tries to do so by deliberately refusing to allow the mind to dwell on anything else. An emotion cannot be induced by an intellectual effort; and, besides, the same emotion cannot be roused often by the same stimulus. The mind is numbed by familiarity. One soon becomes used to the colouring of a room, however striking; the change of key that sent a thrill down the spine like a douche of cold water on first hearing becomes a mere insignificant noise if it is often repeated. So the unvarying round of Cowper's existence, instead of maintaining his emotional state, hastened its departure. The regular sequence of prayer and meditation ceased to stir him just because it was regular. He was trying to do an impossible thing, and he was trying to do it in the way that of all others would fail the soonest. Of course, it was partly the fault of the Evangelical creed, which, as we have seen, made an emotional condition into a moral virtue. But its average adherents did not in practice carry this doctrine to a logical conclusion: the pressure of ordinary life was too strong to allow them to think about their souls all the time. So their emotions were often refreshed by new stimuli. It only shows the strength of the original experience, that, concentrating exclusively on it, Cowper should have felt its effect for as long as he did. But it could not last for ever; and already before he left Huntingdon a change in his feelings had appeared. He began to notice periods of spiritual stagnation within himself, during which the things that had most moved him in the days of his conversion stirred no response at all. He could not keep his attention on the passages of the Bible he loved best; prayers that he had once not been able to say with a steady voice, so exactly did they express the most poignant and intimate experiences of his life, hymns in which he had been used to pour forth his whole soul in thanksgiving, now slipped from his lips almost without his realizing what he was doing. The great phrases of Evangelicalism, Election, Reprobation, Final Perseverance, the very sound of which had been enough two years before to thrill him like the sound of a trumpet, were now so dulled by repetition as hardly to convey any idea at all. " Oh, that I retained my first love," he said sadly to Mrs. Madan, " that it was with me as when I first came forth from the furnace, when the name of Jesu was like honey and milk upon my tongue and the very sound of it was sufficient to sustain and comfort me."

These periods of lethargy did not last long. But they were distressing while they lasted; and he had never known them before. What could be the cause of them ? Perhaps God wished to save him from the danger of being over-confident; or perhaps He was trying his faith. All the saints had trials. He hoped this was the cause, not any fault of his own, and that he would be able to stand the test. If he did, perhaps the periods of lethargy would stop. But though he made every effort, they went on. He welcomed the change to Olney with enthusiasm. A new home under the personal supervision of one of the burning and shining lights of the Gospel, might prove just what was needed to make his troubles disappear. For a few months his hopes were fulfilled. The change of scene and life was a stimulus. His new work gave him too much to do and too much to think about to allow him to worry about himself; while his whole spirit was revived by the impact of Newton's personality. He became confident, hopeful; at moments he knew again the religious ecstasy of two years before. But it was not quite the same ecstasy: he had become self-conscious about it. No longer did it flood his mind, compelling and unbidden, carrying him away whether he would or no. He watched for the least sign of it, tended it, savoured it to the last drop, and when it was gone lingered over its memory—sole witness in a drab world to the living reality of his salvation. Nor was it induced, as before, regularly by the regular incidents of his religious life; but capriciously, by some chance accident—a detail in a service, a phrase in a book hitherto unnoticed, which brought the truth home to him afresh by suddenly presenting it from a new angle.

" The Lord has dealt graciously with me since I came, and I trust I have in two instances had much delightful communication with Him. Yet this opportunity of access was intimated to me in such a way as to teach me at the same time His great care that I might not turn it to my prejudice. I expected that in some sermon or exposition I should find Him, that the lips of His excellent minister would be the instrument by which the Lord would work upon and soften my obdurate heart, but He saw my proneness to praise the creature more than the Creator, and though therefore He gave me the thing I hoped for, yet He conveyed it to me in a way which I did not look to. On the last Sabbath morning, at a prayer meeting before service, while the poor folks were singing a hymn and my vile thoughts were rambling to the ends

of the earth, a single sentence—' And is there no pity
in Jesus' breaſt ? '—seized my attention at once, and
my heart within me seemed to return answer, ' Yes, or
I had never been there.'   The sweetness of this visit
laſted almoſt through the day, and I was once more
enabled to weep under a sense of the mercy of God in
Jesus.   On Thursday morning I attended a meeting
of children, and found that passage ' Out of the mouths
of babes and sucklings ' haſt thou ordained praise,
verified in a sense I little thought of, for at almoſt every
word they spoke in answer to the several queſtions
proposed to them my heart burned within me and
melted into tears of gratitude and love."

In these moments all the old confidence returned,
and he upbraided himself for his inability to endure the
smalleſt trial with unfaltering heart.   But he could
not feel this confidence long.   It was induced by
change of scene and society, and when he got accustomed to this change it went.   The faſt was that he was
" through " with Evangelicalism.   Its appeal to him
had been a purely emotional one, and his emotion had
ceased to respond to that kind of appeal.   As we have
seen, the quickening of the spirit that had attended his
firſt arrival at Olney was never able to reawaken his
response to those expressions of his religion which he
was already bored with.   It could only ſtir him to
respond to some aspeſt of it he had not noticed before.
And this response was pale, flickering, premeditated,
compared with the soul-shaking thrill of his firſt
vision.   Within a few months of his arrival at Olney
all the old disquieting symptoms began to reappear.
When he tried to say his prayers he could not keep his
mind on what he was doing : after a few moments he
would suddenly recolleſt himself, and then, in a second
revulsion of feeling, he would upbraid himself for his
lack of truſt in God's mercy.   He had loved to meditate on his solitary walks—the sights and scenes of the

K

country, which were what he thought most lovely in the world of sense, combined with the thought of that Gospel which was what he thought most lovely in the world of spirit, to soothe his soul in a celestial harmony. Now he could not concentrate on the Gospel at all, except to think how little gratitude he felt for it. How he had loved, in the old days at Dr. Cotton's, with lighted eye and flushed face, to detail the story of his conversion to anyone who could be brought to listen! Now, the moment religion was mentioned in conversation he found his attention begin to wander; and if Newton asked him to tell his story to hearten up some fellow Christian, he felt nothing but a dull nausea at having to say it all over again. Writing about it became as bad as talking. Minutes would pass as he sat, the ink drying on his pen, trying in vain to work himself up into the state of mind in which he could deliver a comfortable religious homily to Mrs. Cowper or Mrs. Madan. And then he would suddenly remember how, two years ago, his pen would have been too slow to keep pace with the flowing tide of his thought: once more a sense of guilt would strike him, and he would lay his letter aside. He could not bear to fall below the standard he had set himself then—to do so would be equivalent to a confession of his own decline —so he gradually ceased to write at all.

Sunday, too, became intolerable to him. In the old days he used to look forward to it as the climax of the week's devotion, the day in which, undistracted by worldly care, he could give himself up to thoughts of God. Now he felt it as the climax of nothing but his own inadequacy, a day in which nothing was allowed to distract him from realizing what a failure his religious life was. The twenty-four hours passed like twenty-four days. That spent in church was the most unendurable. When he first came to Olney Newton's influence had revived his enjoyment of it;

but soon it was as little comfort as anything else. He knelt, and bowed, and sang, and responded, as the service demanded, but the words had no more significance to him than if they had been in Sanskrit. His eye roved listlessly round the congregation, all, as he thought, uplifted in an ecstasy of devotion. But no longer, as on that first Sunday at Huntingdon, did his spirit rise with theirs. Indeed, the contrast between their feeling and his own only made his depression worse. Not only was his spiritual life a failure—it was a far greater failure than that of anyone else.

Prayer, meditation, conversation, correspondence, church, one by one the doors through which the light of salvation had penetrated to his heart were shut against him. But it was not without a struggle. Desperately, assiduously, with every art and energy of which his nature was capable, he did battle with his fears and his boredom, tried to find reassuring relief for his dark moments, cried shame upon himself for succumbing to them so easily, adjured himself to take heart once more. Perhaps, he would still comfort himself, his faith was being put to the test: he was required by an all-wise Providence " to walk through a romantic scene with mountains, deep and dark valleys, caves and dens " ? Or perhaps he was guilty of some secret sin and was now suffering its punishment. Could it be that he had been spiritually proud, convinced that he was immune from temptation ? Or had he not trusted wholly in God, but relied on his own good works to save him ? If he really examined himself, unburdened himself of his sins, his troubles would probably disappear. And he must always remember that his own troubles were trivial compared with those that Christ had undergone for his sake. He set to work diligently to examine his smallest action and thought for a sign of worldliness or vanity, cut himself off more rigorously than before from any

interests that might turn his mind from the narrow
path.   He spent hours on his knees, striving to get
his soul into a proper state of contrition.   It was in
vain : his depression did not disappear.   His mind
was so dazed with self-analysis and self-torment that
he hardly knew if he was contrite or not.   He hoped
God did.   Not for a moment could he revive the
faintest glimmer of his old ecstasy, not for the briefest
instant did his heart glow with the old love, burn with
the old faith.   He could only pray to God for help ;
but the help did not come.   He began to wonder if it
was ever coming at all.   He had done all he could,
and to what purpose ?   Push, coax, wedge as he might,
one by one the doors creaked on their hinges, swung
to, shut.   Without confidence, he resigned himself to
God's mercy.   He was His own interpreter, and he
must make it plain.

Now an event happened which removed his last
resistance.

Cowper had not seen much of his brother during the
last few years.   They had long ago agreed not to
argue about religion ; but as William did not really
care to talk about anything else, such an agreement
prevented them from taking much pleasure in each
other's society.   Since he had been at Olney he had
actually only been over to Cambridge once, when
John was ill.   And then, terrible to relate, he had found
his counterpane littered with plays.   John came more
regularly to Olney ; but his visits were far from being
an unmixed pleasure.   William felt he ought not to let
them interfere with his Evangelical duties, but it
embarrassed him to perform them if he felt John was
sitting by disapproving.   Besides, since John was a
clergyman it might hurt his feelings if he were not
asked to take family prayers.   And yet, since he was not
converted, this was impossible.   It was all very up-
setting.   John, for his part, carefully conformed to

the habits of the house, and avoided all controversial topics. But one trembles to think what his decorous academic mind muſt have thought of a household whose time was divided between irregular piety and unreſtrained philanthropy; where maſters and servants alike were liable at any time to burſt out with intimate revelations about the ſtate of their souls; and in which every detail of daily life was direᶜted by a fanatical sea-captain, with a passion for asking personal queſtions, and without a degree. Altogether he felt it a great relief when the time came for him to climb into the coach and drive back to the peace and the port of Cambridge.

But fate had decreed that, before he died, he too was to be uprooted from the placid seclusion in which he had loitered away his life, and pass through the fires of heaven and hell. In March 1770 William was for the second time summoned to Cambridge by the news of his brother's illness. When he arrived the doᶜtor told him he was dying. Under the shock all William's dying faith flared up once more. Loss of faith and lethargy of spirits were alike forgotten. He only remembered that his brother was dying, and that unless he died in grace he was damned. He was not yet in grace; but Providence had clearly brought William there to save him. And now began a ſtrange drama. Day after day, night after night, cut off from the world in that quiet college room, alone he wreſtled for the soul of the dying man, implored God to soften his heart, himself with breaking voice urged his brother to hearken to the Divine message. At firſt his efforts were vain. Daily John grew weaker: soon it would be too late. William's suspense grew unbearable. Three times in a night he would ſtart up thinking he heard a cry. Was it John's dying groans, or the exultant yell of fiends come to carry off his soul? Or was it some celeſtial intimation for his own ear?

Holding his breath, he listened; and then rushed to the bedside, and once more implored John to believe: once more in vain. Could it be that God meant him to fail? But within the depths of John's own spirit forces were working on his side.

John Cowper's life had followed a calmer course than his brother's. But his nature was very similar —a bundle of nerves, a prey to superstitious fears, afraid of life. And, faced for the first time with a real crisis, in the shape of a dangerous illness, his true self came to the surface. It is said that already, before he fell ill, his composure had been ruffled by a strange incident. Years ago, when he was a schoolboy, a vagrant gipsy in a tattered red military coat had told his fortune. He foretold various events of youth, but had said that he could see nothing for him after the age of thirty. John had not paid much attention to his words; but a short time before his illness, as he was sauntering in the College garden, his eye was caught by a red coat. Looking up, he saw, as he thought, the very gipsy, peering at him through the gate. Before he had time to say a word, the man had disappeared. The sight of him brought the whole incident back into his mind. With a thrill of fear, he realized that every prediction hitherto had been fulfilled. What then could it mean, that the predictions stopped at thirty? Could it be there were no more to make, that what he thought was the gipsy had been an apparition come to forewarn him of his end? Any fears he may have had were increased by his illness; and as he lay in bed he began to review his past in the light of approaching death. It was a discouraging spectacle. All the things he had cared for seemed equally valueless. He felt that his whole view of life must have been wrong. Perhaps William's view was the right one. But he had had no experience that could enable him to feel as William felt. A drab melancholy invaded his spirit. And then one evening as he lay there, suddenly, in the span of a second, the heavens opened and the Divine Light irradiated his soul. He gave a cry which brought William to his bedside; he clasped his hand in silence, and after a little he said, " Oh, brother, I am full of what I could say to you." The nurse asked him if he needed any lavender or hartshorn. He replied, " None of these things will serve my purpose." William said, " But I know what would, my dear, don't I ?" He answered, " You do, brother." At last he had seen what William had seen. And, like William, he had believed.

For six days more he lingered in a still, unearthly ecstasy. Only on one occasion did he reveal a trace of his old unconverted self. It was roused by the thought of Newton. " I shall rejoice in a conversation with him hereafter," he confessed to William, " but I could not bear it now." On the eighth day he sank into a torpor, on the tenth he died.

William's prayers had been answered. He returned to Olney in tremulous exultation, and listened with rapture to Newton expatiating from the pulpit on John's holy death. But the strain which his nervous system had sustained was to prove disastrous to him. Alone in a strange town, he, who had never moved a step from home for three years, had watched his only brother die, himself for half the time in an agony lest he should be going to eternal perdition. He had not even been supported by comfort from Olney. Mrs. Unwin, for reasons unknown, had hardly written ; and this was an added worry to Cowper, who began to think he had offended her. While Newton only wrote to tell Cowper, with his usual plain-spoken trenchancy, not to deceive himself into thinking good works could save his brother : unless he was in grace he would certainly go to hell. The consequence was that whatever was left of Cowper's nervous resistance

was destroyed.   Within a few weeks of getting back to
Olney the fitful flame of religious emotion which had
flickered up for the last time by John's bedside was
extinguished;   and he found himself incapable of
making the slightest effort to recover himself.   With
mechanical lips he continued to repeat the words of
his belief, but they no longer meant anything to him.
Evangelicalism had finally and absolutely ceased to
stir his emotions.   He had drained it to its last drop.
He was not going to get any happiness from it ever
any more.

It was not only his religious happiness that left him.
With it went all other pleasures too.   According to his
belief, religion was the only source of genuine happiness, so that if he found he had been made happy by
anything not specifically religious he was logically
forced to connect it in some way with religion, to look
on it as a channel of the Divine Grace.   The pleasant
domestic life with the Unwins was the prototype of the
corporate unity of Christians living together in faith
and charity.   Natural beauty was the expression of
the Divine perfection in things sensible.   As long as he
still cared about his religion this way of looking at
things accentuated his enjoyment;   for it suffused the
most trivial moment of pleasure with a glow of transcendental emotion.   Every quiet evening by the fire,
every cowslip by the roadside, whispered to Cowper's
spirit intimations of a blessed immortality.   But when
he lost his pleasure in religion he lost his happiness in
these things as well.   It was not only that his conscience
would not allow him to be happy if his spiritual
condition was not such as to deserve it;   he could not
feel pleasure in doing anything without remembering
that in former days such a pleasure would inevitably
have culminated in a moment of religious rapture;   and
the fact that it did not do so any more took away such
enjoyment as he felt.   He paid the proverbial penalty

of one who puts all his eggs into one basket. When the basket broke, all the eggs were broken too.

The outward ordering of his life did not alter with the change in his inner man. He taught in Sunday School, visited, attended sermons, even said his prayers just as he had when he first came to Olney. But the motive that had guided his life into such a course was dead. He went on automatically because he did not know what else to do. His mind alternated between a leaden lethargy and a yet more leaden gloom. Hardly for a minute did he forget his bonds and quicken into feeling once more. Only sometimes, as he wandered amid the woodland solitudes, which lately had brought such happiness to his heart, but now no longer, his response to the beauty around him would mingle with his memories and his sense of present misery to well up and flow away in a gush of lyrical emotion,

> "O happy shades ! to me unblest,
>   Friendly to peace, but not to me,
> How ill the scene that offers rest,
>   And heart that cannot rest, agree.
>
> This glassy stream, that spreading pine,
>   Those alders quiv'ring to the breeze,
> Might soothe a soul less hurt than mine
>   And please, if anything could please.
>
> But fixed unalterable care,
>   Foregoes not what she feels within,
> Shows the same sadness everywhere,
>   And slights the season and the scene.
>
> For all that pleased in wood or lawn
>   While peace possessed these silent bowers,
> Her animating smile withdrawn
>   Has lost its beauties and its powers.
>
> The saint or moralist can tread
>   These moss-grown alleys, musing slow ;
> They seek, like me, the secret shade,
>   But not like me, to nourish woe.

> Me fruitful scenes and prospects waste,
>   Alike admonish not to roam ;
> These tell me of enjoyments past,
>   And those of sorrows yet to come."

By a strange paradox, his frustration became for a
moment its own fulfilment, and his sorrow sighed
itself away in song.   But though these sudden glory-
ings in affliction might relieve his feelings, they did not
make him happy.   For to be happy one must believe
in the solid stability of what one holds valuable.   And
the only thing Cowper held valuable, the pearl of great
price to obtain which he had sold all that he possessed,
had melted into air within his hand.   Such an event
would have been dangerous to Cowper's nervous system
at any time ;   for it might always cause the despondency and self-depreciation bred in him in childhood
to resume their sway over him.   But it was far more
dangerous now than it would have been when he was
twenty-four.   For the faith he had now lost was the
only thing that stood between him and definite madness.   John Cowper and Dr. Cotton had been wrong
in thinking Cowper's religion a sign of mania.   But
they were quite right in thinking that Cowper himself
was not normal.   The delusions of 1763 had never
wholly left him.   He would be haunted for days
together by a strange dream.   Sometimes, as when he
was agitated whether he should go and live with the
Unwins, his mind would be obsessed by some phrase
or sentence, which he took to be a message from God.
Lying in bed in the early morning—always a bad time
for neurotics—these phrases intruded themselves so
insistently on him that he thought they were spoken
by a voice.   But his faith had given him control over
these spiritual disturbances.   It taught him to welcome
them if he judged them to be of God, to despise them
if he judged them to be of the devil ; at any rate not to
pay much attention to them, since his salvation was

already decided.   But now that the light of his faith
was extinguished, his inflamed fancy could make him
its slave whenever it chose.   The truth was that the
fundamental cause of his madness had never been
rooted out of his mind.   His conversion had neutralized
the effect of his sense that he was singled out from the
rest of mankind by the curse of God, but it had done
nothing to make him realize that it was the figment of
his imagination.   So that when he lost his faith he was
as open to its attack as he had been in 1763.   Indeed,
his state of mind in 1772 was that of 1763 over
again.   His nervous resistance had been sapped by
the strain of bereavement; he was the victim of
visionary fears; he was disgusted with his own
spiritual condition; and he had lost all living sense
of the value of anything.   For the second time the
foundations of his sanity were undermined.   Within
eighteen months he was mad for the second time.

But as he descends to his inferno, once more the
smouldering clouds rise and hide him from our sight.
Such scanty records as we possess cannot enable us to
follow the steps of his journey.   Now and again the
clouds lift, and we catch a glimpse of his face; but it
is distorted beyond recognition by the flames of misery
and madness that leap around it.   The actual form
of his insanity arose, ironically enough, from that very
doctrine of salvation which he had been confident
would remove all fears from him for ever.   The soul
was apprised of its salvation, he held, by a sudden
feeling of religion—felt itself to be in grace.   He had
known the feeling once.   But he knew it no longer;
and he was convinced that, in spite of any efforts, he
never would again.   Could it therefore mean that he
had fallen from grace, that he had forfeited his salvation?   Hastily, in horror, he brushed the idea aside.
But, do what he would, it returned, and began to eat
into his mind, till he could think of nothing else.

For the second time in his life Cowper was possessed by the fear of his own damnation. It was inconsistent of him, since it was one of the first articles of his faith that no one could fall from grace. But Cowper's fear was the result not of logical process, but of mental disease; so that its inconsistency made no difference to him. Like all mad people, he thought himself different from anyone else in the world, and therefore that no analogy from the life of anyone else could apply to his. Even if it was God's usual law that no human soul should fall from grace, yet, for some Divine purpose of His own, God had designed his, Cowper's, to be of all souls ever created the one exception. It was only too easy for him to believe this. Did it not agree exactly with that sense that he had been marked out from his fellows by the curse of God which had tormented him ever since childhood ?

His lethargy turned to anguish; and daily his anguish grew blacker. Fits of despair would sweep over him, when he would not speak or even look up, almost every night his sleep was broken by awful dreams. And as always when he was agitated, he began to hear voices. Newton and Mrs. Unwin watched him with dismay, and did their best to help him. It was odd that Newton did. For his enthusiasm for religion led him in general so far as even to look favourably on religious mania. Once he had sent a girl into fits by his preaching, and had refused to express any concern, on the ground that fits might be the means ordained by Heaven to lead her to grace. However, he did realize that Cowper's delusions were due to disease; and he threw himself into the task of curing him with the same ardour with which he threw himself into everything else. Unfortunately, neither nature nor circumstance had qualified him for the rôle of mental alienist. He knew Cowper liked writing verses; so, in order to distract his thoughts to more pleasant fields, he proposed that they should collaborate in writing some hymns "for the use of plain people, with the imagery and colouring of poetry, if admitted at all, only in a sparing form." Cowper dutifully carried out his part of this bleak task. Hymns are, however, of necessity all about the Christian's desire for salvation and fear of damnation, and so they only made him worry more about his soul than ever. Newton also tried taking Cowper over to his house to divert his mind by a bright, cheering talk, but there again he was incapable of talking about any subject except religion; and Cowper's mind remained undiverted. Impassioned adjuration did no good either. Newton used to hold forth for hours about the mercy of God as they paced up and down the leaf-strewn garden paths of the Vicarage. For the time Cowper would be convinced, but in a few hours he was as bad again as before. Newton began to despair. " Dear Sir Cowper was as much in the depths as ever," he wrote to his sister. " He led me to speak last night from Hebrews xi. 10. I do not think he was the better for it." When Hebrews xi. 10 failed, what was one to do ?

Mrs. Unwin's placid firmness was far better suited than Newton's apostolic zeal to deal with Cowper's difficulties. And, indeed, when he was feeling really miserable, her presence was the only thing that gave him the slightest comfort. Yet even she could only soothe him temporarily. She did not know enough about mental diseases in general, or Cowper's in particular, to do him any lasting good. Actually, poor lady, she was, through no fault of her own, the cause of an event that may finally have sent him off his head. For some time past the little household at Orchard Side had been dwindling. Two years before William Unwin had left to take up a living at Stock; and now Miss Unwin became engaged to be married to a Mr. Powley. It was a most desirable match. For not only was he a clergyman, but he had actually been sent down from Oxford for holding Evangelical prayer meetings. Nor could Cowper much regret the departure of Miss Unwin, whose early shyness of him had hardened into suspicion. But propriety would not permit him to go on living with Mrs. Unwin alone. To part was unthinkable to either; and so, in the autumn of 1772, they agreed to marry. Can it be that the prospect of so momentous, so intimate a change in his life, the basic horrors of his existence, the thought of his mental disease, and perhaps his physical imperfections, swept back into his mind and thrust his tottering reason finally from its throne? It does not seem unlikely.

At any rate, from this time events moved rapidly to their catastrophe. On January 24, 1773, Newton was woken at five in the morning by a messenger from Mrs. Unwin asking him to come over to Orchard Side at once. He hurried through the raw darkness to find Cowper in a fit of raving madness brought on by some peculiarly horrible dream. After some hours the fit passed; but it recurred. And from this time on he was treated as an invalid. He was moved to the Vicarage, where, he had a fancy, he felt more at ease. Doctors were sent for, and Mrs. Unwin never left him. But not yet was he quite defeated. In his more lucid intervals he still clung with a feeble, unconquerable pertinacity to the Lord who saved him. In an awed wonder Newton listened to him as he lay half dead on his bed, after some frightful bout of mania, whispering with the last painful breath of his spent forces that he welcomed his sufferings, and that if he could get rid of them by stretching out his hand he would not do so without God's approval. For he knew God was good and he trusted in Him. But he could not hold out for ever. Another shock, the few frail strands of faith to which he still clung were torn from his bleeding fingers and he fell headlong into the abyss. On the night of February 24th he had a dream. What it precisely was no one knows; but in it, amid circumstances of unspeakable horror, he heard from the lips of God Himself the certain and irrevocable sentence of his damnation. The next morning the last vestiges of sanity had left him. He did not know where he was or who was speaking to him. Cowering back on his bed in that pleasant Vicarage room, he saw only the distorted faces of the demons, heard only the roaring of the flames of hell open to receive him.

Once again the powers of darkness had beaten him. Risen in the storms of madness, in the storms of madness the short, strange day of his faith had sunk to its setting. And it has been a commonplace of subsequent literary history that the madness was brought on by the faith. A commonplace, but not a truth; Cowper's madness finds its origin far deeper in the sufferings of childhood, it may be in inherent physical defect. All his life it was hung over him. And religion, so far from being the cause, was the most considerable of the remedies by which he tried to get rid of it. It failed. And once he realized that it had failed, it is true that the emotional tension encouraged by Evangelicalism, and the personal responsibility for its own state which it placed on the individual soul, did increase Cowper's nervous agitation and so accelerate the advent of his madness. But though it accelerated it, it did not make that advent more sure.

On the contrary, it had been far nearer curing him than any other remedy. The life of active interests and cheerful social amusements so naïvely recommended by subsequent historians he had tried without any effect; because such a life did not try to deal with he causes of his malady at all. Of course, Evangelicalism did not go to the root of it, for it had not the necessary scientific knowledge; but it did face its deeper problems. It did seek to fight the enemies of the spirit with spiritual weapons, to expel, not merely to evade them. And the consequence was that 1763 to 1767 was the one happy period of his mature existence. Under the shadow of later years he would look back and ask himself if it had not been part of another life. In wonder he gazed at the world of familiar things transfigured by a golden and unearthly radiance; himself in the midst, free and fearless.

CHAPTER IV

THE next two years of Cowper's life are a lurid blackness, spasmodically lit up by flashes of more lurid light.
The structure of his nervous system was overturned,
the coherence of his thought destroyed, as they had not
been even in 1763. It was not only that he had
succumbed a second time, and therefore of necessity
minded far more than he had the first. But his collapse
came as the result of a far severer shock. His first
madness had been the culmination of a slow decline of
spirits from a happiness at best but partial. This was
the sudden and complete failure of a force in whose
ability to protect him he had believed implicitly. All
his life he had sought such a force; at last he
thought he had found it, and he attached himself
to it with all the unquestioning trust he had never
been able to give to anything else. Then it collapsed.
And in proportion as it had made him happy, its
collapse made him wretched. It was as if he had been
foully betrayed by an old and beloved friend. The
bottom was knocked out of his universe. His whole
scheme of things had been turned upside down; and
obscurely he felt that all his other values were turned
upside down with it. The one supreme good had
proved false: how should lesser goods prove more
genuine? The only coherent thought in the inchoate
quagmire of agony in which he writhed was a dim
obsession that he must not trust to anyone or anything.
From Newton and Mrs. Newton, at times even from

Mary herself, he shrank in wild-eyed horror. He refused to touch any food they brought him, for fear it was poisoned. Had he not loved them next his faith ? Then they must be next his faith in falseness. Dr. Cotton was called in to help him ; but Dr. Cotton was associated in Cowper's mind with the happiness of his conversion, and he turned away from him with dull suspicion. Suicide itself, which had seemed to him the unforgivable sin, now began to present itself to him in the strange guise of a Christian obligation. It struck him that Abraham had reconciled himself to God by the sacrifice of what he held most dear—his son : might not he reconcile himself to God by the sacrifice of what he held most dear—his own life ? Once again he tried to hang himself. Once again he failed. But this time he had no reaction against it. He only felt that he had lost the last despairing chance of redeeming himself, and he sank into a dumb lethargy of despair. He came down to meals and went for walks and worked in the garden, with bent brows and tense, fixed stare, oblivious of all around him. Only when he was asleep did he forget his troubles. Mrs. Unwin, tiptoeing into his room with shaded candle to see how he was resting, would wonder to see the lined brow smooth, the worn face relaxed in a childlike smile, while at intervals he murmured in a drowsy happiness fragments of those hymns and prayers in which of old he had been wont to express his unsullied trust in God. When morning came he would be as bad as ever. He only knew the normal world in dreams : awake he lived in a nightmare.

It seemed impossible that he should ever rise a second time from such an abyss. But he did. For all his hyper-sensitiveness Cowper was not without vitality. Indeed, his very sensitiveness, his quicksilver responsiveness to circumstances and suggestion, could only have belonged to a nature in whom the

pulse of life beat high.   You muſt be very much alive
to feel as much as that.   His spirit, so fragile, so
dejeéted, so palpitatingly naked to pain, yet bore
within it a small, welling fountain of vitality that, unless
completely deſtroyed, could never long be kept from
flowing.   Cramped by physical disability, clogged by
nervous inhibition, shut in by external circumſtances,
it yet within a short time began to gush forth and
force a passage for itself to the daylight.   Nothing
happened to alter his conviétion that he was damned ;
but slowly, gradually, impelled by nothing but the
sheer impulse to live behind them, his torn nerves
began to mend, his spirits to resume their equilibrium.
All the same they could not have done it alone.   Cowper could never have endured through his period of
chaotic despair long enough to let the myſterious forces
of life within him begin to work unless he had had
something or someone to support him.   In a word,
he would never have recovered if it had not been for
Mrs. Unwin.

From the moment he became ill she gave herself up
body and soul to his service as calmly and unobtrusively and decisively as she did everything else.   It
was not a light task.   At firſt, Cowper as often as not
was a moaning, gibbering maniac ;   later sunk in a
ſtupor.   Sometimes he shrank away from her in
suspicious horror, more often sat for whole days
together without showing a sign of pleasure at her
presence.   Yet he could not bear her to be away from
him for a moment.   Every minute of every day she
watched with unrelaxed attention for the firſt signs
of one of his fits of mania, that she might soothe it
before it grew uncontrollable.   Often she never left
him even at night : when she did she never knew if
she might not be woken up to ſtop him killing himself.
The days lengthened to summer, contraéted to winter,
lengthened to summer again.   And ſtill the crisis

was not passed, and still her task went on. It was a terrible strain. Her health was impaired for ever.

She had other annoyances to put up with. The parishioners of Olney thought her connection with Cowper an odd one, and they said so. But Mrs. Unwin was unconventional, as only the simple-minded can be. She had always been accustomed to do what she thought right regardless of difficulty. And she never thought about what other people would think of her, because she never thought about herself at all. Nor was she encouraged to do so by her religion. Her Evangelicalism was not the religion of respectability. It had the virtues as well as the defects of its exclusiveness. If it taught her to shun the pleasures of the world as wicked, it also taught her to scorn its censures as trivial. It shone out, the sole and heavenly light by which she should guide herself in a dark world. It was the fanaticism of her faith that enabled Mrs. Unwin to go through what she did. Nor did its narrowness matter. Depth, not breadth, was what she needed. Against the surrounding blackness her plain, determined figure assumes the heroic proportions of an Antigone.

She saved Cowper: the mere consciousness of a tangible human relationship gave him a solid foothold on existence when all the rest of the ground seemed collapsing beneath him. The feeling that someone loved him, and someone sane and good, made him want to cling to life when he was far too distracted to be affected by a more abstract motive. He held on to Mrs. Unwin's hand like a child in the dark, and after two years a few faint streaks of light began to appear. He grew calmer, began to take an interest in things around him; in May 1774 he was well enough to go back to Orchard Side.

Newton could not pretend he was sorry to see him go. Not that his Evangelicalism had been any less

practical than Mrs. Unwin's. He had put up Cowper
in his house for a year. He had put up Mrs. Unwin
too, in face of the outraged public opinion of his parish.
And he had refused to let either of them pay a penny
for their keep, because he thought a Christian minister
ought not to take money for doing good. But he had
found it a strain. It was no joke to have a lunatic
living in one's small house for a year, especially such
a gloomy lunatic. " Yesterday, as he was feeding
the chickens," he writes with a certain pathos, " some
incident made him smile. I am pretty sure it is the
first smile that has been seen on his face for sixteen
months." Such a guest certainly detracted from
those amenities that the most Evangelical of clergymen
had a right to expect of family life. And there seemed
no reason why Cowper should ever go. By 1774 he
was physically quite well, and there was his own house
waiting for him, just across the garden. But when
Mary suggested they should return there, he only
burst into tears. The robust-minded Newton found
it indeed hard to sympathize with such an attitude,
especially as Cowper was putting him to considerable
expense. Try as he might, as week succeeded week
and month succeeded month he could not help remembering this. " Upon the whole, I have not been weary
of my cross," he reflected when at last they had gone,
" yet sometimes my heart has been importunate and
rebellious."

For the second time Cowper had begun to emerge
from the black cloud of madness. But this second
recovery was of a very different kind from the first.
That had broken over him in a great wave of joy that
had washed all the horrors of madness clean out of
his mind, and quickened him to an intensity of spirit
he had never known before. But his second madness
had inflicted a deeper wound on his nervous system—
far too deep, in fact, to disappear in a moment. And

now he felt no sudden change in his spirits. He still believed he was damned. So little hold had he on reality that for years after this he could never be sure if the Newton he saw was really Newton or some phantom masquerading in his shape. Only his vitality was so strong that in spite of injuries it had begun in time to force him towards recovery. Even if he was to be damned in the next world he found some enjoyment in things in this ; and he began to feel he had better take his pleasure as he could and while he could. Resolutely averting his eyes from the painful subject of his soul, therefore, he began to concentrate on the interests and happenings of every day.

First he could only do this sporadically. His whole being had been so shattered by his illness that he was incapable of apprehending happiness except in snatches, and those far too seldom for him to string together on them any scheme of existence. Most of the time he lay like a man rescued from drowning, in a sort of twilit coma, neither sad nor happy, only relieved to be free from the struggling agony of the moment before. A chance phrase or thought would as often as not recall his spiritual condition to him ; the world would grow dark around him, and he would bury his face in his hands. But now and again the sight of some natural beauty would breathe a whiff of happiness into his heart ; his eyes would brighten, and he would look around. Or his wasted lips would part in involuntary laughter at some prank of cat or dog playing in the garden. All his moments of enjoyment came from Nature or animals. The keenest pleasures of his childhood had been connected with them ; and now, at this his third re-birth into the world of sense, it was the pleasures of childhood that first stirred a response within him.

One day, a little time after they had come back to Orchard Side, a neighbour arrived with a tame hare he thought Cowper might like to keep as a pet. He was delighted with it. For hours every day he would watch its antics and try to tame it. The good people of Olney, delighted that something had at last given pleasure to the poor gentleman at Orchard Side, all began to give him hares. This was too much of a good thing. Cowper thanked them all with his usual politeness, but only kept three of their presents. For the next few years these hares—Bess, Puss and Tiny—were a dominating interest in his life. His sympathy had always enabled him to enter into the lives of those he saw around him. And with the hares he had entered into a life from which all the painful problems of human existence were necessarily absent. In their company he escaped for a moment from hell—not into heaven, but into Eden before the Fall; into a life physical and sylvan, innocent of the knowledge of good and evil; a remote Hans Andersen garden world, where a blade of grass was as big as a bush and the greatest enemy was a hornet and the garden wall was the end of the cosmos. The hares—bold Bess, timid affectionate Puss, who pulled at his coat with his teeth to make him go out, and surly Tiny, who gambolled with an expression of dignified disgust on his whiskered features—grew as individual and entertaining to him as his friends; only they were without that disturbing human attribute, the soul, the very name of which made him feel depressed. He never tired of observing their habits, noticing how Bess liked to spend the morning asleep among the cucumbers, and Tiny always frisked most wildly when the sky grew dark before a storm. He had work to do for them too: to get their food, bread and lettuce in the summer, and bread and shredded carrot in the winter; to shake out their straw beds; to shut them up for the night. He made them each a little wooden hutch, and devised a little entrance into the drawing-room through which they could run in and out from these hutches in the evenings.

All this was a great step forward. For the first time since his illness he had found happiness, not in capricious moments of emotion, but in a regular interest outside himself. The daily tasks imposed something of order on his life without regard for his moods; while the light manual labour of carpentering and cleaning diverted his attention, without tiring his brain. From now on he took a steady turn for the better. The hares had so intensified his love of animals that he began to keep more pets. Goldfish, guinea-pigs, birds, a cat and a dog—Mungo—successively made their way into the house, till poor Mary must have felt she was living in a menagerie rather than a human dwelling. Then Cowper took to gardening again. There was not much garden at Orchard Side. But he sowed and weeded and watered every inch of what there was; was always out if the weather allowed, sweeping the paths or planting the neat rows of mignonette and lavender, whose scent was to blow so deliciously in at the window when the summer did come. At first all his garden was out-doors. Then someone gave him some pineapple seeds; he got a frame for them and finally a little greenhouse. Besides the pineapples, he grew geraniums in it and orange blossom, and even a New Zealand flower called the Broallia, which both he and Mary thought " the most elegant flower they had ever seen." Lord Dartmouth, who came over one day to see it with Newton, thought so too; so that they felt they must be right.

Cowper threw himself into gardening and keeping hares with the same passion with which he had thrown himself into Latin-verse writing when he was fifteen, and religious exercises when he was thirty-two. But they could not occupy his whole attention, and as he got better he began to look about for occupation that would take up more of his time. Carpentering was his first choice. He used to do odd jobs about the house, mending cracked windows and rickety table legs, and he made a stool and a chair as a present for Mary. He enjoyed the work very much, but it hurt his eyes, so he had to give it up. Drawing attracted him next: by its help he felt he would be able on the rawest winter day to dwell for a little amid those summer scenes that had such power to soothe his soul. He had a master at hand in a Mr. Andrews, who lived near by. Olney was no centre of the visual arts, and most of this poor gentleman's time was spent in carving scythes and draped urns for tombstones. But he also taught people to draw. Cowper gave himself up to his new pursuit with his wonted enthusiasm, sat all day before his easel drawing dabchicks and mountains, and by the end of a few months had become sufficiently proficient to present Mr. and Mrs. Newton with two sketches for their parlour wall. But, as he might have expected, the work began to hurt his eyes, as much as carpentering had done. And he was forced to give it up too.

And now what was he to do? Idleness left him vitally open to nervous attack, yet there seemed nothing he could do that would occupy his time. Suddenly he thought of literature. Even since he was a child he had amused himself by writing occasional verses. Why should he not attempt something more ambitious? The idea took hold of him as no other had done. Not only would composition occupy his mind, but he might by means of it teach valuable moral lessons. For even in his present condition of mind, when the whole subject of religion looked black in his eyes, his conscience was worried by the thought that he was not in some way trying to further the cause of God. Once more he took up a new task with tremendous energy, and within a few months he had finished two long poems. He worked so hard, in fact, that Mary thought he was making himself ill, and begged him to stop. He submitted; but the lack of occupation brought on such an alarming fit of depression that she very soon besought him to take up his pen again. He was never to lay it aside till his last illness. Thus, as a chance diversion of convalescence, did Cowper begin that work which alone has kept his name clear from those mists of oblivion which enshroud most of his contemporaries. At the age of forty-nine, unintentionally, he entered on the career of a famous poet.

The effect of his new work on his life was immediate. At last he had found an occupation which really filled his time. Gardening, carpentering, drawing, had at best only been able to occupy him while he was actually working at them, and as he got more accustomed to doing so, they had not been able to hold him even then. While his careful fingers worked, his mind wandered, wandered irresistibly as Fatima to the forbidden door of his spiritual condition. But he could not write without thinking about it all the time he did it. And he would go on thinking about it when he was not writing at all. His life was therefore no longer a darkness lit up by spasmodic and capricious flashes. It had structure and purpose, and though there were dark moments in it, they did not break up this structure and purpose. Besides, writing gave him a means of self-expression, an outlet for his rising energy, a satisfaction for his starved vitality, which accelerated his nervous recovery sevenfold. Soon he felt strong enough to turn his attention to the world of human beings. He began to write regularly to Hill and Unwin again, to take an interest in the life of Olney. By 1780 he had managed to weld the shattered, scattered fragments of his life and thought into some

sort of permanent pattern. The mists of madness
have parted on a new phase of Cowper's existence.

It was not at all like the one on which they closed.
The unearthly light and unearthlier darkness have
vanished, and we are back into the plain daylight
of the eighteenth century, the busy, sequestered
domestic world of Berkhamsted and Southampton
Row. On Cowper himself neither his Evangelicalism
nor his madness had left much outward trace. Long
absence from society had, indeed, given his manners a
shy, old-fashioned ceremoniousness; but this only
added an individual and delightful flavour to the irony
and sweetness which they enshrined. And to women
especially, his anxious courtesy was charming. He
was grown a little fat and a little bald : was he not
nearly fifty! But there had always been a sober
foppishness about him which had made him take care
of his appearance. Even at his most religious, he
would always write to William Unwin to get him a
" smartish " stock-buckle or a new-fashioned cocked
hat. And now, dressed for the afternoon in blue coat
and green satin waistcoat, with his scanty hair rein-
forced by some from the barber and done in a bag
with a black ribbon, and carrying a snuffbox in his
hand, he looked, as he said, " a very smart youth for
his years."

Nor did the outward ordering of his life offend
against the conventional standards of his neighbours.
The holy singularity of which he had been so proud
at Huntingdon was gone. Instead of vigils and
meditations and prayer meetings, his time was taken
up by the thousand trivial necessary avocations of
house and garden that occupied the people around him.
His life was still very regular, its unvarying round
modified only by the seasons. In winter, when the
greater part of his work was done, it was spent mostly
in one room—the little wainscoted parlour of Orchard

Side, thirteen foot square, with its spindle-legged chairs and its view of the street and its print of Cowper's old friend Thurlow over the chimney-piece. It was here, at the civilized hour of ten, in his dressing-gown and cap, that he had his breakfast, and Mary poured out his morning cup of steaming, scented bohea for him. He used to sit on for a little after breakfast, reading while she sewed. If something struck him in his book he would read it aloud to her; then they relapsed into a placid silence. Next he must see after the greenhouse and the hares and the birds and the cat. And now he must sit down to the two or three hours' writing which made up his very reasonable working day. His writing-table was an old card-table; but of course it had never been used as such since it had come into the possession of this godly household. It was not very good for writing on, as it was so low. Cowper had painfully to heave an atlas on to it every time he wanted to work. He and Mary ate off it too; but it was no better for that than for writing. It had little shallow hollows round the edge, originally meant for counters, and Cowper and Mary always forgot about these when they were covered up by the tablecloth, and put their glasses down on them. So that they were always spilt, and often broken. Still, it was the only table in the house that was the right size, and they made the best of it. A walk followed, then dinner; and then possibly another walk, sharp, through the frozen or muddy lanes, with the sear leaves rustling round Cowper's feet, and Mungo leaping before him. Nobody in those days was so silly as to go out if the weather was really bad. Indeed their clothes did not permit it. And during the bad weather of 1781 Cowper and Mary hardly stirred from their tiny house and tinier garden from November to February. But Cowper was far too regular in his habits to forego his daily

exercise, and on bad days he used to swing dumb-bells
or skip or play a decorous game of battledore and
shuttlecock with Mary. As the short winter's day
faded to a close, once more he heaved the atlas on to
the table, and sat down to read or write. Sometimes
as he sat there in the gathering dusk, where the firelight set the room aſtir with shadows, the paper would
drop from his hand and he would sink into a drowsy
reverie. Idly he fancied caſtles and foreſts in the
crumbling coals, discerned portents in the fantaſtic
filaments of soot that formed and fell on the bars of
the grate. And then his attention would wander,
and he would sit gazing with fixed, absent eyes, loſt
for a short moment perhaps in some country of his
desire—green blossoming woods of spring, or by the
glittering sea. Suddenly a noise would penetrate
his consciousness—the wind rattling the window, or
the maid coming in with the tea. Blinking his eyes
in the unaccuſtomed brightness of the candlelight,
he would shift his position and return to earth. And
now began that moment of the day that Cowper liked
beſt—tea-time on a winter's evening. He liked tea
better than any other drink—it gave him juſt the
mild ſtimulus that his nerves required. And the
little meal in the cosy, candlelit room, alone with his
beſt friend, and the winter's night shut out by curtains,
was the very incarnation of that innocent security
which all his life had been his idea of perfeĉt happiness.
The rain might drum on the window, the wind whiſtle
along the deserted ſtreet; it only emphasized the
warmth and comfort inside, where the kettle hummed,
and the cat lapped up its milk, and Cowper and Mary
laughed over the day's happenings. They were
interrupted by the twang of a horn and the hollow
sound of the galloping of hoofs outside. It was the
poſt arriving at the " Bull Inn." And a few minutes
later a rush of cold air would blow into the house as

the door opened to admit letters and newspaper—that newspaper that brought to Olney the news of Mr. Fox's last speech, and the Duke of Devonshire's last rout, and Mr. Wilke's last enormity. After tea, the little door in the wall was unlatched, and for a short time the room was alive with the scampering of the hares. Then Cowper and Mary settled down to a quiet evening. She always worked, either knitting his socks or embroidering.

> " The well-depicted flower,"

as Cowper put it,

> " Wrought patiently into the snowy lawn
> Unfolds its bosom. . . ."

Sometimes he read aloud, sometimes copied out what he had written in the morning, sometimes, if he was tired, just wound her wool for her. But whatever they were either of them doing, it generally ended in conversation—long, delicious conversation, now gay, now serious ; and now their voices would soften in tender reminiscence, now hush into a silence more intimate than speech. A country supper of eggs and radishes, enlivened by a modest glass of wine, rounded off their evening. And then, candle in hand, they said good-night. Summer days passed in much the same occupations as winter. But they were spent for the most part outdoors, reading or working in the garden ; and Mary and Cowper often took a walk before supper.

They were not confined exclusively to each other's society. The " County," indeed, they did not see much of. To do so entailed keeping a carriage ; and, anyway, Cowper had very little in common with the card-playing, ball-going County ladies, and still less with the red-faced, two-bottle, fox-hunting Squire Westerns who were their husbands and brothers. His

pets had given him a hatred of all forms of sport.   He
attacked cruelty to animals unceasingly both in prose
and verse—not always his best verse—

> " I would not number in my list of friends
>   (Though graced with polished manners and fine sense
> Yet wanting sensibility) the man
> Who needlessly sets foot upon a worm.
> An inadvertent step may crush the snail
> That crawls at evening on the public path,
> But he that has humanity, forewarned,
> Will tread aside and let the reptile live."

But to find friends Cowper did not need to fly high
or far.   Newton, indeed, was with him no longer.   He
had not been so successful at Olney as he had intended.
After the first shock of surprise had worn off, the
people had ceased to pay much heed to his vehement
ministrations, and in spite, possibly because of, the
fact that he redoubled his efforts, they came in time
actively to dislike him.   His unpopularity reached its
climax when he announced from his pulpit one autumn
Sunday that he hoped no one would illuminate their
houses or make a bonfire on the approaching 5th of
November.   Not only did many people stick candles
in their windows who had never thought of doing such
a thing before, but a large crowd of infuriated revellers
marched down to attack the Vicarage.   Newton was
for defying these Sons of Belial like the prophets of old ;
but the prayers of his panic-stricken wife persuaded
him to take the more pacific course of paying them to
go away.   His pride was doubly wounded.   And when
in 1779 he was offered the Parish of St. Mary Woolnoth in London he accepted it.   His resilient spirits
soon recovered themselves at the prospect of the
greater scope for his talents and enterprise afforded by
a London parish.   " I am about to form a connection
for life with one Mary Woolnoth, a reputed London
Saint in Lombard Street," he remarked humorously.

His departure did not mean as much to Cowper as it would have done ten years before. Since his illness each of them felt the other's company a slight strain. Cowper could not bear to mention the subject of religion; and he knew Newton cared to talk of nothing else. So that, though he was still very fond of him, he felt awkward in his presence; and even when he wrote to him, as he did regularly after he had left, it was in an embarrassed, self-depreciatory tone, as if apologizing for his inability to provide what Newton had a right to demand. Newton, for his part, had not lost his affection for Cowper. But his dominating nature resented the feeling that anyone had escaped, however unwillingly, from the orbit of his influence; and temperamentally he had no sympathy with defeatism. He could not help thinking Cowper would be all right if he would only make an effort. And he told him so. This in its turn irritated Cowper, who felt Newton was not making the slightest attempt to understand him. All the same, when the moment of departure actually arrived, all Cowper's other feelings were overwhelmed in a gush of regretful emotion. His timid, constant nature, fearful of the future, tenacious of the past, felt any change a painful wrench. And, besides, Newton and Mrs. Newton and the whole Newton household were bound up in his mind with that period of his life which, however tragic its termination, was yet its only period of joy and of hope. " The Vicarage looks a melancholy object," he wrote to Mrs. Newton. " As I walked in the garden I saw the smoke issuing from the study chimney, and said to myself, ' That used to be a sign that Mr. Newton was there, but it is so no longer.' The walls of the house know nothing of the change that has taken place. The bolt of the chamber door sounds just as it used to do; and when Mr. Page goes upstairs, for aught I know the fall of his foot could

hardly be distinguished from that of Mr. Newton.
But Mr. Newton's foot will never be heard upon that
staircase again. . . . Though in many respects I have
no more sensibility left in me than there is in brick
and mortar, yet I am not permitted to be quite unfeeling
on this subject."

Even when Newton was gone, however, Cowper was
not deprived of clerical society. Fashionable or fox-
hunting parsons were even more dreadful in his eyes
than fashionable or fox-hunting squires; but Newton
had managed to make Olney a little centre of " faithful " ministers. Mr. Scott, the curate of Weston,
was an example of the extraordinary force of his
personality. Till middle life he had lived the respectable, unimpassioned life of the orthodox Church of
England clergyman. Then, going into a cottage one
day by chance, he found Newton praying by a dying
man. The faith that glowed in his eyes, the ardour
that rang through every modulation of his voice, so
affected Scott that from that very day he became a
strong Evangelical. Cowper saw a certain amount of
him. He was a scholar, and used to drop in to ask
advice on a point of style in some commentary he was
writing. And once a fortnight at least the little
parlour at Orchard Side was filled with the huge form
and exuberant personality of Mr. Bull, the Nonconformist minister from Newport Pagnell.

The Reverend William Bull was one of those strong,
independent, eccentric characters that England, and
rural England especially, seems to produce at all
times as frequently and effortlessly as those writhen
and sturdy oak trees which they so closely resemble.
He was the son of a yeoman; and a strong religious
experience when he was a child had decided him to
enter the Independent ministry. He had taught
himself Hebrew, been ordained, and had spent the
rest of his life at Newport Pagnell, where he divided

M

his time between ministering to his flock and working
in his study. This lonely and self-dependent course
of life, in which all his natural idiosyncrasies had
been allowed to develop unmodified by conventional
influence, had streaked every aspect of his character
and habits with a kind of quaintness. He had a rich,
fiery, winning personality, and imagination and humour
and learning as well. But his imagination ran riot
in fantastic flights; his humour was extravagant and
uncouth; and his learning was a lumber room of
curious information and ideas—valuable and worthless
indiscriminately heaped together—more like that of
some seventeenth-century savant, Browne or Burton,
than the regulated classicism of eighteenth-century
scholarship. His amusements were eccentric, too.
He had a niche cut in his garden wall, where he would
sit and contemplate, almost completely surrounded
with brickwork within three or four inches of his
nose. And he measured the circumference of his
small plot of garden, and then took exercise by walking
doggedly round it every day, marking each round by
moving a bit of shot along a groove in the wall till
he had walked five miles. His life revolved round
religion; but his religion, like his learning, seemed
to belong less to the eighteenth than to the seventeenth
century: it was mystical and disordered, given to
expressing itself in wild vagaries of the imagination,
even in jokes. He was an eloquent preacher in a
style of his own, full of homely metaphors and allusions,
and so much in earnest that the very mention of the
Passion was enough to fill his eyes with tears. But
in the midst of the most emotional passage, perhaps
on the Passion, he would stop to bawl objurgations at
someone trying to slip away from church before the
sermon was over. He was naïve, too. Once he was
persuaded to visit Scotland. He enjoyed himself,
but was very much concerned not to be ensnared by

the worldly splendours he saw there. Cardinal Beaton's palace he said was fine, but not as fine as heaven; he was at pains that people should realize he could not think of comparing it to heaven. But in spite of his peculiarities he was by far the most interesting person living near Olney. After all, it was something to find someone with humour and imagination and learning, however eccentric his habits. Cowper met him with Newton, and took to him immediately. He had that infectious vitality that always attracted him; and soon it was a recognized thing that Bull should dine at Orchard Side once a fortnight. His idiosyncrasies appeared even in his personal relationships. Sometimes he would be robustly mirthful, at others subdued, melancholy and confiding; but Cowper liked him all the better for this. To be made a partner of another's mood gave him just that assurance of intimacy without which friendship was no pleasure to him. He was more put off by Bull's smoking, a habit which, as a symbol of exclusively male society, he had always detested; but he grew even to like it, so much did it seem part of those happy evenings when dear " Taureau," as he affectionately called Bull, sat puffing away beside him in the garden of Orchard Side, or, more rarely, in the dusky, casemented library of his own house at Newport Pagnell.

But the great of Olney—clergymen and schoolmasters—were not the only people in whom Cowper took an interest. From the sash-window of the parlour, year after year, he used to watch the sleepy, desultory life of the country street, and note with unfailing, amused interest its distinctive figures: Palmer the draper, standing in the doorway of his shop, Wilson the barber, strolling along, a wig box on his arm, such a strict Sabbatarian that he refused to dress even the hair of a lady of title on Sunday; so that she had, poor thing! to have it done the evening before, and sit up all night for fear of disarranging it : Nathan Sample, the maltster, who, though less regularly religious, was always ready to declaim against the Papists. Every morning, just as Cowper was cleaning his teeth, he would see old Geary Ball shambling past the window—Geary Ball, once a burning and shining light of the Gospel, but now only regular in his attendance at the bar of the " Fox and Grapes." And after him, perhaps, might strut a pursy figure, with thumb on hip and *blasé* expression on his face—a lacemaker whose name Cowper never knew, but whom he called the " Olney misanthrope," because in all the years he had seen him he had never observed him speaking to anyone.

Nor did he merely look on at Olney life. He took part in it as well. It had got about that he had been a lawyer, and the front door of Orchard Side often opened and shut to admit some shopkeeper anxious to learn some point of law, but less anxious to pay a professional lawyer to tell him. " They cannot be persuaded," said Cowper ruefully, " that a head once covered by a legal periwig can be deficient in those natural endowments that it is supposed to cover." Then he took part in charitable work. It was he who, when the Olney lace-makers were starving, wrote to Mr. Smith, the rich Nottingham banker, for help ; and when Mr. Smith very generously sent fifty pounds, it was Cowper who distributed it. Again, he was one of the prime movers in establishing the Sunday School in 1785. Indeed, it was high time; for in spite of poor Newton's efforts, the children of Olney, even those of seven years old, were profane. Cowper and Mary had often hastily to turn aside when they met a party of them, lest their sensitive ears might be offended by the frightful language they might hear.

Indeed, life at Olney was not without its incidents.

Out of the window one day Cowper saw a scene of Hogarthian farce. The beadle was flogging a man for stealing, the magistrate beating the beadle for not hitting hard enough, and an angry virago beating the magistrate for beating the beadle. On another night one of the hares ran away : a terrible excitement ! Half the town was out after it. It ran two miles, and a man caught it in a back yard, and Cowper rewarded him with the large sum of six shillings. In 1784 came the Election, and the candidate—" a most loving, kissing, kind-hearted gentleman "—came to solicit Cowper's interest, and surprised them all in the middle of tea, and kissed Mrs. Unwin and the cook. The monotony of the daily round was also varied now and again by visitors. William Unwin came, which was pleasant, and Mrs. Powley, which was less so. Cowper noticed that she never laughed at any of his jokes ; he concluded she had no sense of humour. Actually she believed him to have robbed her mother of £1800 ; so perhaps she was throughout the visit in a state of scarcely suppressed indignation. Newton came to stay once or twice too. His company, we know, Cowper felt to be rather a strain. But he enjoyed having Mrs. Newton, and still more Miss Catlett, Newton's niece, whom he had adopted, a cheerful child of thirteen or fourteen. " Euphrosyne, the laughing lady," Cowper called her, and " Oh, Miss Catlett," he would say, looking across the table with a gentle twinkle in his eye, " oh, Miss Catlett, will you have a cutlet ? " Other visitors came to Olney besides those who came to Orchard Side. Once, in 1738, a menagerie arrived, with a real live lion. The keeper would have put his head in its mouth, only Cowper besought him not to unless he had another to spare. And in the April of 1784 Lord Houghton's regiment was billeted in Olney, and the band gave a concert one morning just outside Orchard Side. Bright glinted the sun on red coats and pipeclayed breeches, shrill and sweet came the sound of bugle and fife on the chill spring air. Regardless of the cold, Cowper hung out of the window, striving to catch every note. He wondered if he was wrong to enjoy it so much. In the days of his conversion he would certainly have thought so; but his life was so starved of æsthetic experience, that the little regimental band filled him with a rapture not to be resisted.

Starved, did I say? I was wrong. For though the achievements of conscious art did not come his way, their place in his emotional life was more than supplied by the works of Nature. He had always loved natural beauty, but never with such an exclusive intensity as now. It was to it he had turned first of all when he began to recover, and as his energy increased he only turned to it the more. Cut off as he was from the satisfactions of mysticism on the one hand and those of active life on the other, all the capacity for joy inherent in his highly-strung nature had to pour itself down this one narrow channel. The fact that it was narrow only made it flow the stronger. "Oh, I could spend whole days and moonlight nights," he exclaimed, "in feeding upon a lovely prospect! Mine eyes drink the rivers as they flow." His was not the visionary Wordsworthian feeling that loves the visible world as the incarnation of a Divine eternal Spirit. Even the religious tinge with which it had been invested in the days of his conversion had now vanished, though he still prefaced any expression of his feeling by an acknowledgment to God. But in reality a great deal of Cowper's pleasure arose from the fact that natural beauty belonged, like his hares, to that part of life into which the dismal problems of the soul did not enter, that it had no need of a remoter charm ungathered from the eye and asked for its appreciation only the immediate instinctive pleasure that it stimulated. Indeed his enjoyment gained an exquisite, intolerable poignancy from his conviction that it had no significance in that world of spiritual values which, in his view, was the only reality, that all this tangible, palpable, ravishing beauty he saw around him was really but the shadow of a shade, which within a few brief years would be lost to him for ever.

And if he did not love Nature in the way Words-worth did, neither did he, like Keats, love it because it fed his imagination, because he could use those aspects of it he thought the loveliest to create the land of his dream. He loved it with an objective, self-effacing love, for what it was; and every aspect of it was beautiful to him. There was no sound in Nature that was not harmonious outdoors, he said, after sitting out one sunny morning in the garden. Bees, dogs, even geese, he loved them all—except perhaps a donkey; and even the donkey he disliked because it had been braying close to him just when he was trying to work. And what he felt of natural sounds he felt of sights and smells as well. Actually the country of his preference, humdrum, overgrown Buckinghamshire, was not very pretty. But it was the country he knew best, and therefore he liked it best. With all its intensity, Cowper's love of Nature was of a piece with the rest of his feelings, an affection rather than a passion. He loved it as he loved Mrs. Unwin, quietly, patiently, tenaciously, without moods or explosions, with a strength that grew with the passage of years, cemented by habit, hallowed by a thousand tender recollections. And he knew the object of his love as one can only know an old friend. It presented no detail so tiny that he did not remark it, no fleeting alteration that escaped him. With the delicate accuracy of a micro-scope, he would note how already, in September, the sycamore showed red against the varying green of the surrounding trees; how the cock waded with altered, hampered gait through the winter snow; the curious, sweet, amber smell the earth gave forth in hot weather; the squirrel's winter nest of wool and leaves hidden in the recesses of the hollow elm. Cowper had walked so long and so often in the woods that the animals did not mind him. The rabbits did not cease to gambol as he passed, and the ring-doves cooed at his approach.

His preoccupation with detail was increased by the fact that the range of his observation was so limited. It was confined, indeed, to the garden and his daily walks; and the walks he could go were few. There was a sequestered field he liked, especially on the hot summer days, where he lingered listening to the black-birds beneath the flickering shade of a group of poplars which reflected themselves in the waters of the Ouse, winding between them. One melancholy day he arrived to find the grass and a few stumps naked to the sunshine. The trees had been cut down.

" The poplars are felled," sang Cowper, " and farewell to the shade
And the whispering sound of the cool colonnade."

After this his walks were almost entirely limited to the Wilderness of Weston Park—a country house about a mile from Olney. It belonged to a Mr. Throck-morton, who gave Cowper the keys. It was one of those civilized wildernesses that Capability Brown devised to satisfy the longings of a society weary at times of play and masquerade, but shrinking from the grossness of rustic reality : elegant Arcadias in a style of conscious irregularity, a discreet English version of the baroque pastorals of Trianon and Bayreuth; deliberately winding walks that opened as by chance on lovely calculated vistas; smooth-swept swards where an eighteenth-century lady might com-mune with Nature and not soil her silken skirts; artfully disposed groves " sacred to retirement," where

the Gibbonian philosopher might meditate in comfort
on the pleasures of rural solitude. Weston Wilderness is a small example of the style; but it is none the
less charming for that. The artificial always looks
best in miniature. It is a feathery plantation only
about half a mile square, but it is divided up into a
network of narrow walks thickly planted on each side,
to make it seem three times its real size. And there
is a Gothic temple in it, and an avenue; and now and
again one comes on a little sculptured urn with an
inscription on it to the memory of one of the Throckmortons' dogs. It is a forlorn place now. The
paths are piled with leaves; the grass waves knee-
high; the carving on the urns is blurred with moss.
But it still retains a charming flavour of the past.
Amid a prosaic agricultural landscape, it stands like a
fragment of the eighteenth century strayed by some
strange accident of time and space into an age not its
own; and as one passes between the classical piers
that form its entrance into the green twilight of its
walks one seems to be stepping back into 1780, and
half expects to meet Cowper's lanky figure, flecked
by shifting gleams of sunshine, pacing the turf towards
one. Perhaps his ghost does walk there—with a
spectral Mungo barking soundlessly at his heels.
Certainly the whole place is instinct with his spirit.

He had always liked Nature best slightly tamed,
and there was no moment of the year when the
Wilderness was not beautiful to him. It was lovely
on a sunny, breezy May morning, when the trees were
in early leaf, grey willow and silvery poplar and glossy
maple, with guelder rose and laburnum and bending
lilac flowering beneath them, and violet and mezereon
at their root; and the birds sang and the squirrels
chattered and scampered

"In anger insignificantly fierce;"

or at the late end of a summer's day, when all was indistinct in the warm dusk, and the scents of evening were fresh in the air. Exquisite summer evenings, when Cowper and Mary loitered home to supper contentedly weary, their arms full of honeysuckle, and the young moon going up the sky before them. But the Wilderness was lovely in winter too: on calm, crystal mornings after snow, when Cowper's figure slanted, blue and grotesquely long, across the glaring whiteness, and Mungo leapt and rolled and buried his nose in the powdery cold, and beneath the thick branches of the central avenue the moss was still green, and it was so quiet that you could hear the bells of Clifton Church, now loud, now soft, away the other side of the valley; or on winter afternoons, when already at a quarter to four Cowper would gaze between the leafless boughs across the furrowed fields, sparkling with frost, to where on the horizon blazed the tremendous conflagration of sunset.

He enjoyed the walk back from the Wilderness as much as the Wilderness itself; through the gate and past the fountain, and down the narrow path, ankle deep in thyme, to the rustic bridge. Then came the shrubbery, with its moss-house and alders, and then up to the Cliff, where he would stop to get his breath. It was not really a cliff, but a ridge overlooking the valley of the Ouse. Cowper would stand with the wind blowing the hair about his face staring across the glittering loops of the river, far away into the hazy distance towards Steventon; then his eye would rove round, pausing for a moment, maybe, where the smoke rose from a thatched roof solitary in the middle of an elm wood.

The " Peasants' Nest," as he called it, had always caught his imagination. He liked to fancy himself living there—a rustic hermit, alone with birds, animals and trees. With pensive eyes he gazed; then with a

half-smile he would remind himself that he had once
visited the cottage and found it extremely uncomfortable, with no water supply. It was the healthy
side of Cowper's self-distrust that it never allowed his
imagination to become self-indulgent or self-deceptive,
as the romantic imagination was so often tempted to
be. With modest amusement he would prick the
bubble of his daydream, and turn towards home.

He spent even more time in the garden than in
walking. It was not just when he was gardening—he
liked to sit there as well. At first this was a little
difficult. The narrow strip of ground, closed in as it
was by high walls, was insufferably hot if it was sunny,
and if it was not sunny it was cold. But it was
intolerable to be forced to spend a lovely morning in
the stuffy parlour, distracted by the street noises.
No wonder he hankered after the seclusion of the
" Peasants' Nest." Then one day in 1780 he conceived the idea of taking the plants out of the greenhouse and sitting there. He hung the wall with mats,
put down a carpet, a table and a comfortable chair,
and arranged a little row of myrtles in pots at the
entrance to serve as a sunblind. Thenceforth he sat
there morning, afternoon and evening, from May to
the end of September. These summer days in the
greenhouse were the pleasantest in the whole year to
him. Whenever he speaks of them the sentences
begin to lilt and dance as to some sylvan orchestra of
piping birds and rustling leaves.

" We have not envied you," he writes to Bull away
on a visit. " Why should we envy any man ? Is not
our greenhouse a cabinet of perfumes ? It is at
this moment fronted with carnations and balsams,
mignonette and roses, jessamine and woodbine, and
wants nothing but your pipe to make it truly Arabian,
a wilderness of sweets." And again, " Our severest
winter, commonly called the spring, is now over, and I

find myself sitting in my favourite recess—the greenhouse. In such a situation, so silent, so shady, where no human foot is heard, and where only my myrtles presume to peep in at the window, you may suppose I have no interruption to complain of, and that my thoughts are perfectly at my command. But the beauties of the spot are themselves an interruption, my attention being called upon by those very myrtles, by a row of grass pinks just beginning to blossom, and by a bed of beans already in bloom; and you are to consider it, if you please, as no small proof of my regard, that though you have so many powerful rivals, I disengage myself from them all and devote this hour entirely to you."

It was not odd that he liked it so much. It combined the two things to which he now looked for happiness—domestic life and natural beauty. The garden was only a few feet away from the noise and sordid bustle of Silver End, but Cowper heard nothing but birds and bees, saw nothing but flowers and waving treetops. For all his senses could tell him, he might have been in the depths of the country : indeed, it was like a bit of the country—a plot of remote, leafy silence, set as if by enchantment at his very door, where he could escape from the harsh hurry of the world, and where, as he sat through the placid hours, all the troubles of his jangled nerves would dwindle to a green thought in a green shade. And yet there was none of the roughness of the really wild about it. However fiercely the sun might beat down, it was cool in the greenhouse; if a summer storm came up the sky, all Cowper knew of it was a few claps of thunder and a sudden sharp patter of rain on the roof above his head. And the whole atmosphere of the neat, old-fashioned garden, tended by his own hand, and the neater little outdoor room, with its well-worn, well-kept, well-remembered bits of furniture, and dear

Mary within easy call, breathed cosy, cheerful, civilized security. The different elements that go to give its character to this phase of Cowper's existence sum themselves up in his garden life. If he rises before our mental eye, it is in the greenhouse on some golden September afternoon; a tranquil figure writing at his desk, with his linnets twittering in a cage above his head, and the dog slumbering at his feet; while outside the air is sweet with mignonette, and the sunlight filters greenly in through the myrtle leaves, and patterns itself on the carpeted floor.

It was a life before all things sequestered—a refuge, a sanctuary, an escape. It is true that with his recovery his interest in the great world and its doings had returned. With what delighted expectation did he open the rustling folds of the newspaper! With what zest he read its contents and expounded them with appropriate comments to Mary! The American War, the Gordon Riots, the controversy over George III and his Parliament—he had his views on them all. His point of view was the typically respectable one of the period. He was a Whig, nurtured in the tradition of 1688, convinced that our Constitution was the culminating achievement of an all-wise Creator; and George III's attempt to tamper with it struck him as so much sacrilege. On the other hand, he could not wholly approve of Fox and the Opposition: not only were they most unevangelical in their private lives, but they had an unnatural tendency to take up the cause of foreigners. For Cowper gloried in the name of Briton. The Americans in his eyes were simply rebels against the cause of God. As for the French, they were to him, as to most of his contemporaries, the despicable swarm of grinning, posturing frogs, as we see in Hogarth's picture of Calais Gate; three of whom any Englishman ought to overcome single-handed. If they defeated us in the war it could only be through treachery; and their typical representative was Vestris, the professional dancer, Vestris, whose unmanly prancings had roused all Paris to frenzies of enthusiasm. For such people Cowper could only feel contempt. This jaunty Chauvinism sits oddly on his nervous, complex character.

Yet for all his outward excitement, he was not deeply interested in politics. His attitude was that of the spectator seeking diversion rather than that of the interested actor. As he said to Newton, " You will suppose me a politician, but in reality I am nothing less. These are the thoughts that occur to me when I read the newspaper, and when I have laid it down I feel more interested in the success of my early cucumbers than in any part of this great and important subject. If I see them droop a little I forget we have been many years at war." His interest in books was similarly limited. He read a great deal, both to himself and aloud to Mary—on summer afternoons in the greenhouse, and by the crackling winter fire. But he would not read anything philosophical—it demanded too serious an attention—or poetry—it competed with his serious work. No, what he liked was something picturesque and full of incident—Clarendon's *History of the Rebellion* or, still better, *Captain Cook's Voyages.* " My imagination," he remarks of the last, " is so captivated that I seem to partake with the navigators in all the dangers they encountered. I lose my anchor, my mainsail is rent into shreds, I kill a shark, I converse with a Patagonian ; and all this without moving from the fireside." The truth was he had never so far recovered his mental health as to lose that horror of the world that had originally inspired him to leave it. Even if Olney had no very pleasant associations for him, it was yet a haven ; and the very idea of being sent back into the whirlpool of active life made him shudder. Only now and again, by way of varying the monotony of his daily round, he liked to take a look, as in a magic mirror hanging in the recesses of his sanctuary, at the pageant of the great world, past and present, moving now bright, now dark, before him. When he had seen enough, he covered it up and returned to the comfortable reality of the garden and the hares and Mary.

But the dangers that his mode of life was primarily designed to avoid were those that came not from the crowd, but from solitude. He wished to escape the pressure of this world, it is true, but, far more imperatively, the pressure of the next. Not that he had ceased to be an Evangelical. Every idea or event or practice he heard or read of was weighed in the " experiential " scale—weighed and generally found wanting. Public schools, foreign travel, rouge, ballooning—did they further the cause of God ? On the whole, he thought not. Ballooning was, he admitted, a difficult question. There was nothing morally wrong about it, but he could not believe that God, Who had given man two legs to walk with and had created the earth to use them on, could really approve of his neglecting these endowments to career about the sky in a machine of his own invention. The question of rouge presented no such difficulties. It could only be used from two motives—to deceive or to attract the male, and either, though perhaps pardonable in a wretched unenlightened French-woman, must be reprehended in an English lady. But indeed England was now wallowing in a slough of vice and luxury. It was an additional reason for retirement if one was needed. The way the Sabbath was broken —and by the most distinguished people in the land, the Duke of York and the Duchess of Devonshire— made him shudder. But even their shortcomings did not rouse him to such angry eloquence as did the growing prevalence of sacred music. He had it for a fact that a London clergyman gave concerts in his church on Sunday afternoons—concerts without words. " I believe that wine itself, though a man be guilty of habitual intoxication, does not more debauch or befool the natural understanding than music, always music; music in season and out of season, weakens and destroys the spiritual discernment, if it is not done in an unfeigned reverence to the worship of God and with a design to assist the soul in the performance of it, which cannot be when it is the only occupation—it degenerates into a sensual delight."

And he had heard, too, that a lady, anxious to dissuade her daughter from indulging in the dangerous delight of walking in Ranelagh, called in this very clergyman to support her, and he had actually said in front of the daughter that he saw no harm in it. Such were the alarming results of promoting Sunday concerts ! As for the Handel Festival at Westminster Abbey, Cowper did not know whether it made him laugh or cry. That a number of people, all in danger of eternal damnation, should collect together and sing about it, that they should do it in honour of a music-monger, a fellow sinner like themselves, and that they should do it in a church, was beyond any folly that he could have dreamed of. Newton sought to recall these people to a sense of their true situation by preaching a course of sermons on the words of " The Messiah." Cowper applauded his intention ; but he could not expect it would do much good. Clearly the American War was a judgment inflicted on England for her wickedness. But was it a sufficient punishment ? When he thought of the sacred concerts and the Handel Festival, Cowper began to doubt it. Only final perdition seemed adequate to such offences And indeed, in the summer of 1785 he thought there were great signs that it was not long to be delayed. The weather was unnaturally stuffy, he saw several

shooting stars, and the moon shone dull and small like
"a red-hot brick." Such phenomena could not be
without significance. Altogether, he felt he would not
be surprised if the world came to an end before the
year was out.

But though he still judged mankind by Evangelical
standards and envisaged his future in the light of
Evangelical ideas, the religious conceptions which
underlay these ideas he tried as far as possible to
forget. His Evangelicalism was ethical: it consisted
wholly of ethical judgments on men and events; it
expressed itself in an easy, conversational style,
altogether different from the Biblical phraseology, the
fiery emphasis, that had characterized his utterances
in the days of his conversion. The purely religious
aspects of his creed ever since his illness he had striven,
with the pertinacity of desperation, to put out of his
head. He would not go to church or attend family
prayers; and when others stood with bowed heads
during grace, he sat down, knife and fork in hand,
deliberately averting his mind from the subject.
Newton wanted him to write a book about religion,
but Cowper told him that though he did not mind
making short references to the subject in verse, he
simply could not let his mind dwell on it for as long as
would be needed for a prose work. And if people
tried to talk about it to him, or argue about it in his
presence, he first tried to change the subject, and
if that failed, left the room. For of course there
was a reverse side to the homely monotony of his
life—a reverse side of blackest horror. Within the
centre of his consciousness remained unaltered the
conviction that he was damned, that every day that
passed brought him a day nearer to an eternity of
torment; and he had fixed his eyes exclusively on
such things as could still give him pleasure, had
laboriously devised from them the whole elaborate

N

scheme of occupation and habit and amusement which was his mode of life, in order to distract himself from the frightful fate that awaited him. But the certainty of that fate remained like a dark pit in the grassy garden world of his every day.

He looked at it as little as possible, but sometimes he could not help it. One day, for example, when he was in the garden, he heard an old breeches-maker who lived in a neighbouring cottage, singing at his work.

> " Oh, for a closer walk with God,
> A pure and heavenly frame,"

he sang in aged, quavering tones,

> " A light to shine upon the road
> That leads me to the Lamb."

It was one of Cowper's own hymns ; and as he listened he recalled with an anguished twinge of regret how trusting and hopeful he had been when he wrote it. Now he trusted and hoped no longer, and never would again. Others might take comfort from the words : they only made their author more sadly conscious of his own despair.

He had other moments of more sensational depression ; in winter especially, when he sat for weeks together, cooped up in that dark, poky house, with the rain drumming on the panes outside and nothing to keep his mind from brooding on itself. January was the worst month, January, that included the anniversary of the awful dream that had finally shut him out from hope. His sick, suspicious nerves fancied that there was something fatal to them in the month ; and for weeks before his heart would be beating in an agony of apprehension. Would he go mad again in January ? When he thought about it rationally such a fear seemed nonsensical ; but he could not stop it from worrying him. Until February was safely begun he was in a fever. In these moments of discouragement Cowper turned once more to Mary. Calmly and unobtrusively as ever, she bore his burden, and in time it passed. But he was never so far recovered as to face his fears and have them out and examine them in the light of reason. He would not listen to argument. Mary, Newton, Bull—all his friends—reasoned with him and reasoned again, in vain. In 1782, Newton, optimistic as usual, sought to see if the force of example would have more success, and wrote Cowper a letter describing the strange case of Simon Browne. This was a Nonconformist preacher residing in London during the earlier years of the century, who, like Cowper, had, for no sensible reason, become convinced he was damned. He made every effort to escape his fate, even going so far as to write to Queen Caroline asking her to intercede with God on his behalf; as he felt that a person of her exalted rank would have more chance than a nobody like himself of engaging the attention of an overworked Creator. Whether the Queen granted his request we do not know. It would have been a great favour on her part if she had, as she was more than half an atheist. At any rate, the prayer was not granted, and poor Mr. Browne died without hope. Newton thought that the patent absurdity of his story would lead Cowper to realize the equal absurdity of his own. However, Cowper only replied with polite acrimony that the cases were different. " I could point out to you," he said, " some essential differences between his state of mind and mine which would prove mine to be by far the most deplorable. I suppose no man would despair if he did not apprehend something singular in the circumstances of his own story, something that discriminates it from that of every other man." This was always the burden of his case: he was unique. As he says on another occasion : " My friends expect I shall see again. I admit the validity of this reasoning in every case but my own." The truth was that about this particular subject he was still mad, the victim of an obsession—an obsession which blinded him to reason or common sense. The pit remained dark in the middle of the garden, and he still walked round it with averted eyes.

His condition of mind reflects itself in his letters and poems. The letters are the best things he ever wrote, the finest achievement of one who had cultivated to the highest point of perfection a natural genius for intimacy. They are unpretentious—he hated consciously well-written letters, and even thought that a letter should be destroyed after the recipient had read it—but they are not in the least like notes dashed off in the intervals of a busy life. They are composed in a lucid, unforced, graceful English—the very perfection of the plain style, by no means to be attained in a hurry. Every corner is rounded : there are no abrupt transitions : the briefest note begins and ends with a charming, easy turn of phrase. They are beautifully differentiated, to suit the temperament of his correspondent : serious to Newton, sensible to Hill, playful and confiding to Unwin. They do not tell much news, for there was little to tell ; but rather follow whatever whims and thoughts happened to chase each other across Cowper's mind as he sat in the garden, or by the candle-lit table on a winter's evening. No letters show such variety of mood. The stream of sparkling, limpid sentences flows on, now in sunshine, now in shadow ; and now it dimples in humour, now lingers sombre under the shade of melancholy boughs.

The poems are not so good as the letters, but they reveal other things about Cowper. One realizes from them that he was an amateur who wrote as a distraction. Only very rarely do his verses attain that complete felicity of expression, that indissoluble marriage of

word and thought that characterizes the work of those
to whom their art is the undisputed centre and fulfilment
of existence.   But when he speaks about any subject
he cares about the authentic accents of poetry come
into his voice ; and as his peculiar mode of life had
given him tastes not common among poets, he had a
real vein of his own.   His is almost the only domestic
poetry : " I sing the sofa," begins his most considerable
poem, and the line might stand advertisement to one
whole aspect of his achievement.   He sung the sofa,
of the respectable country home of his day, and the
tea-table by the sofa, and the chest of drawers opposite
the sofa, and, leaning against the sofa, the chessboard
with its carven armies, and the gay needlework on the
sofa cushions and the woolly lap-dog that leapt up from
them to bark at an intruder.   The animals he loved
play a large part in his poetry.   He writes fables about
them—" The Dog and the Water-lily," " The Retired
Cat "—fables which are made to point a neat moral, but
which vividly portray the peculiar tricks and idiosyncrasies of their furred or feathered protagonists.
Turning to human beings, he is still domestic ; writes
lively occasional verses to Mary, on a nosegay he had
picked for her, or to Newton, on his return from
Ramsgate, celebrates in mock ballad style the mis-
adventures of a muddy walk.   With gentle, penetrating
satire he painted the bores who come to call—the
emphatic speaker who " dearly loves to oppose, in
contact inconvenient, nose to nose."   Or the wearisome
tellers of anecdote :

> " 'Tis the most asinine employ on earth
>   To hear them tell of parentage and birth
>   And echo conversations dull and dry
>   Embellished with ' *he said* ' and ' *so said I.*'
>   At every interview their route the same,
>   The repetition makes attention lame.
>   We bustle up with unsuccessful speed
>   And at the saddest part cry—Droll indeed ! "

Or sometimes, his voice changing to a tenderer tone, he will sing for a while the simple affections and sorrows of family life. Such writing may never glow with the white-hot temperature of the greatest poetry; but its author has caught an aspect of life not often touched on by poets and crystallized it into art.

Cowper writes beautifully of Nature too. With exquisite precision he isolates the characteristic features of the landscape, "the clouds that flit or slowly float away,"

> "*Hypericum all blooms*, so thick a swarm
> Of flowers like flies clothing her slender rods."

The streams that

> ". . . chiming as they fall
> Upon loose pebbles, lose themselves at length
> In matted grass that with a livelier green
> Betrays the secret of their silent course."

Or the robin in winter

> ". . . flitting light
> From spray to spray. Where'er he rests he shakes
> From many a twig the pendant drops of ice
> That tinkle in the withered leaves below."

No other writer has "caught" the character of the landscape of southern England so exactly. And yet Cowper is never consciously English, as some later writers have been. He describes England because he wants to describe the country, and it is the only country he knows. He does not even bother about an appropriately rustic style, but employs the formal Miltonic diction he had been brought up to think correct for serious poetry. Yet this seems to make his descriptions all the more genuine, as the water-colours of his contemporaries Girtin and Cozens, for all their conventionalized style of drawing, their faded classical graces, communicate the spirit of the English

countryside as the life-like snapshots of later impression-
ists never do.   It is the visitor who notices local terms
and typical " bits " : the inhabitant knows the place
too well to be conscious of such external features.

Cowper writes well, too, when he gives rein to the
ebullience of his florid eighteenth-century patriotism,
the gallant stirrings of emotion roused in him by some
heroic event or personage :

> " Weigh the vessel up
> Once dreaded by our foes
> And mingle with your cup
> The tears that England owes.
>
> Her timbers yet are sound
> And she may float again
> Full charged with England's thunder
> And plough the distant main."
>
> But Kempenfelt has gone,
> His victories are o'er,
> And he and his eight hundred
> Must plough the waves no more."

Is there not a fine martial clang about that ?

But now and again, misled by conscience, a most
unreliable guide in æsthetic matters, Cowper adopts a
tone of religious reprobation, girds against the wickedness of the world and summons people to throw themselves upon the mercy of God.   Immediately all the
light fades from the page, and it becomes pompous,
wordy and uninspired.   For Cowper has left the
realm of his real feelings.   Though he still thinks
Christianity true, he has ceased to feel anything for
it ; he does not care a pin if the world is wicked or
good.   As for the mercy of God, as far as he himself
is concerned he profoundly disbelieves in it.   He may
tell people they ought to think of such subjects, but
they are the subjects that he spends his whole life
trying to forget.

With growing success. The ordered life of Olney was so unvaried, each day so exactly like the last, that often it seemed to him that time was standing still. But in reality it hurried all the faster. A year there passed as quickly as a week of more diverse existence. "My days steal away silently," he said, "and march on as poor mad King Lear would have made his soldiers march, as if they were shod with felt." And with time came change. Beneath the level, uniform surface went on a steady, persistent process of alteration. Cowper was regaining his mental health. Not that he was getting more amenable to reason: if you argued with him he listened as little as ever: but other forces than reason were working for his recovery. Gradually, stealthily, the movement begun in 1776 was advancing, his natural vitality was re-asserting itself with a growing force. He felt no sudden change of mind or conviction; he simply began to think more and more about the outside world and less and less about his own internal problems. The pit remained unillumined; but it was diminishing in area, and grass and trees were encroaching on its slopes. In 1779 his predominant condition had been one of dull despair varied by fits of anguish and rarer snatches of enjoyment; by 1780 these moments recurred often enough for him to construct a relatively normal system of life around them, and he had glimpses of an altogether more light-hearted condition of mind. "I wonder that a sportive thought should ever knock at the doors of my intellect, much less gain admittance," he remarks to Unwin. "It is as if Harlequin should intrude himself into the gloomy chamber where a corpse is deposited in state. His antic gesticulations would be unseasonable at any rate, but especially so if they should distort the features of the mournful attendants into laughter. But the mind long wearied with the sorrow of a dull, dreary prospect will gladly fix its eyes on anything that will raise a little variety in its contemplation, though it were but a kitten playing with its tail." By 1781 happiness had become the rule rather than the exception. His fits of actual anguish were few, and in between whiles their memory cast only a faint shadow over his life. He was further taken out of himself by the publication of his first book. Cowper always denied he was ambitious, said he only wrote for pleasure and did not care what the critics said. Indeed, how should he care, seeing that he was only too painfully aware that all the glories of the world were vanity ? But in fact when his book was accepted by a publisher he could not contain his pleasure ; and when it first appeared before the public, he was in an agony of apprehension as to how it would be received. Of course he had really a large fund of natural ambition which he had always repressed, partly in consequence of bad health, but still more because he was convinced he was born to be a failure. He said he did not care for honours, because he feared he was never going to get them. Actually, though his first book made no great stir, it was decidedly no failure ; and his growing interest and pleasure in life were so far encouraged. However, before the book was out another force had come into his life that was to affect him more profoundly.

One afternoon in July 1781 Cowper was staring idly out of the parlour window when his attention was caught by the sight of two ladies emerging from the bulging, bow-windowed little draper's shop opposite. One he knew : she was Mrs. Jones, wife of the clergyman of the neighbouring village of Clifton. Her companion was unknown to him. But there was something about her appearance by which he was immediately and strangely attracted. Moved by an impulse foreign to his usual retiring character, he besought Mrs. Unwin to find out who the lady was, and ask them both in to tea. She complied; the invitation was accepted; and the unknown proved to be Mrs. Jones' sister, a Lady Austen, widow of a baronet called Sir Robert Austen. Now that the object of his interest was actually in the house Cowper's mood underwent a strong reaction. He became even shyer than usual, lingered for several minutes outside the parlour door trying to screw up enough courage to go in; and when at length he did so was so overcome with confusion that he could barely stammer out the first formal words of greeting. A few minutes' talk with Lady Austen, however, and all his embarrassment had vanished. She had an easy, intimate manner, and a vivid, responsive personality. Her dark eyes sparkled with laughter at the least hint of humour, softened with concern at a suggestion of sorrow. And her own contributions to the conversation were alive with shrewdness, wit and infectious gaiety. She seemed to take to Cowper at once; when she rose to go it was with many protestations of hope that they would meet again. Cowper was only too willing. Not only was she far and away the most dazzling figure that had appeared at Olney for years, but he felt her peculiarly sympathetic to himself. And the very next day he and Mary were trudging along the water meadows, thick with yellow irises, towards Clifton. Their visit led to a return visit to Olney; and soon the rigid ritual of Cowper's existence, unvaried for twelve years, was broken up in favour of a succession of engagements to walk and dine and drink tea in the company of the ladies of Clifton Rectory. They even had a picnic. It was a decorous kind of picnic. At mid-day the ladies and Cowper started off to walk about a mile to a spinney, where, suitably waited on by their servants, they had dinner in a summer-house. But a masked ball could hardly have been a more sensational variation to Cowper's usual course of life.

He enjoyed himself immensely. "Lady Austen's lackey and a lad that waits on me in the garden drove a wheelbarrow full of eatables and drinkables to the scene of our *fête champêtre*. A board laid over the wheelbarrow served us for a table; our dining-room was a root house lined with moss and ivy. At five o'clock the servants dined under a great elm on the grass at a little distance, boiled the kettle, and the said wheelbarrow served us for a tea-table. We then took a walk into the wilderness about half a mile off, and arrived home again a little after eight. We had spent the day together from noon to evening without one cross occurrence or the least weariness of one another—a happiness few parties of pleasure can boast of." In the pleasant warmth of such gentle gaieties Cowper's and Lady Austen's early liking for each other ripened into a close friendship; and by the end of the summer she was talking of selling her house in London and coming to live with Mary and Cowper at Olney.

Throughout the whole affair she had been the active party. One cannot, indeed, imagine her passive in anything. She was all quick-silver and electricity, a live, high-strung, compelling personality, with an intense desire to please and considerable powers of doing so. Though she was not at all uncultivated, people were the principal interest of her life. She was quick to sum up character, to detect foibles, to appreciate charm and originality, to get into the key of another's mood, to say the things that pleased, to avoid the things that jarred. And her feelings were as responsive as her mind. She could not be in company without her spirits rising in a bubbling fount of vivacity; the smallest service would fill her eyes with tears of gratitude. When she took a fancy to someone it was immediately and enthusiastically. She had the defects of her qualities. She was overexcitable, indulged her emotions, liked to dramatize her life, to see herself as the heroine of a situation. And like most people whose charm is an important factor in their lives, she was an egoist: demonstrative herself, she exacted demonstrations from her friends; and though she forgave easily she was easily hurt. She had been married and widowed young, and since then had divided her time between London and France. And she had all the polish and experience that come from so varied an existence. But at the time she appears in Cowper's story she was in strong reaction against the great world. " She had seen much of the world and accounted it a great simpleton," said Cowper. For the time being, at any rate, she was in love with the pleasures of retirement; and it was in pursuit of them she professed to have come to stay with her sister and brother-in-law. But she was too young, too energetic, and too exclusively interested in people, to be genuinely attracted by a life of self-sufficient seclusion; and the truth was that she had come to the country because she was restless. She had no settled position and no responsibilities and nothing to do. She was ready to throw herself into the first friendship that came her way. Cowper, too, was the very man to attract her. He had always had great charm for women, and Lady Austen was far too quick to be put off by his stiff provincial manner. Indeed in her present mood it only added to the attraction she felt. Cowper incarnated for her the happiness of country solitude, so preferable to the bustling, strident vanity of the world she had left. Her inflammable fancy caught fire the moment she met him; and she devoted all her arts and energies to cementing the connection.

He seconded her willingly. The romantic glow which had haloed her figure when he first caught sight of it out of the window had not faded on closer acquaintance.   He was by temperament peculiarly susceptible to the subtle sweetness, the intimacy, the feminine shimmer, of an accomplished, charming woman ; and this susceptibility had been sharpened by the fact that for many years he had seen so little of them.   Lady Austen was a lot of other things he liked as well— vital, spontaneous, humorous, and tender-hearted. Nor, with all her arts and experience, did he feel her to belong to a different and more worldly existence than he did.   If he talked of serious subjects she immediately became admirably serious herself ; and he was pleased to find that she disapproved of Sunday concerts as much as he did.   It is possible that her views became stricter when she was with Cowper.

But at moments he felt a little nervous, a little self-conscious, about his relationship to her.   It was certainly delightful, but very unlike any that he had ever had with anyone before : and he was not at all sure what it might lead to, or what other people might think of it.   With a comic anxiety he assures and reassures his correspondents that she is quite as much Mrs. Unwin's friend as his own, that he likes her in great part because she is so fond of Mrs. Unwin. What Mrs. Unwin herself felt is not so clear.   The summer had been certainly more amusing than usual, and Lady Austen, charming to everyone, was especially charming to her : she was not likely to be anything else to Cowper's closest friend.   But Mary must have felt that the character of their lives, of their time-honoured tête-à-tête, would be enormously changed by the addition of a third, especially such a lively third.   It is hard to believe that she regarded the idea with unmixed feelings.   Certainly William Unwin, to whom the whole affair was communicated, was dubious.   He wrote to say that he had heard Lady Austen's financial position was uncertain, and that they ought most emphatically to find out about it before

engaging themselves to her, anyway. Cowper wrote
back a vehement letter assuring him that her financial
position was impeccable; and added that he was in
favour of her coming to live in Olney chiefly because
it would be so much pleasanter for Mrs. Unwin to
have a woman friend near at hand. Anyway, he
wound up, Lady Austen would not be able to come
for nearly-two years, so that there was no need to get
excited about it. Indeed for the moment the whole
affair remained vague; and in October Lady Austen
went back to London. Before she left she proposed
that Cowper and she should open a regular correspondence. It was to be with him rather than with Mary,
he carefully explained to William Unwin, " because
writing does not agree with your mother." Lady
Austen also suggested that they should address each
other as brother and sister. Cowper was quite willing;
it seemed to place their relationship on an admirably
safe and sensible basis, encouraging to intimacy, discouraging to dangerous sentimentality. Alas, he was
wrong! It is one thing when a woman asks a man to
look on her as a sister after he has made love to her.
It is quite another when she does it before. In the
present instance it was nothing less than the thin end
of the wedge of love. Any vague apprehensions that
Cowper may have felt at the beginning of his connection with Lady Austen were to be justified. Week
after week he wrote and she replied; and gradually, to
his horror, a more impassioned note began to creep
into her style.

One cannot blame her. Cowper's position in
regard to such matters was so queer. Passion had
always been foreign to him; and now mental troubles
and his association with Mary together put any
idea of a love affair quite out of the question. On the
other hand, the only relationship he cared to cultivate

with anyone was an intimate and tender friendship; and it is almost impossible for an unattached man and woman to live in intimate and tender friendship without one of the two beginning to look on it as a dawning love affair. The very fact that Cowper was so little open to passion made this more likely, for he was careless how far he pressed the intimacy. He felt no danger himself, and so could not remember that she might not feel the same. For all his shy good-breeding, his manner towards women was remarked on for its "tender gallantry." He had the kind of temperament that always prefers a tête-à-tête to a general conversation. He singled out the object of his interest by a thousand small personal attentions, small personal solicitudes, small personal confidences. He loved to laugh with her at some joke private to themselves, to recall with sentiment some memory they shared together.

All this was bound to make a difficulty in any friendship he had with a woman; but the circumstances of his connection with Lady Austen made these difficulties peculiarly acute. He saw her as a glittering goddess who had suddenly descended from a sky-borne chariot to illuminate his drab life, and this made him feel his relationship to be different not in degree but in kind from any other he had known. This feeling appeared in every word he said to her.

" Dear Anna," he writes to her in December,

> " Dear Anna, between friend and friend
> Prose answers every common end,
> Serves, in a plain and homely way,
> T' express th' occurrence of the day—
> Our health, the weather and the news,
> What walks we take, what books we choose,
> And all the floating thoughts we find
> Upon the surface of the mind.

> But when a Poet takes the pen,
> Far more alive than other men,
> He feels a gentle tingling come
> Down to his finger and his thumb,
> Deriv'd from Nature's noblest part.
> The centre of a glowing heart!
> And this is what the world, who knows
> No flights above the pitch of prose,
> His more sublime vagaries slighting,
> Denominates an itch for writing.
> No wonder, I, who scribble rhyme
> To catch the triflers of the time
> And tell them truths divine and clear
> Which couch'd in prose they will not hear,

> .   .   .   .   .

> Should feel that itching and that tingling
> With all my purpose intermingling,
> To your intrinsic merit true,
> When called t' address myself to you."

This is not quite a love poem, but it is very near to one. And it expresses exactly the state of Cowper's feelings. In a respectable, rarified sort of way, he was a flirt. He did not wish, as we know, a declared love affair; indeed, he avoided it. But he preferred a personal relationship that involved a slightly raised emotional tension, that moved in an atmosphere tinged with half-hidden, half-hinted romantic sentiment.

Lady Austen's ardent temperament understood no such half shades. She did not actually make a confession of her love to him; indeed, she may not actually have confessed it to herself. But she answered his hints of sentimental regard with open protestations of affection; and finally, early in January, he got a letter from her in which, after celebrating his virtues in a strain of lyrical rhapsody, she ended by prophesying their friendship would attain a culmination of unique and supreme felicity in the near future. Poor Cowper became very agitated. Clearly he would have to do something at once to damp this rising flame; but it was an embarrassing task. She was so touchy. Only a few weeks before, she had taken violent offence at some slighting reflection she professed to have found in one of his letters; and he had been forced to write an elaborate apology and explanation before she was pacified. He hardly dared to think what her feelings would be if he ventured openly to rebuke her. However, her wrath was a less disturbing alternative than her love, and, sighing, he sat down at his table and composed a letter. It was in a lofty vein. Solemnly, he bade her remember that he was an erring mortal; that by exaggerating his perfections she was in danger of falling into the sin of idolatry; and, starting off with such false hopes, a closer acquaintance with him would certainly fill her with disappointment. It is to be doubted whether a strain of apocalyptic exhortation is that best fitted in which to deal with the fragile affairs of the heart. Mary, it is true, thought Cowper's letter admirable; but she may have had her own reasons for approving of it.

Not so Lady Austen: nor did she. She was even angrier than Cowper had feared. Within a few days he got a letter back from her, of such a violent kind that he could only suppose she had made up her mind to sever their connection for ever. He stifled a few involuntary pangs of regret and resigned himself to the inevitable. After all, there was a brighter side to the affair. It might have been a great strain to have her always in the house. She was so very vivacious. He remembered that, in some ways, it had been quite a relief when she went away in October. He and Mary had felt exhausted at having to maintain a level of conversation so persistently sparkling.

Meanwhile, however, Lady Austen's volatile feelings had suffered a revulsion. Her wrath had died down as quickly as it had flared up. And now she

o

could only remember how much she liked Cowper, and seek about for some means of making it up with him. She had been working three pairs of ruffles for him, and by way of opening negotiations she sent them to him by the hand of her brother-in-law. Cowper could not reſtrain his pleasure at this sign of goodwill. He did not thank her directly, but he asked Mr. Jones to do so : and to show that, for his part, he bore her no malice, he sent her in return a long-promised copy of his firſt book. But his cooler temperament could not so soon forget the paſt: his peaceful disposition was nervous of reopening a connection liable to such ſtorms. This diffidence was increased by the next news he heard of Lady Auſten.

" She is to spend the summer in our neighbour-hood," he wrote. " Lady Peterborough and Miss Mordaunt are to be of the party : the former a dissipated woman of fashion, and the latter a haughty beauty. Retirement is our passion and our delight. It is in ſtill life alone that we look for that measure of happiness we can rationally expect below. What have we, therefore, to do with characters like these ? Shall we go to the dancing school again ? Shall we caſt off the simplicity of our plain and artless demeanour to learn—and not in a youthful day either—the manners of those whose manners at the beſt are their only recom-mendation, and yet can in reality recommend them to none but the people like themselves ? "

It was very sad. Enchanting creature though Anna might be, it was clear from the company she kept that, contrary to his firſt impression, her background was too different from his for their friendship ever to reſt on a firm basis. Essentially he feared she belonged to another world, even if she did disapprove of Sunday concerts.

Still, there were signs that he had not completely resigned himself to her loss. William Unwin had taken advantage of the formal reconciliation to go and inspect her for himself, under cover of a call of courtesy. It is significant that he was disappointed in her, and told Cowper that she was strange and stiff in her manner towards him.   Immediately, Cowper blazed up in her defence.   There must have been some misunderstanding, he wrote; she was ordinarily most forthcoming.   It was no good: he could not conceal the fact that he liked her, that he longed for her friendship again.

His longings were satisfied.   There was no more talk of Miss Mordaunt and Lady Peterborough— baleful priestesses of the Moloch of fashionable life. In the summer Lady Austen came back to Clifton alone; and within a few days of her arrival she had hurried over to Orchard Side, rushed into the house, and flung herself with a torrent of smiles and tears into Mary's arms.   She had come determined on peace. She explained, she apologized, she forgave, she captivated; and Mary herself admitted that there was no resisting her.   Before the visit was over they were once more, officially at least, on the terms of the previous summer.   Cowper and Mary did, indeed, feel a little awkward, but Lady Austen did not; and after a few weeks' constant intercourse they did not either.   The quarrel was as forgotten as if it had never taken place.   There was no doubt it was more amusing when she was there.   Once again the monotony of their daily round was brightened by a ceaseless course of gentle diversion.   Actually they were prevented by the weather from enjoying so many of the delightful outdoor schemes, walks, expeditions and picnics as they did last summer: there had not been such a bad summer for years.   During weeks together the meadows between Olney and Clifton were in flood. However, Lady Austen was not the woman to be daunted by a trifle like that.   She got hold of a donkey, and day after day, mounted on its back, she splashed through the water to come and discuss and joke and tell tales with her dear "brother." Even when the weather made it impossible for them to meet, she managed to brighten his life. She wrote to him, and got him a small printing press; so that he could while away the time in clumsily stamping out, in blurred, uncertain type, a letter or a copy of verses for her.

The summer was not without its more sensational incidents. One evening when Cowper was sitting peacefully in the parlour he was startled by a knock at the door; and he rushed out to find Lady Austen being supported up the steps, apparently in great pain. She had come to Olney Church for the afternoon service, and had suddenly been taken ill there. She was put to bed, and a doctor was sent for, who reported her to be suffering from "bilious colic." Any one of a bilious habit should be thankful that they do not live in the eighteenth century; for colics then seem to have been formidable affairs. Twenty-four hours later, after an afternoon in which Lady Austen had appeared her usual lively self, Cowper was called into her room, to find her in a violent fit of convulsive hysterics. However, this may not have been due to the sort of illness so much as to her highly-strung temperament, which could not but show itself, even in her ailments. It would be fanciful as well as ungallant to suggest that she was influenced by a desire that Cowper should come in and comfort her. Anyway, two days later she was well enough to ride back to Clifton on her donkey.

So passed the summer; and now the autumn was here. And Lady Austen determined not to leave her "brother" again. But where was she to live? There was no room for her in Orchard Side. However, as usual, she had a plan. One evening, as they were sitting calmly at Clifton, she suddenly suggested that they should all set up house in the deserted Clifton Manor House. Cowper looked at her with mingled fear and delight. That he and Mary should break up the twenty-year-old order of their existence and start life in a new house at a month's notice—only Anna could have conceived of so fantastically bold an idea. Still, he could not help being attracted by its very boldness; and in his next letter he mentioned it to William Unwin, in an airy, half-laughing way, as if he were nervous that he might not like it. However, William Unwin was less suspicious of Lady Austen than formerly. She had tactfully told Cowper that she thought Mr. Unwin was the most elegant figure she had ever seen: and Cowper had passed the information on: which perhaps accounts for the modification of William's views. The scheme proved impracticable; but it was settled, instead, that Lady Austen should take the Vicarage which was, of course, quite near to Orchard Side, and which the Vicar—a man of large family and small means—was only too willing to let. In October she moved in, and for the next eighteen months it was her home.

She had got what she came for. Cowper and she hardly spent a moment of the day apart. A door was cut in the wall between the two gardens, and immediately after breakfast he walked across to " pay his respects " to her. Later she nearly always accompanied him and Mary on their walk; and sometimes, when Mary was tired, Lady Austen and Cowper went alone. During the week they had dinner together alternately at Orchard Side and the Vicarage: they were still sufficiently Evangelical to deny themselves such a dissipation on Sunday. From dinner on they were together till bed-time. Cowper enjoyed the change in his life. " Lady Austen," he told a correspondent, " was the cleverest and most entertaining woman in the

country." Her wit and vitality doubled the amusement he got out of his ordinary relaxations—talking
and walking and reading aloud. And besides, she
could play deliciously on the harpsichord. His letters
begin to sparkle with gentle gaiety. " How different
is the complexion of your evenings and mine ! " he said
to Joseph Hill. " Yours spent amid a ceaseless hum
that proceeds from the inside of fifty noisy and busy
periwigs ; mine by a domestic fireside, in a retreat as
silent as retirement can make it, where no noise is made
but what we make for our own amusement. For
instance, here are two rustics and your humble servant
in company. One of the ladies has been playing on
the harpsichord, while I, with the other, have been
playing at battledore and shuttlecock. A little dog, in
the meantime, howling under the chair of the former,
performed in the vocal way to admiration. This
entertainment over, I began my letter and, having
nothing more important to communicate, have given
you an account of it. I know you love dearly to be
idle, when you can find the opportunity to be so ;
but as such opportunities are rare with you, I thought
it possible that a short description of the idleness I
enjoy might give you pleasure. The happiness we
cannot call our own, we yet seem to possess, while
we sympathize with our friends who can."

In a word, his life was still as secluded from the rush of
the outside world as he could desire. But Lady Austen's
presence gave it a liveliness and a colour that made
him ten times stronger to resist his spiritual enemies.
For these had not ceased their attacks. Indeed, in the
autumn of 1782, Mary was in terror lest he might go
mad again. Not only was the winter-time coming on
—-always a dangerous time—but it was just ten years
since his second attack ; exactly the same length of
time as had elapsed between that second attack and the
first one. This was just the sort of fact, as Mary,

with her long experience of Cowper, well knew, to
send him mad. His mind was such an inchoate mass
of superstition and fear that if he thought it was time
for him to go mad again, he would do so.

Sure enough, as the autumn went on, Cowper was
seized with fits of gloom. In the middle of a conversation he would suddenly fall silent: his jaw would
drop, and an expression of anguish would overcast his
features. With impotent dismay Mary watched him.
Her patient, tenacious, self-denying character, so
wonderfully able to give support in a tragic crisis, had
not the resource to forestall such a crisis by diverting
Cowper's mind from the dangerous slopes it was
descending. However, Lady Austen had. One
evening, when he was particularly downcast, she
offered to tell a story which, she said, had amused her
as a girl. Mary begged her to; but Cowper only
preserved a stony silence. Undaunted she began, and
with all the spirit and humour she could muster,
recounted the sad adventures that befell a linen-draper
of London in his efforts to celebrate the anniversary
of his wedding. Cowper listened to the first incidents
with his face still fixed in an expression of dejection.
But Lady Austen was nothing if not high-hearted.
She went on; within a few minutes a smile began to
steal across Cowper's face, and by the end of the story
he was in peals of laughter, all the heartier from the
fact that they came as a reaction from profound
depression. He was so amused, in fact, that he could
not sleep, but lay awake putting the story into verse.
Next morning he read the verses aloud: this time it
was the ladies' turn to laugh. He retired to the greenhouse—it was still early in October—and set to work to
finish the poem. As he polished off each passage he
gleefully sent it across the way to provoke the laughter
of his friend, Wilson, the barber. When the whole
thing was finished it was sent away and published in a

broadsheet; and within a few days all London was laughing over the story of John Gilpin. Cowper was delighted at its reception; but it gave him a slight qualm too. He, who had hoped to shine through the world as a light of the Gospel, had only succeeded in becoming famous as the author of a comic poem. He was still more distressed to learn that his rivals for the chief share of the public interest were the antics of a performing pig and the unedifying confessions of the notorious Mrs. Bellamy. " Alas! " he said rue-- fully, " what is an author's popularity worth in a world which can suffer a prostitute on one side, and a pig on the other, to eclipse his brightest glories ? " All the same, he had reason to be grateful to John Gilpin, for he had saved him from going mad. Owing to Lady Austen's tact, winter passed and spring, and he was safely back in summer, without his spirits having passed through anything worse than a mild melancholy.

She stimulated him to write other things besides. She often wanted words for music; and Cowper would employ a dull morning in composing a copy of verses to be sung to the tune of " The Lass of Pattie's Mill," or " The March in Scipio." She believed strongly in his powers, and thought he could attempt something more ambitious. One day he was declaiming against Pope's translation of Homer : it was a favourite theme with him.

" Why don't you write a translation yourself ? " she said.

The idea sank into his mind and later bore fruit. Another day she urged him to write something in blank verse.

" I have no subject," he said.

" Write about anything," she returned impetuously. " Write about the sofa."

He took her at her word. And a few days later, began a poem which started, as required, about the sofa, but gradually blossomed into something bigger; in fact, into the biggest work he ever wrote: "The Task," a long, meditative poem of several thousand lines, into which he poured more or less at random the chief conclusions and reflections and observations that remained to him from fifty-five years of troubled life. His genius had always been meditative, and the subject absorbed him as no other had. He grew happier every day—happier, indeed, than he had been since his last illness. He felt all the sense of well-being and self-satisfaction that comes through regular, hard, congenial work: and all the time he was not working he spent delightfully talking and walking, reading and eating and laughing with Lady Austen. He hardly had time to write a letter. "Yours, more than I have time to tell you," he scribbles off to a correspondent. "The ladies are in the greenhouse, and tea waits."

It was a delightful life; but it did not, it could not last. The circumstances that had made his relationship with Lady Austen impossible fifteen months before remained unchanged. It was no easier than it had been then for a man and a woman to spend almost every hour of every day together for months without danger to the deeper feelings of either. And while still avoiding the boiling-point of passion, Cowper still liked to keep the emotional temperature decidedly warmer than that of mere friendship. Indeed, since he had safeguarded his position by declaring it openly to her, he sailed nearer the wind of a love affair than ever. He had carefully explained to her that she should look on him as an unromantic and imperfect fellow mortal. He had carefully explained to everybody else that she was more Mary's friend than his. Surely, therefore, he need not fear any misunderstanding. But his tender and gallant manner was just as tender and gallant as before. Indeed, more so. He gave her a lock of his hair, and she had it set in a diamond brooch : and he wrote some lines to celebrate the occasion :—

> " The ſtar that beams on Anna's breaſt
>   Conceals her William's hair,
> 'Twas lately severed from the reſt
>   To be promoted there.
> The heart that beats beneath the breaſt
>   Is William's well, I know ;
> Another prize and richer far
>   Than India could beſtow.
> She thus his favoured lock prefers
>   To make her William shine ;
> The ornament indeed is hers,
>   But all the honour mine."

Such language might well have kindled hope in the moſt discreet of women—and Lady Auſten was very far from being that. Her charaćter had not changed, any more than Cowper's. She was ſtill susceptible, ſtill uncontrolled, and ſtill peculiarly open to Cowper's kind of charm. The long winter of 1783, when she spent whole days indoors, with nothing to diſtraćt her from thinking about Cowper, was enough to revive the ſtill-glowing embers of her passion. By the New Year Cowper was beginning to feel the atmosphere uncomfortably hot. Apart from anything else, her intereſt in him was so inconvenient from the praćtical point of view. He could only work in the morning ; but in the morning she liked him to come and see her. Now that he was fairly ſtarted on a long piece of work, he wanted to give up these visits ; but she was dreadfully wounded if he even suggeſted not coming. The situation was getting very difficult ; he would soon be compelled to bring matters to a crisis. Before he could force himself to the fearful task, however, he was foreſtalled by someone else. No man in the world can live permanently in the same house with two ſtrong-willed women, both violently in love with him. Indeed, only a man of supreme taćt and dexterity in personal

matters could have done it as long as Cowper did.
Mary had submitted to Lady Austen's presence as
long as she felt it held no danger for her ; for she was
glad of anything that amused Cowper.   But in time she
did begin to suspect danger, and then the very same
qualities that made her Cowper's slave in most matters
made her his master in this.   Her love was intense,
self-sacrificing and exclusive.   She would die for him,
but she would never share him.   When she thought
there was a possibility that she might have to, she took
action at once.   What actually happened we do not
know ; but in the spring of 1784 it was made clear to
Cowper that he must choose between Mary and Anna,
and also that he must choose Mary.   Not, indeed, that
he would have hesitated to do so.   Constancy, gratitude,
the claims of old friendship, these had always been far
and away the strongest motive powers in his life.   And
to Mary he was bound by every tie that gratitude and
affection could form.   Had she not seen him through
the brief, strange summer and bitter winter of his
days ?   Was it not by her help that he had lived to see
the sun shine once more ?   She had dedicated her life
to him ; for him she had risked the sacrifice of her
small fortune and her good name.   If he were to spend
the rest of his life in her service he would hardly
recompense her for what she had done for him.   Anna,
on the other hand—ravishing creature though she
might be—had only known him for two years, and he
was not bound to her by any bond of gratitude.   From
the point of view of the highest principle, there was no
question what he ought to do.   And anyway, with all
her charms, Anna could be very tiresome.   He made
his decision quickly.   Sitting down once more at his
table, once more he wrote her a letter.

Of all the pages torn by an undiscriminating fate
from the records of Cowper's life this letter is the most
tantalizing.   He was very proud of it himself.   He

said that it made it unmistakably clear that they must separate; but that it did so in a tone both " tender and resolute." Lady Austen herself, in later years, admitted that it was an admirable letter. Not at the time, however. Yet once more her hasty passion blazed up: she threw the letter into the grate; and within a few days had left for Bristol. In a flurry of dust her coach rattled away out of Olney, and out of this history. For it was the end. This time there was no reconciliation. Within the next five years she came twice to stay at Clifton; but she never saw, or spoke or wrote to Cowper again. A few years later she married a Monsieur de Tardiff, and went to live in France. Did her love for Cowper linger for long after they parted? Did she ever, amid the hard glitter of Napoleonic Paris and the lawful embraces of Monsieur de Tardiff, cast a wistful eye back to her brief Arcadian yearnings, and the peaceful evenings of Olney? So the historian wonders and conjectures; and is ignorant. Lady Austen's exit from the stage of Cowper's life on that May morning was as abrupt and complete as had been her entrance.

Cowper did not waste time in fruitless regret. For all their similarity of taste, for all her exquisite sympathy with his moods, at the bottom of his heart he had never lost the feeling that she was different from him, a brilliant, exotic bird of paradise who had alighted, by chance, in his quiet country garden. It had been pleasant for a few dazzling moments to watch her preen her feathers and flutter her wings; but he had always known that in the end she would fly away. So that when she actually did so, he remained cheerful. Her departure was a pity, but it was to be expected. Lady Austen, had she seen him, would certainly have upbraided him for heartlessness. But in reality she had no cause to repine. She had affected his life profoundly. And it is the measure of this effect that he could face life with much equanimity when she was gone. Four years ago such a loss would have depressed him, however certainly he had expected it; for his spirits then were too weak to stand the loss of any support. But his connection with her had increased his power of resistance ten times over. Apart from anything else, the fact of having two delightful women in love with him must have added to his self-confidence. And the complications arising out of their rivalry, tiresome though they might seem at the time, diverted his mind from morbidly brooding on itself. But Lady Austen had exercised a more direct and individual influence on his recovery. Her mere presence revived his interest in life: she was so flamingly excited about everything that happened that anyone who was with her could not help catching fire too. The books Cowper read, the subjects he talked about, the poems he wrote, all seemed more absorbing when she was there. It was on his work, above all, that her influence was so important. Cowper had always worked better under direction. He was hard-working and enthusiastic once he had got something to do; but timid and unenterprising about getting it. Lady Austen's sympathetic imagination supplied him with subjects: her confidence in his powers gave him the impetus to take them up. Before she came, the locomotive of his genius had never properly started: by the time she had left it was running at full speed; and Cowper was too occupied in guiding its course to vouchsafe her more than a passing glance of farewell.

There was nothing now to distract him from his work. He was able to spend a large part of every day in writing. He had found a refuge even more secluded than the greenhouse: a summer-house at the extreme end of the garden. It was an extraordinary little erection of lath and plaster and red tiles; as Cowper truly said, just like a Sedan chair, with barely room in it for himself and a table. On one side, the door opened on to the roses and honeysuckle of the garden ; on the other, he could gaze through a window at the grey-lichened trunks of the fruit trees in a neighbouring orchard. Cowper loved the summer-house. " It is a place in which I fabricate all my verse in summer-time," he wrote. " The grass under my window is all bespangled with dewdrops, and the birds are singing in the apple trees, among the blossoms. Never poet had more commodious oratory in which to invoke his muse."

However, summer came to an end, and he had to write indoors. But still he worked on through murky morning and candle-lit evening, and still, as he worked, his spirits steadily rose ; still, the return of nervous health, begun so haltingly fifteen years before, got faster and more irresistible. By May 1785, when " The Task " was just at the point of completion, it achieved such a speed and momentum as never before. Hard work had proved the very best thing for him. One of the strongest forces against Cowper's recovery had been his fatalistic submission to evil ; and this had been encouraged by his habit of life. For years his whole existence had perforce been one of inert and idle submission to circumstances. But during the last fifteen months he had been working ; and working not just to pass the time, but to achieve a desired object. This could not fail to put him in a more active frame of mind, to make action, rather than submission his first involuntary response to events ; and the action that inevitably presented itself to him was struggle against his nervous enemies. Besides, he could embark on his struggle with more hope of success than of old. No one can bring a long, ambitious work to a successful conclusion without gaining confidence in his own powers. And over and above all this the sheer excitement of creation had keyed up his spirits to a pitch at which they could not but be hopeful.

The black pit of his fears shrank to the size of a pin-point. He could not understand it, still less could he account for it, but he felt more cheerful every day. Unexplained, unexpected movements of delight began to stir in his consciousness, and for the first time there stole into his heart the thought that all his fears might come to an end, that he might be saved. On he worked : ever tenser grew his emotional excitement. And then, actually, the incredible happened. He woke up one morning in May 1785 to find that the burden of fear which had been the central fact of his existence for thirteen years had rolled away. He felt he could believe what Mary and Newton had always said. God loved him, as He loved other created beings ; and, all being well, He would save him in the end. He felt no dazzling ecstasy as in 1763 : the sky was not yet clear of clouds. But that grey pall, now dark, now faint, which since his illness had overcast every inch of its surface, was rent apart at last. And he saw the sun.

For three dream-like days, days ever to be remembered, the mood lasted. And then once more the clouds covered the sky. Facts fell back into their former proportion ; the old fears resumed their power ; the old convictions recovered their force. The truth is, that if the mind runs on one line of thought over a number of years, it makes a sort of rut for itself ; and though it may be lifted out of that rut by a violent emotional excitement, after this excitement passes it tends to fall back into it. Cowper's mind had, as we have seen, been dominated by his conviction of damnation ever since 1775. The organization both of his outward and his inward existence, his interests, his occupation, his general habit of mind, had grown up in the light of this conviction ; and except when he was swept away by a great gush of creative energy, it was very difficult to live according to the forms of such an existence without unconsciously accepting the views on which it was based. Reason, no doubt, should have told him that if he had been able to reject these views for three days, he should be able to reject them always. Nothing had happened at the end of three days to make them more probable. But reason, as usual, weighed little with him ; for his belief was the result, not of a logical process, but of disease. After all, his nerves had been so injured, it had been so long before they had even begun to mend, that the process of their recovery was necessarily irregular. He might have moments of relief, but at first he must expect a relapse to follow them.

Such a relapse was disappointing. " The heavens," he said, " only opened to shut again." But, oddly enough, he did not feel deeply discouraged. Perhaps in his heart of hearts he had never expected happiness to last. Anyway, any other feeling was far outweighed by his pleasure in the realization that he could even for a moment be hopeful. He had taken his damnation for granted so long that any more sanguine mood, however short-lived, was a bright sign. He wondered if happiness might not come again, and come to stay. Certainly, his general condition of mind continued to improve ; even if he did not feel as he had during the three days, he felt better than he had before them. It is true that he still became irritable if anyone suggested that he was better: indeed, his spirits still went through dark periods. But they were grey rather than black. And his mind was far too absorbed by his work to succumb to their influence, as he had been used to do. Whatever his conviction about his damnation, he thought about it less, and about other things more. In every way he was more normal.

He was so much more independent than he used to be. " The Task " was finished by October 1787, and he had to arrange for its publication. Newton had been his intermediary with his publisher for the first book ; but for some reason Cowper now thought that he would prefer to do it through Unwin; and he did not even tell Newton he had written a book until it was just coming out. Newton was extremely hurt. He had never been able to bear the thought that Cowper was escaping from his influence, and this seemed to point unmistakably to the fact that he was. He wrote to him in that tone of Christian forbearance which is only employed by those seriously out of temper, and demanded an explanation. Ten years before such a letter would have shaken Cowper to the earth. That he, the despised and rejected of God and man, should have so provoked one of the paladins of the celestial army, would have been intolerable even to think of. However, now he only wrote back a calm note, giving his reasons for his action, but offering no apology. Newton replied, less Christian and more censorious. And now it was Cowper's turn to lose his temper. Really, Newton was too interfering. He had half a mind to tell him frankly what he thought of him. On second thoughts he refrained. But he did not give way ; and in the end it was Newton who made the first overtures for peace. Cowper in an attitude of dignified defiance is a comic thought. Still, the fact that he should be able to take one up was a healthy sign.

His old interest in the classics, too, had returned— returned after an absence of twenty years. In the days of his conversion he had looked upon them as pagan vanities ; and since then, except for an occasional glance at an old Virgil, he had never had the heart to take them up again. Now he wrote off to Unwin to ask him to send him a Homer. He enjoyed reading it enormously. But he did not merely read it. He was at a loose end after " The Task " was finished ; and, as always, when he had nothing to do his spirits began to sink. Suddenly he remembered Lady Austen's

P

suggestion that he should translate Homer. He took up the *Iliad*, and started on one book as an experiment. It was so successful that he went on. For the rest of the winter he was completely absorbed in this work. For the second time Anna had saved him from a bad winter. Poor Anna! Let us hope that Cowper had the grace to miss her a little!

Perhaps he did not, though. Already new friends had sprung up to take her place. One evening when he was sitting in his room, a Mr. Bagot was announced to see him. It turned out to be a Bagot who had been a friend of his at Westminster. There had been several brothers, and one was now a bishop; one of the very few bishops, as it happened, of whom Cowper conscientiously could approve. His caller, William Bagot, had become a clergyman too. Cowper was delighted to see him. He loved to recall with tenderness the happy days of the past, and he liked a friend ten times better if he had known him a long time. Besides, Mr. Bagot was a scholar. There was no one in Olney with whom Cowper could discuss the niceties of Homeric scholarship, and he now poured forth a flood of opinions and questions. Bagot did not live in the neighbourhood; he had merely been staying with one of his brothers, who did. But the connection was not allowed to drop when he went away. Whenever he visited his brother he used to come over to see Cowper; and between whiles they corresponded about Homer.

Cowper had also got to know the Throckmortons, the owners of Weston Park. The present owner was not the same as he who had originally given Cowper the key of Weston Wilderness. He had died lately, and had been succeeded by his son, John. To him Cowper wrote, asking if he still might keep the Wilderness key. And he received an answer which not only granted his request, but invited him and Mrs.

Unwin to come and see a balloon sent up in the park
a few days later. In spite of Cowper's doubts as to the
morality of ballooning, he accepted the invitation.
The balloon, however, failed to go up; but Cowper
and Mary enjoyed themselves as much as if it had.
Both Mr. Throckmorton and his wife were very kind.
Singling them out from all their other guests, they led
them into the house to drink chocolate, asked them to
use the garden as well as the park to walk in, and
repeated over and over again their wish to see more of
them. Cowper liked the idea. He thought both Mr.
and Mrs. Throckmorton charming. It was true that
they were Roman Catholics, born of the breed of that
Scarlet Woman who preached that works were worth
as much as faith. But it is the measure of how much
Cowper's Evangelicalism had modified that this fact,
which twenty years ago would have made him shudder,
now made no difference to him at all.

All the same, he felt shy. After all, the Throckmortons lived in such very grand style. It would be
pleasant to go and see them once in a while; but anything like a common social life seemed impossible.
So, though he was cordial, he made no decided movement towards cultivating a friendship with them.
Mr. Throckmorton was also shy; and for a year or two
the acquaintance remained at a standstill. In the
summer of 1785, however, for one reason and another,
they met more often than usual. And now Cowper
was in a much more active condition of mind—willing,
nay anxious, to follow up the acquaintance.

These new additions to his list of friends did their
part in accelerating his recovery. He was living more
like an ordinary man than before, and he became more
like an ordinary man. And now an important event
happened. "The Task" came out. It was a quiet
time in the literary world, and it had a huge and
immediate success. At one swoop Cowper soared to

the top of the tree of contemporary poetry. Preachers, politicians, literary pundits united to praise him. Olney became a famous place, the summer-house and the greenhouse celebrated objects. Mrs. Throckmorton brought over a party of fashionable ladies down from London to see them. Cowper feared they would be very disappointed when they did. Things seem much more attractive when described in poetry than they are in reality. But he showed them everything, with gratified care, made them each a neat bunch of myrtle, and took the opportunity to repay a small part of Mrs. Throckmorton's hospitality by giving her some cuttings of a special kind of canary lavender for her own garden.

Nor was she the only one of his friends to congratulate him. One morning he was excited to receive a letter in a familiar hand. He tore it open, to be faced with the demonstrative, opinionated, entertaining, helter-skelter style, the heavily underlined writing of Harriet Hesketh. She had read his poems; she thought them perfectly delightful; she had felt she must get into communication with him again. Cowper was overjoyed. If Bagot's visit had unsealed the fountains of tender recollection, how much more did this ! Harriet was associated with some of the pleasantest days of his life. The drawing-room of Southampton Row; the walks to Ranelagh; that summer in Dorsetshire—all the forgotten beloved scenes of the past crowded in a glowing haze of memory before his mind's eye. He hurried from the table and wrote off an enthusiastic letter of thanks. Harriet was now a widow, comfortably living in London, with nothing much to do, and she talked of Cowper and his poems to all her friends. Soon her letter was followed by others, from other members of Cowper's family.

And the letters were followed by gifts. A silver snuff-box and several bottles of Madeira from Harriet, and a beautiful desk, inlaid with ivory and silver, from

an anonymous donor.   Harriet asked him about his
financial position.   He admitted he was pinched.   She
wrote round to her relations, and soon his income was
increased by a hundred a year.

This was very pleasant : he had disliked feeling
that he was indebted to Mary.   But his renewed
friendship with Lady Hesketh was still pleasanter.   It
engaged his attention as no personal relationship had
done since his first meeting with Lady Austen five years
before : he neglected all his other correspondence in
order to write to her.   She took as intense an interest in
him as he did in her.   When he sent her a chicken as
a present she was in an agony lest such a present might
have involved a sacrifice on his part.   He reassured her.
And with growing enthusiasm and more and more
adjectives and exclamations and endearments, the correspondence continued.

At last, Lady Hesketh suggested coming to stay, in
June.   Cowper's excitement knew no bounds.   His
letters became lyrical with joy.   " I have nothing to
do but wish for June ; and June, my cousin, was never
so wished for since June was made.   I shall have a
thousand things to hear, and a thousand things to say,
and they will all rush into my mind together, till it will
be so crowded with things impatient to be said that for
some time I shall say nothing. . . . After so long a
separation, a separation that of late years seemed likely
to last for life, we shall meet each other as alive from the
dead."   And again, " I shall see you again.   I shall
hear your voice.   We shall take walks together . . .
you shall sit with a bed of mignonette at your side and
a hedge of honeysuckle, roses and jasmine ; and I will
make you a bouquet of myrtle every day."

But as the time of her visit drew near, one difficulty
after another sprang up to prevent it.   First, there was
the question of the house.   She refused to come to
Orchard Side, as she wanted to spare Cowper's income ;

but it was difficult to find lodgings with enough rooms
for the three servants without whom Lady Hesketh
could not think of travelling. The linen-draper had
rooms to let, with a charming sitting-room, but they
contained no bedroom for Lady Hesketh's woman.
A lace buyer near the church had good bedrooms, but
no sitting-room for the cook and footman. The
Vicarage alone was big enough to hold her retinue
comfortably, but it was completely unfurnished.
However, after a little discussion a Quaker of the
neighbourhood offered to supply furniture for five
months for the very moderate sum of five guineas,
including two large armchairs and a " superb bed "
adorned with a bedspread of linen with a picture of
Phaeton kneeling before Apollo printed on it. The
little household at Orchard Side gave itself up to busy,
delighted, excited preparation for the coming visit.
Mary began fattening up her chickens, Cowper got
ready a fine passion tree in a tub to fill up the unused
fireplace of the Vicarage parlour. The weeks passed,
and then, only a fortnight before she should arrive,
Lady Hesketh wrote to say that her coach was broken
down and she must wait for it to be mended. Cowper
nearly burst into tears. For the whole day he sulked
and complained, deaf to Mary's consolations. It was
the last delay; however. The coach was soon put right;
Lady Hesketh wrote a last letter imploring them to
make no grand preparations to entertain her; and on
the 20th June, 1786, amid peals of bells from the
church tower, she drove into Olney.

As might have been expected, when he knew she was
actually on the road Cowper had been seized with a fit
of nerves. He was so excited at the thought of meeting her that he wondered if it might not prove too much
for him. A thousand fears began to stir in his troubled
brain. Even if it did not make him ill, the meeting
might prove a disappointment. He had acquired few

lasting convictions in his melancholy fifty-four years
of life; but one of them was that anticipated joys
generally proved disappointments. When she arrived
it seemed for a moment as if it was going to be justified.
A cloud descended on him, and during the whole
afternoon he sat, glum and stiff, his eyes fixed on the
ground, barely opening his mouth. For once, however, his fears were not realized. Within a few hours
he had got his spirits back. Lady Hesketh was just
the same as she used to be, just as lively and warm-
hearted and managing and enthusiastic and respectable,
just as full of jokes and advice and demonstrations of
affection and orthodox opinions. Even her brilliant
complexion had not altered. Her presence made a lot
of difference to Cowper. It was not the same sort of
difference as Lady Austen had made. In his relation
with Lady Hesketh there was no hint of romance.
She was his cousin, and he felt for her that comfortable,
friendly regard, founded on a common origin, cemented
by common memories, that one feels for a relation.
They understood each other by instinct. They had
the same prejudices, the same conventions, the same
jokes. Lady Hesketh was always throwing Cowper into
fits of laughter, especially when she told him " the
story about the Gloucestershire Attorneys." He saw a
great deal of her. Unlike Lady Austen, again, she
did not interfere with his work. During the morning
he was left completely alone, but the afternoon they
spent together, walking, or driving in her carriage.
If they walked, Lady Hesketh used to carry a velvet
bag full of pennies with her and scatter them to the
village children—a homely charity, after Cowper's own
heart. They dined together and spent the rest of the
day in each other's company. If it was fine, they sat
in the garden, if wet, indoors, " comfortably round
one dining-table, without stirring, till after supper,"
says Lady Hesketh. " Our friend delights in a large

table and a large chair. There are two of the latter comforts in my parlour. I am sorry to say that he and I always spread ourselves out in them, leaving poor Mrs. Unwin to find all the comfort she can in a small one, half as high again as ours, and considerably harder than marble. However, she protests it is what she likes; but I hope she is sincere. Her constant employment is knitting stockings. . . . Our cousin has not, for many years, worn any other than those of her manufacture. She sits, knitting, on one side of the table, in her spectacles, and he on the other, reading to her, in his." Lady Hesketh used to listen while he read aloud. If he wrote, she copied out the manuscript of his translation.

But she did not merely enhance his life as it was. Her practical, feminine nature, anxious to do good to her fellows, and sure she knew how to do it, thought Cowper needed society. His nervous attacks were, to her common-sense eye, due to his abnormally solitary life with these queer, religious people. So, day after day, the wheels of her chariot rolled out of Olney, bearing her and Cowper and Mary to pay a visit at Weston or Gayhurst.

Cowper was very well able to make himself agreeable, and he enjoyed these visits. Mary, too, strongly approved of these excursions. Her patient, loving observation had long ago told her that Cowper was the better for variety. Was it not this knowledge that had made her put up with Lady Austen for so long? When it came through Lady Hesketh, she welcomed it. It was a great comfort that she liked Lady Hesketh so much. From the first she had been pleased by the tone of her letters. " Please tell Lady Hesketh that I truly respect and love her," she had said to Cowper. Lady Hesketh sent her a silver snuff-box. When they met the favourable impression produced on both sides by these amenities had been confirmed. After all, Mary had no reason to be jealous of Lady Hesketh. William Unwin liked her too. He had paid a formal call on her in order to form his own impressions, as he had before on Lady Austen ; and, as before, he had been dubious. Lady Hesketh's complexion was so very brilliant for a woman of her age. Could it be real ? Cowper earnestly assured him that it was. He had seen it come and go. William came to stay during Lady Hesketh's visit, and was completely won over to her. Never indeed had four people got on so famously. " Now we want Mr. Unwin," said Lady Hesketh, the day after he left. " Her reason for saying so," quoted Cowper to Unwin, " was that we had spent nearly half an hour together without laughing, an interval of gravity that does not often occur when you are present."

One of Cowper's friends, however, was not so pleased at the new developments in his life. Since the disagreement over the publication of " The Task," Newton had watched Cowper's career with growing suspicion. He had been disagreeably surprised to learn that Cowper was spending his time in translating the writings of the heathen. Cowper, fearful that he might not like it, had made as little of it as he could, merely referring in a casual way to the fact that, by way of passing the winter days, he was making an English version of the old Asiatic tale of Homer. Newton felt not altogether satisfied. He said to a friend that in the days of his conversion Cowper would no more have thought of doing such a thing than of putting the tale of " Jack the Giantkiller " into Greek. Nor were the Throckmortons, a Roman Catholic family of social habits, the friends he would have expected or approved for a sincere Evangelical. In 1786 he began asking questions about them. Cowper assured him that they were charming people and that he was certain the acquaintance was blessed by Providence. For a second time Newton felt not altogether satisfied. And now, as the summer advanced, what should he hear but that Cowper was off every afternoon on some party of pleasure in the Babylon of Bedfordshire County society. He wrote off hurriedly, demanding an immediate explanation. Cowper was not so concerned to please the susceptibilities of Newton as of old. He told him what he had done, and defied him to see any harm in it. Actually, as he was careful to point out, his conviction of his own damnation had not altered. Newton need not worry. He was ſtill fundamentally miserable, and Mrs. Unwin ſtill spent hours praying for him. This was reassuring news; but Newton's fears were not really removed. He had heard for a fact that Cowper had been seen in a green coat and had even taken part in an archery competition. In face of such facts no amount of plausible explanation could set his mind at reſt.

Cowper might say he was miserable, but, in fact, his recovery progressed daily. It was not only what Lady Hesketh did which raised his spirits. It was the fact that she did it. She returned to Cowper's life, a figure from his dead youth, that blissful period before he had gone mad; and in her company he unconsciously tended to fall back into the habit of mind of those days. Old jokes, old names, were ever on his lips, and old thoughts began to creep back into his mind. Harriet, especially, had been a cheering influence, even in the paſt. Was it not she who had brought him back to happiness at Southampton? And in her company his outlook ſteadily brightened. It had brightened before, but now for the firſt time improvement of spirits began to show itself in outward form. He spoke of himself in his letters, except those to Newton, not as one surely damned, but as one who, though not yet admitted to salvation, cherished a conſtant hope that one day he would be. In response to Lady Hesketh's request, he even began to say grace at table.

Shortly before she came, Mr. Throckmorton had told Cowper that Weston Lodge, a house of his in the village, had fallen vacant, and he wondered if Cowper would like to take it. For himself he had rejected the idea as too revolutionary, but he told Lady Hesketh about it in case she might like to take it herself. In her turn, she rejected the proposal. But she took up the idea of Cowper living there with passion. She thought that his depression arose in great part from his living at Olney in a gloomy little house, associated with, and inseparable in his mind from some of the gloomiest experiences of his life. If he could live somewhere else, and somewhere like Weston, where he would be near pleasant and only mildly religious friends, she thought it probable that his morbidities would vanish away. It remained to be seen, however, if the house was a suitable one. One afternoon they all drove over to see it. Even in its vacant state it compared very favourably with Orchard Side. It was certainly a most incongruous setting for spiritual disorder, a neat, square, sunny house, in a style at once unpretentious and well-bred, with window-seats and low white panelled rooms and a shallow, charming staircase. And its situation was in keeping with its appearance. The front, unlike that of Orchard Side, looked forth over the open fields, and the back on to its own walled garden that rambled up the hill, half useful, half ornamental, with currant bushes and damask roses mixed till it was bounded by the tree-tops of Weston Park. So that it was quiet. But it was not lonely. If one walked a few yards down the road on one side, one came to the classic gates of Weston Park, and on the other to the straggling end of the village of Weston, with its thatched cottages and gardens gay with hollyhocks: the perfect English village of idyllic imagination, where red-coated huntsmen jingle gallantly to the Meet on a soft autumn morning, or, on a glowing evening in summer the cumbrous hay-carts creak home with sun-bonneted children perched atop.

Lady Hesketh was determined Cowper should have the house. And though he could not have made up his mind on such a change by himself, he was really very glad when she made it up for him. There was a little difficulty finding the money. But Lady Hesketh helped them: and early in October they moved. When the actual moment for going arrived, Cowper minded as much as he had always minded a change. He had lived at Olney for nineteen years, and he was bound to it by the tentacles of a thousand memories. There, in the distant days of his conversion, he had joyfully prayed and praised; there his second madness had fallen on him; he had recovered there; there played with his hares and written his first book; there met and laughed and quarrelled with Anna; there known his first belated taste of fame. Many of these recollections were sad, but he felt as much bound to the place by sad as by happy recollections. Change is painful to man because it puts him in mind of his mortality. "This," he tells himself, "was once the present and now it is vanished; and so will vanish everything else." His sorrows seem among the deepest and most permanent things in his life; and thus, their disappearance strikes him as proportionately telling evidence of the frailty of things mortal. As he drove away from the house, Cowper's eyes were dazed with tears. He happened to go into Orchard Side again two months later. In the cold light of the winter afternoon the plaster hung from the ceiling and the dust blew up and down the floors. It seemed impossible to believe that only a few weeks before here had been the friendly, warm abode of human beings. The sense of mortality swept over him once more, and

with a double force.   His mind reverted to the theme
of its most sombre meditations.   " Such and so dismal," he said to himself, " is the condition of a soul
deserted by God."

However, his melancholy soon left him when he was
back at Weston Lodge.   It was so cheerful to do one's
work in a newly-furnished room, looking south; much
more cheerful than in a dingy room looking north.   Now
and again he would pause for a moment and look out of
the window, and his eye would light, not on a dull row
of houses, but on green foreground and blue distance.
Then his view would be blocked perhaps by the head
and shoulders of Mr. Throckmorton, turning in at the
gate to pay a morning call.   Cowper's life was full of
mild social events.   He dined with the Throckmortons
several times a week, and in the afternoon Mrs.
Throckmorton would sometimes call, and her husband
or the chaplain used to meet him in his rambles in the
wilderness, now only a few easy steps from the door.
There was no doubt the change was a success.   " I
think every day of those lines of Milton," he writes,
" when congratulating myself on having obtained,
before I am quite superannuated, what he seems not
to have hoped for sooner :

> ' . . . And may at length my weary age,
>   Find out a peaceful hermitage.'

For, if it is not a hermitage, it is a much better thing ;
and you must always understand, my dear, that when
poets talk of cottages and hermitages, and such-like
things, they mean a house with six sashes in front, two
comfortable parlours, a smart staircase and three bed-
chambers of comfortable dimensions—in short, such
a house as this."   Could it be that Harriet was right :
that his melancholy had been but a temporary illness,
from which he had now recovered ?   And that such

moments of depression as he had lately experienced were fancies called up by the gloomy memories associated with his old dwelling? Could it be that the storms and breaking seas of his life's day were behind him, and that now, as evening drew on, his battered bark was to be permitted to rock to rest, softly in a sunlit harbour?

CHAPTER V

ALAS! Cowper's hopes were vain. In the middle of November news came to Weston that William Unwin had been taken suddenly ill at Winchester. A week later he was dead. A lifetime of patient resignation to evil, and the desire not to make things worse for Mary, stopped Cowper from giving way to grief. Bull, who rode over on a visit of condolence, was amazed how calm he managed to appear. But in reality he was suffering under a great shock. It was not only that he had been especially fond of William. He had come to the age when man can ill bear the loss of anyone he cares for: for he feels it to be the sign and prologue to his own dissolution. Besides, he cannot well spare a friend when he is too old to make new ones and too weak to live a life of solitary independence. The circumstances of Unwin's death, too, were particularly painful to contemplate. He left a young wife and two small children. " I cannot think of it," said Cowper, " without a heartache I do not remember to have felt before." A mood of lassitude and dejection took possession of his spirits. He lost all pleasure in society, would sit for hours at his table, unable to bring himself to work at anything.

So passed December; and now January, fatal January, was here. Sure enough, the old symptoms began to reappear. His sleep was troubled by dreams, his waking hours by accusing voices. In his present condition they were fatal to him. His shaken nerves could muster up no power of resistance. Every day he grew rapidly worse. Melancholy swelled to obsession, obsession to delusion. Finally one terrible night once more in dream he heard the voice of God raised in wrath against him. " I will promise you anything," it declared, and again, " I will promise you anything." To Cowper this could only have one meaning. It was the firm and final declaration of Heaven that any hopes of salvation he had cherished were vain, and any good God might seem to promise him was not to be believed. The foundation of such confidence as he still possessed was swept away ; and the whole structure of habit and security which he had managed to erect on the broken remnants of his old life fell to the ground. For the third time in his life Cowper was a raving maniac.

Six weeks had sufficed to destroy the work of thirteen years. At first sight it seems astounding. But the truth was his recovery had been more apparent than real. The seat of his malady had never been touched ; the infected area had never been examined, much less cleansed ; he had never lost any of his delusions. Only his intense vitality had enabled him to achieve a partial return to mental health in spite of these handicaps. Whatever his delusions, he managed to prevent them dominating his thoughts. But he was like a man breathing through one lung. And, like a man breathing through one lung, he could only go on if he was subjected to no extra strain. In Unwin's death for the first time he sustained a severe shock ; and, most unluckily, at that very time of year when he was always at his weakest. The consequence was that he immediately succumbed.

The disease followed its old course. Once again he tried to kill himself. Once again he shrank from all other friends, and clung only to Mary. In one respect it was a worse attack than before, for it came after a period of so much hope and he felt proportionately discouraged by it. On the other hand, this time it lasted much less long than before. There was no period of gradual recovery. One day in July he returned to his right mind; and by September he was working and writing letters and dining out, to outward appearance just the same as he had been before the attack.

It was to outward appearance only. His inner man had in that time undergone a change only less decisive than his original conversion. He had completely and finally lost his capacity for hope. Of course he had despaired many times before : in the throes of madness and when he felt madness coming over him. But now he did so when his health and spirits were improving, in cold blood, and with clear eyes, in the light of a sort of perverted reason. Why should he hope ? All the methods to which he had trusted to defend him against the enemies of his spirit—religious, medical, social—all in turn had failed him. He could not face being disappointed again. He had better not hope. Indeed, had he not received a specific warning not to do so ? Of course God was omnipotent, and might reverse His decision and save him. But why should He ? Everything went to show that his old convictions were right. He was the single created soul predestined to fall from grace. What was God's purpose in so predestining him he could not tell. The only reason he could think of was that He did it to demonstrate His omnipotence, even over His own laws. Such a view would have been impossible to anyone with a living devotional life. No one who still felt God to be the principle of peace and love in their own life could also have believed He could act so

Q

unjustly. But it was far too long since Cowper had experienced any spiritual happiness for this to move him. He saw no reason, indeed, to doubt the truth of the Calvinistic doctrinal system. Only now, after his third collapse, he could no longer conceal from himself the fact that to his sinful eyes it did appear inexplicably cruel and unjust. Nor was it his own sad history alone that brought this home to him. All Evangelical England was at this time ringing with the horrors exposed by the first anti-slavery agitation. Cowper brooded on the fate of these thousands of wretched heathen, created, as it seemed, only that they might be tortured in this world and damned in the next. His creed told him that it was all a part of the beneficent plan of an infallible God ; but he could not even begin to think how this could be so. If such was the will of God, why should it be unlikely that He should damn the soul of a single worthless sinner like himself ? No ; reason and observation alike forbade him to hope.

The strange thing was that, in spite of this, he was not sunk in a black despondency. But though he had lost all heavenly comfort, on earth he was not yet comfortless. Mary's devotion during his last illness had added another strand, if another strand was needed, to the strong cord that bound Cowper to her ; and now that all hope of Divine succour had finally left him, her figure loomed out, the single citadel of support on his horizon. His relationship to her was far and away the most important thing in his life. It alone stirred a movement of happiness in his deeper feelings ; it alone promised not merely distraction from sorrow, but was in some degree its antidote. Without Mary, Cowper would have felt too weak to face life at all. With her at his side, his lot could not be for long wholly without alleviation.

Nor had he lost his power of enjoyment. The amazing vitality that had enabled him—shattered, fragile creature as he was—to survive a third attack of violent melancholy madness, still rose within him. He found that he still responded to the world around him with interest, with delight. In a spirit of sad philosophy, therefore, he abandoned himself to the pleasures of the moment. This, too, was not a new attitude for him. He had adopted it after his last attack; but, like his despair, it was for the first time the expression of deliberate and cold-blooded decision. Even if he was going to go mad the next January, he thought to himself, what was the advantage in worrying about it in June?

" The present is a dream," he said, " but one wishes to make it as pleasant as one can."

Two things in particular made it pleasant. One was his work. Translation was an ideal employment for someone in his condition; for it gave him regular occupation without making too severe a demand on his creative energies. And he found it very soothing for a large part of every day to exchange the society of his own stagnant thoughts for that of the active and unintrospective warriors of Troy and Greece. He had also recovered his enjoyment of the amusements and incidents of ordinary life. There were more of them at Weston than at Olney. The world he lived in there was less of a hermitage: it was more the ordinary world of the English country gentry of the day; the world depicted with so precise an irony by Jane Austen —distinct from fashionable London society on the one hand, and more sharply from that of rich farmers and families in trade on the other—a small world of rigid conventions and easy labours and mild amuse-ments and regular habits, where all the men were clergymen or squires, and led much the same life

whichever they were; and the women copied out
extracts and played the harp; a world whose serious
occupations were looking after the land and sitting
on the Bench and getting married, whose pleasures
were sport and cards for low stakes, and small talk all
the time, and now and again a ball. Cowper never
went so far as to attend a ball. When Mrs. Throckmorton gave one at Weston Park he excused himself
as too old. But he joined her archery club, and wore
its green coat and buff waistcoat with ingenuous delight.
The Throckmortons were inevitably the centre of his
social life; Mr. Throckmorton placid and pink-faced, his
wife sharp-featured and with lively eyes, as they live for
us in the elegant chalk of Downman to this day. There
was nothing about them of the scandal-mongering,
fox-hunting ladies and gentlemen that Cowper detested.
They were quiet and well-bred and cultivated. Cowper
could not contain his admiration when he saw the
drawings of the Pantheon Sir John had made in Rome
when he was there on the grand tour. And his
library, too, was a model of what a gentlemen's should
be. He asked Cowper to use it as if it were his own.
There was, indeed, no end to the kindness of the
Throckmortons. All through the winter they sent
Cowper braces of partridges, and when Mrs. Throckmorton learned that he no longer had a greenhouse,
she gave him complete control of hers. As for
invitations, they never stopped. Hardly two days
went by that one could not see Cowper and Mary
picking their way through the few yards of muddy lane
that separated them from the Park. The Throckmortons were seldom alone. As Cowper sat down
at table his eyes would travel along a whole row of
faces; county neighbours over for the day or relations
staying in the house—brothers and aunts and red-
cheeked children in sprig-muslin frocks or skeleton

jackets, nephews or nieces, as the case might be. Cowper enjoyed all this company : he felt he was getting a glimpse, as from a secure window, at the great gay world. Not that he was a mere spectator. Now that he was a famous poet his every word was received with respectful interest ; and in the pleasant warmth of this attention he blossomed into a raconteur. Characteristically his stories were generally against himself—the ludicrous figure he cut when he had been pursued by a bull or torn his trousers in a public place. He told them with an exquisite zest of appreciation. Before the story was well begun, his gentle eyes had begun to twinkle, his thin lips to expand in a smile ; and by the time the point was reached he was in a fit of laughter so infectious that no one who heard him could fail to laugh too. And he liked playing with the children. One day they persuaded him to get into a wheeled chair, and then whirled it at a break-neck and terrifying speed from one end of the house to the other. Such are the penalties inevitably consequent on kindness to children.

His intercourse with the Throckmortons was not confined to their house. Now and again Mary and he mustered their resources, made careful preparation, and had the family to dinner. And more often, if her husband was away, Mrs. Throckmorton would come in and share their ordinary simple meal. She had become a great friend. Cowper liked Mr. Throckmorton very much ; but, as usual, it was the woman in whose company he took most pleasure. In almost every letter he writes at this time we catch a glimpse of her neat, vivacious figure—Mrs. Throckmorton coming in for the afternoon to copy out his translation for him ; Mrs. Throckmorton coming back from mushrooming, her sweeping skirts inches deep in mud ; Mrs. Throckmorton stopping with some visitor

at the garden gate. If Cowper saw her from the
window he would hurry out and bring the party in.
Ten years before an unexpected stranger interrupting
him at work would have upset him for the day. Now
he stood and talked unconcerned, even if he noticed a
visitor stealing a glance at the sheets of manuscript,
the ink still gleaming wet upon them, that littered the
writing-table. The Throckmortons were away two or
three months in the year ; and then Cowper wrote long
letters to " Mrs. Frog " as he called her, giving the
news of village and garden and nursery, telling her
how he had had some children still staying on at the
Park to tea, or how Mr. George Throckmorton's
fiancée, Miss Stapleton, had come and played spillikins
with him. This Miss Stapleton became as close a
friend as Mrs. Throckmorton. She sang beautifully ;
and this to Cowper, so sharply sensitive to æsthetic
pleasure, and as ever so starved of it, shed an ideal light
over her figure. Some of the most exquisite moments
of his life at this time were due to her. She sang his
own songs ; and as he sat in the quiet parlour listening
to the familiar words as they floated up on the sweet,
true voice, a thousand emotions of joy and regret and
tenderness stirred in his heart. One summer evening
after she had finished he walked out into the garden.
All around, the trees were loud with the song of the
nightingales. Miss Stapleton's voice was still echoing
in his ears; it was as if the nightingales had taken
up the tale of her melody. For a time he listened
entranced, then, as the twilight gathered, he turned
homewards. He wrote a little poem about the
incident. His friendship with the Throckmortons
was always inspiring him to occasional poetry. He
constituted himself as a sort of poet laureate to the
family—composed epitaphs for their dogs, Fop and
Neptune, to be carved on urns in the Wilderness, and

wrote verses congratulating Mrs. Throckmorton on her beautiful handwriting, or lamenting the death of her bullfinch.

The Throckmortons were his greatest friends; but they did not make up the limit of his acquaintance. We find him at eight o'clock in the morning uncomfortably arrayed in all the stiffness of full dress and wig, to drive over and spend a day with Bagot's brother at Chichely. And he was always walking over to Olney to see his old friends, Wilson the barber, or Palmer the draper. Prone on Palmer's counter he would lie, watching the customers and gossiping. He had made a new friend in Olney, too—the vicar, Mr. Bean. He liked him so well that he even agreed to contemplate a religious subject long enough to write a hymn for the Sunday School. Perhaps he felt that any thoughts suitable for innocent children would be unlikely to remind him of the spiritual condition of a hardened sinner like himself. The hymn shows his views to have been still uncompromisingly Evangelical:

> " Hear, Lord, the song of praise and prayer
>   From Heaven, Thy dwelling-place,
> From infants made the public care
>   And taught to seek Thy Face.
>
> Thanks for Thy Word and for this day,
>   And grant us, we implore,
> Never to waste in sinful play
>   Thy holy Sabbaths more."

We must hope Mr. Bean was satisfied. It can hardly be imagined that the children entered with much heart into these bleak aspirations.

People used to come and see Cowper too, Bagot and Bull, and Mr. Greatheed, the minister of Newport Pagnell, bowling over in his high-wheeled phæton; and one day young Lord Ferrers rode over with his tutor, and had the condescension to partake of a dish of chocolate. Old friends used to come and stay for several days—Newton, the Powleys, Harriet Hesketh. With Newton, Cowper, to outward appearance, was on as intimate terms as ever. But it was only to appearance. Newton was on the look-out for the least sign of backsliding. He was extremely distressed when Cowper told him he was writing some verses in response to a request from a lady on a pen which she had found on the Prince of Wales's writing-table. The very name of so famous and so flourishing a sinner filled Newton's mind with suspicion: could it be that Cowper was going to mention it in terms of compliment? Cowper assured him that, on the contrary, " there was no character in Europe he held in greater abomination." But Newton was not satisfied.

The truth was that Cowper had touched that weak spot in his character that all his self-discipline had not enabled him to remove, his desire to dominate. Because he could no longer dominate Cowper, he no longer trusted him, and any alteration in his mode of life he took as justifying his mistrust. Sometimes, as he compared the wild whirl of carriage drives and village tea-parties in which Cowper now lived with the missionary meetings and spiritual exercises of twenty years before, he even wondered if Cowper was not right about his soul—that he really had fallen from grace. Christian charity bade him hope not. The claims of old affection prevented him breaking with him. But holding such views, it was not to be expected that their intercourse was any longer much pleasure to either. For a long time they had been receding from each other: now a gulf had opened out between them, and although they might clasp hands over it, neither of them was ever to cross it again.

Any failure on the part of Newton was more than compensated for by Harriet Hesketh. Her friendship was an even greater source of pleasure to him than that of the Throckmortons. He looked forward to her letters, and still more to her visits, with passion ; and if either of them was delayed fell into a fever of anxiety. It certainly was a different place when she was there. Her bustling, caressing presence seemed to brighten any room she came into. Cowper basked in its glow. The most humdrum occupations, like unpacking a parcel, were delightful when Harriet sat on the stairs, her voluminous skirts spread around her, and watched and commented. Even to be interrupted by her was a pleasure.

" Should you find many blots and my writing illegible you must pardon me in consideration of the cause. Lady Hesketh and Mrs. Unwin are both talking as if they designed to make themselves amends for the silence they are enjoined to keep when I sit translating Homer. Mrs. Unwin is preparing the breakfast, and not having seen each other since they parted to go to bed, they have consequently a deal to communicate."

She usually came in the winter, and it made a valuable difference to his spirits at that trying time of year. She called him Giles Gingerbread and Jeremy Jago, as she used to do in Southampton Row forty years before. With the youthful nicknames some of the light-hearted confidence of youth came back to him.

Harriet's kindness was not confined to visiting him. As its only link with London, she undertook a thousand commissions for the household at Weston, ranging from canvassing subscribers for Homer to buying " a pound of green wax for a spindle." While as for her presents, Cowper's thanks could not keep pace

with them. She practically furnished the house, as
well as helping to pay for it. As Cowper's eye ranged
round the pleasant walls of his study, from carpet to
bookshelf, from looking-glass to brass-studded armchair, it lighted on nothing that was not a present from
Harriet. The very cap he wore for working in the
morning—that strange turban-like cap—was from her;
and she used to brighten his simple meals by sending
him claret and Madeira. He had a capacity for
attracting presents. A serious-minded lady, Mrs.
King, in the neighbouring village of Pertenhall, read
his poetry and then scraped an acquaintance with him
on the grounds that she had known his brother.
Cowper added her gladly to his list of correspondents.
In return she sent him cake and apples and a brilliant
counterpane of her own making.

She was not alone in wanting to know him. By an
ironical caprice of fortune, Cowper, who had spent
a considerable part of his life in search of retirement,
who had found the humdrum narrowness of middle-
class London insufficiently obscure for his desires,
at the age of sixty, unintentionally, had become a
public figure, one of that minute band who, in each
generation, manage to make their personalities felt
outside their immediate surroundings, to be liked and
discussed and disliked by people who have never seen
them. To pass the time, he had written some verses,
and it had happened. Hurdis the poet wrote to him
for advice; Romney wanted to paint him; the
Dowager Lady Spencer, mother of the magnificent
Duchess of Devonshire, asked to be allowed to call
on him. Fox himself could spare a moment from
the heady, hectic whirl of debate and dice-box in
which his life rotated to contemplate with his usual
unrestrained enthusiasm the unsophisticated pleasures
of life at Olney.

His work gained him more than admirers: it gained him disciples. In the winter of 1786 a young man called at Weston, who said his name was Rose, and that he had come to bring Cowper the compliments of some Scottish professors. It was only a pretext. Samuel Rose, like many of his contemporaries, if we are to believe the verbose mural tablets put up to them by their relations, lived a life " dedicated to the pursuit of virtue." His every act was part of a deliberate and considered scheme of self-improvement. He had worked conscientiously at the University, and now, at the age of twenty, he worked conscientiously at the London Bar. Reflection suggested to him that he would be benefited both morally and intellectually by intercourse with a man of genius who was also a man of virtue. Such a character is notoriously rare, but Rose believed he would find it in Cowper. Unluckily, he had not given that time to the cultivation of the social graces that he devoted to that of solid worth; with the result that his manners were stilted and awkward: and at first it seemed probable that he would go away before any of the desired beneficial intercourse had been achieved. However, in time Cowper's tact and sympathy broke through his reserve. Poor Rose! he turned out to be a very simple-minded young man, naïve and candid, and he confessed to Cowper in a gush of confidence that he had been shy all his life, even of his own father. He was touchingly grateful for kindness; in a short time had lost his heart to Cowper and everything to do with him. " I here feel no restraint, and none is wished to be inspired," he wrote to his sister on a later visit. . . . " We rise at whatever hour we choose; breakfast at half after nine, take about an hour to satisfy the *sentiment*, not the *appetite*, for we talk—good heavens! how we talk! and enjoy ourselves most wonderfully. Then we separate—Mr. Cowper to Homer, Mr. Rose to transcribing what is translated, Lady Hesketh to work and to books alternately. Mrs. Unwin, who in everything but her face is like a kind angel come from heaven to guard the health of our poet, is busy in domestic concerns. At one, our labours finished, the poet and I walk for two hours. I then drink most plentiful draughts of instruction which flow from his lips, instruction so sweet and goodness so exquisite that one *loves* it for its flavour. At three we return and dress, and the succeeding hour brings dinner upon the table and collects again the smiling countenances of the family to partake of the neat and elegant meal. Conversation continues till tea-time, when an entertaining volume engrosses our thoughts till the last meal is announced. Conversation again, and then rest before twelve to enable us to rise again to the same round of innocent virtuous pleasure." It was delightful to find that anything so improving could be so enjoyable. Cowper for his part liked Rose very much, urged him to struggle against his shyness, to see more of the world, and to go and call on Lady Hesketh in London. Rose agreed. But the thought of bearding, so to speak, a lady of title in her own den was so formidable to him that it was months before he could muster up courage to follow Cowper's advice.

Cowper's other disciple was also shy. He was a second cousin on his mother's side, called John Johnson, a Cambridge undergraduate. And, inspired with an admiration for Cowper's poetry, he took advantage of the relationship to propose himself to stay in the January of 1790. He had an eager, ingenuous face that attracted Cowper at once; but for the first three days he sat with bright eyes and blushing cheeks unable to stammer out a word. At last, however, Cowper melted his reserve as he had melted Rose's.

And Johnson was revealed as a warm-hearted, untidy
boy, who threw himself into whatever he was doing,
scribbled poetry, played the fiddle, chattered, giggled,
and tripped up over the furniture with the same charming, clumsy impetuosity. He was, indeed, as clumsy
as a young colt; and, colt-like, when he walked in the
fields would suddenly break into a frisk, a skip or a
gambol. Not that there was anything untamed about
him. His frolics were always gentle and innocent;
if a serious subject was mentioned he became suitably
serious at once; and he was going to be a clergyman.
He had a tender conscience, too. A few days after
he arrived he asked Cowper's opinion on a poem
which he said had been written by one of his friends.
Cowper gave it, and Johnson confessed with shame
that he had written the poem himself. As can be
imagined, Cowper did not find much difficulty in
forgiving such a deception, but it continued to worry
Johnson, who, after he had gone back to Cambridge,
wrote profuse apologies. He would have done anything not to annoy Cowper. By temperament a hero-
worshipper, he met him at the very age when such a
temperament is most susceptible; and he fell under
his sway even more completely than Rose had done,
hung on his every word, counted it his highest privilege
to do him a service. He offered to take back all of the
Homer that was ready to Cambridge in order to copy
it out. This, however, with a wise distrust of the
discretion of undergraduates, Cowper politely but
earnestly refused. But he had grown very fond of
Johnson. He would have been disposed to love
anyone connected with his mother; and Johnson's
spontaneity and gaiety and innocence were just the
qualities Cowper had always liked in people. Besides,
he felt him a little like himself as a young man : it was
almost as if he were his son. Cowper was a born

father, and there is a pathos in the way all his paternal feeling, deprived by an untoward fate of natural outlet, now flowed on to Johnson. How it pleased him to guide his tastes, to direct his studies—characteristically, he told him to give up metaphysics and mathematics as sterile intellectual frivolities—to take pleasure in his successes, to sympathize over his failures, to warn, to exhort, to spoil him. His friendship grew only second in importance to that Cowper felt for Harriet. He longed for them to like each other, and introduced them. It was a great success. They had the same vivacity, the same respectability, the same love of innocent jokes. To Johnson, Harriet appeared lit up by all the reflected glory of Cowper's affection ; while she, for all her fifty years, had not so far forgotten the triumphs of her youthful beauty as no longer to take pleasure in the attentions of an agreeable young man. Of course, she soon had a nickname for him —Sir John Croydon—and she wrote him a great many letters, mostly about Cowper, it is true, but not without a touch of personal archness. Johnson's correspondence was much increased by his new acquaintance. He wrote to her, he wrote to Cowper ; to begin with, he wrote to Mrs. Unwin. Somehow this dropped, and Cowper, very anxious that Mary should not feel left out of it with his new friend, administered a gentle reproof—" One letter of hers," he assured Johnson, " from the point of real utility and value, is worth twenty of mine."

Both Rose and Johnson came often to stay. It was an excellent thing for Cowper, apart from his affection for them ; for they could do things his woman friends could not—help with Homer, or take him for long walks. Cowper's increased social activities had not diminished his pleasure in Nature. Indeed, it grew stronger every year. Long association strengthened this feeling, as it strengthened all his others. There was not a field, a path, a blade of grass that was not heavy with memories for him by now. Whenever he caught sight of Olney spire rising in the distance he thought of Newton and the hours he had spent there with him; if he passed a stile or a tree where he had walked with a friend, involuntarily he would recall what the friend had said to him there. Even things of the intellect had natural associations for him. He always read outdoors if possible, because he knew that should he forget a passage the sight of the field or the glade where he had read it would bring it all back to him. The very passing of time he marked by the way it registered itself on the face of Nature. Lady Hesketh would come "when the leaves grow yellow," a book would be published "before the first roses"; in a moment of melancholy he beautifully warns a correspondent against hoping too much from his friendship, "for the robin may whistle on my grave before next summer." It seemed as if, as his body declined back to the earth of which it was made, his spirit tended insensibly to merge itself in the spirit of earth, and see through her eyes.

Every day of his life, then, at the end of his morning's work, he would go upstairs, carefully put on his wig and shoes and brown overcoat, and sally forth. But it was pleasanter when he had someone to go with him. He generally had, what with Rose and Johnson and the Powleys and the Throckmortons. His acquaintance with Johnson had revived his connection with Donne relations, and they came to stay too: Johnson's sister, even shyer than himself; and her aunt, a placid Mrs. Balls; and Cowper's cousin Rose, whom he had not seen since he had dandled her on his knee when he was a boy. Now she was a precise-featured Mrs. Bodham, but very amiable, and in 1791 she and her husband came and stayed ten days—"a parson's week." Indeed, there were people staying at Weston during the greater part of the year. Never since he left London had Cowper's days been so full, so normal.

Alas! it did not mean that he enjoyed them more. Had not hope departed?—and with hope other interests had lost their power to satisfy his mind. Not even when he was enjoying them most did he look on them except as drugs that might for a moment delude him into forgetting his sad fate, but were powerless to save him. And, strong though the dose might be, the drug did not always work. He had his black moments, and they were black indeed. Now that January had twice proved fatal to him it was an almost unsupportable period. And he began to be worried by an even stranger cause of fear. The moon, the full moon, terrified him: he felt it an unholy power, able to make men mad. With a pathetic flicker of humour he tried to laugh himself out of this.

> "I'll instant write a most severe lampoon,
>   Of which the subject shall be yonder moon,"

he said to Lady Hesketh once-when they drove home beneath the cold brilliance of a winter's night. But he could maintain this mood of bravado only as long as he was in company. When he was alone in his bedroom, where the moonlight stood in livid pools on the floor and filled the walls with dim huge shadows, an unaccountable panic would steal into his heart, and he would remember his damnation and tremble. Newton had feared the moon, too. In these prosaic-seeming Evangelicals of the eighteenth century there lurked a wild atavistic strain. They were not called "enthusiasts" for nothing. And in their prim parlours Artemis the Destroyer could still strike terror.

Cowper felt his fears, too, more persistently dangerous than before. So precarious did his peace of mind become that he even refused for a time to write anything against slavery, lest it might upset him. And when his days were happiest he could pass a night of torment. Indeed, the contrasts presented by his life at this time were extraordinary. Never before had the incongruous strains of which it was made up appeared in such startling, such fantastic proximity. At one moment he might be sitting in the cosy, unromantic little parlour at Weston with Mary and Harriet and perhaps " Mrs. Frog," drinking tea and joking and mildly gossiping; himself the gentle life and soul of the little gathering, to all appearance completely satisfied to discuss how a fox had been killed at Kilwick Wood or if there was to be a new curate at Olney. Then bedtime would come. With smiling, decorous friendliness Cowper would see Mrs. Frog to the door, and retire to his room. He crossed the threshold into a world of visionary horror ; where the comfortable veil of the flesh was torn asunder, where the voice of God Himself could be heard speaking in His wrath, and the flames of hell leapt at the very window, and in the corners frightful fiends crouched, ready to spring. After a few hours of broken sleep came daylight, and then once more Cowper would dress and come down and enter for another few weeks, as it seemed with complete peace of mind, the humdrum world of an eighteenth-century country village.

There is something terrifying about such a mixture. Nightmare and madness seem doubly awful concealed in surroundings outwardly so prosaically calm. If such a mode of life does not bring peace of mind one feels none can. Nothing he can do, nowhere he can go, is of any use to protect man against the invisible onslaught of his soul. However, the mixture was all

R

Cowper hoped for now. Despairing of cure, he devoted all his efforts to keeping as he was, to maintaining the balance between night and day, and if he could get no better, at any rate to get no worse. And for three years vitality and care combined to enable him to do it. It was for three years only. In 1790 the balance began to dip ever so slightly on the side of night. It was partly due to the passage of time. Mere recreation ceases to distract as it grows more familiar; while misery becomes growingly hard to bear. But besides this, Cowper was now near sixty; and he could not forget it could not be long before his death— death! which had been for him the ultimate horror since he was a boy, and which, according to his present views, was to introduce him to an eternity of anguish. In face of such a prospect he was not likely to be comforted by the society of a few old friends and by country walks. Both the one and the other served rather to put him in mind of the flight of time, a flight that every day seemed swifter. "A yellow shower of leaves is falling continually from all the trees in the country," he writes. "A few moments only seem to have passed since they were buds, and in a few moments more they will have disappeared. . . . It is impossible for a man conversant with such scenes as surround me not to advert daily to the shortness of his existence here, admonished of it as he must be by ten thousand objects. There was a time when I could contemplate my present state and consider myself as a thing of a day with pleasure, and I remembered seasons as they passed in swift rotation as a schoolboy remembers the days that interpose between the next vacation when he shall see his parents and enjoy his home again. But to make so just an estimate of life as this is no longer in my power. I would live and live always, and am become such another wretch as Mæcenas, who wished for long life, he cared not at what expense of sufferings."

Nor was this the only way in which the passage of years affected his spirits. For some time he had been a semi-invalid. He suffered from lumbago, from astigmatism, from indigestion; while the strain of his spiritual troubles had shattered his nervous system. The smallest hitch in the ordered progress of his day put him in a fever of anxiety. If Lady Hesketh failed to write he immediately came to the conclusion that she was dying; and once, when he was woken up by a party of drunken revellers reeling past the house, he could not sleep for the rest of the night, and even on the following evening was still too much affected to dine with the Throckmortons.

He was very careful of himself, and studied his ailments with that conscientious zeal which people of uneventful life are prone to devote to their own health. He consulted various doctors. They recommended strange remedies. For several minutes every day Cowper excoriated his naked back with a brush for the good of his lumbago; while at one time he tried to cure his indigestion by taking an emetic every week. He did not like to interrupt his work, so when the strenuous day came round he would sit throughout the morning, basin and manuscript side by side before him, alternately versifying and vomiting. Disagreeable though they were, these remedies did him no good; and now, as with advancing age his power of resistance weakened, his health got worse. He felt feeble and ill all the time; which in its turn made him more liable to depression and less able to throw it off.

Finally, in June 1791, he finished his Homer, and was left with nothing to do. This had always been bad for him, ever since early days in the Temple, and since 1774 one of the strongest chains that bound him to sanity had been regular work. Now it was taken away when he was already disposed to melancholy by failing health and spirits. The effect was immediate, although it was in the summer. By September his nervous condition was definitely beginning to get worse. He realized it, and his daily occupations and interests began to lose such attraction as they still possessed for him. Powerless to sustain him in a real crisis, as he had painfully learnt in 1771, they now proved themselves incapable in the long run of maintaining a hold on his attention, even in a period of comparative mental peace. What he had been told about them in the days of his conversion had turned out to be perfectly true : they were false gods that seduced a man from following the true, only to fail him in the end. And it was also true that the only people he knew who were happy were those with faith. Faith—the humble, unquestioning faith of a village woman who knew no more of the world than she could spell out from her Bible—was better worth having than all that society and learning and fame could offer one ; faith that removes mountains could even give peace to the heart of man. Now, at the end of his life, after trying to keep it out of his thoughts for twenty years, he sought once more the consolation of religion. He had no new experience which might encourage him to think he would get it, not one spark of his old ecstasy lit up his horizon. But his vitality was still too strong to let him resign himself to despair : he still struggled involuntarily towards any gleam of hope. And religion was the only source of hope in which he now believed. In spite of his conviction of his personal damnation, his creed did teach that God's pity was infinite ; so that there was a chance he might be saved even if his condemnation had been declared. Anyway, it was the only chance there was. But unless he could revive his faith, he knew he would not get it. Turning in disgust and disappointment from the pleasures and preoccupations of the world, he sought desperately, hopelessly, anywhere, anyhow, for anyone, who might revive the spark within him.

This search was the origin of a curious episode. Samuel Teedon, the schoolmaster of Olney, was one of those eccentricities who seem to be an unavoidable by-product of a great religious movement. In himself he was the kind of man who is equally incapable of inspiring respect or dislike; a well-meaning, industrious little creature, but trivial, self-important, and silly. He was a dreadful bore, too. If he met you he never left you alone; and his conversation was what one might expect of a feeble intellect that had always known more than the people that it lived among. It consisted of tedious anecdote, diversified by floods of apologetic and irrelevant digression, and couched in a pretentious jargon of his own invention, founded on the view that a long Latin word is always better than a short English one. He called wine " inebriating fluid " and flowers " variegated flora." Nor were his circumstances more prepossessing than his personality. He lived with a handful of squalid relatives; either they or he were always ill, and he was miserably poor. This last added to the horror felt by others for his company. When he was not boring them he was begging from them. So far there was nothing about him to call for special notice. But he had been converted to Evangelicalism. He was the very last man whom it could do good to. Incapable of the devotion which was its virtue he was only too disposed to that hysteria which was its defect. Nor was the narrow, monotonous life of a country village likely to keep this hysteria within check. So far was it from doing so, in fact, that he became

possessed with the idea that he was the especial
favourite of God, Who communicated with him direct
by some spiritual channel unknown.   It seems likely
that he evolved this view with the subconscious
intention of obtaining some compensation for his
failure to stand out among his fellows in other ways.
But Evangelicalism gave him grounds for it by its
insistence that the despised of this world were more
acceptable in the eyes of Heaven than the great.   His
celestial connection certainly did not better his mundane
situation, if we are to judge from a diary he left.
Neither his own health nor that of his relations improved, though he solicited the especial benediction
of Heaven every time either took the smallest remedy.
" Very ill at home," he writes, " but through mercy
cured by drinking very freely of brandy," and again,
" My cousin took some red bark, which I hope the
Lord will bless."   He remained so poor that whenever
he had anything extra to eat he entered it in his diary
with pathetic and detailed precision ; and his religion,
far from making him less, made him more boring to
other people, even to his spiritual directors.   " Went
in the morn to church and heard Mr. B. from ' spare
the rod.'   In the noon went to Weston.   Mr. B.
overtook me, but never spoke, though just by on the
other side of the hedge, and seemed fearful by his own
velocity of my overtaking him."

   Teedon's Evangelicalism had brought him into
touch with Cowper and Mary years before, and he was
always in and out of the house.   Cowper soon found
him as much a bore as everybody else did.   He was
easily embarrassed, and he never knew when Teedon
was most embarrassing : when he expatiated with
unctuous self-appreciation on his spiritual privileges,
when he laboriously pointed out the best passages in
" The Task " to Cowper as if afraid he might have

overlooked them, or when he thanked him in a ſtrain of pretentious compliment for his kindness. " I have wanted all my life," he declared one evening, " to be conneĉted with a man of genius and ability, and," turning to Cowper, " in this worthy gentleman I have found it." " You may suppose that I felt the sweat gush out on my forehead when I heard the speech," said the sensitive Cowper, " and if you do you will not be at all miſtaken." He had not the heart to snub anyone so well-intentioned and so ſtupid. But for twenty years he had avoided Teedon as much as possible.

Now, however, in his desperate effort to retrieve his faith, his attitude towards him underwent a change. Here was a man who had the very faith he longed for, the pearl of great price for which he was ready to sell all that he had. Even if he was tiresome by worldly ſtandards, that ought not to matter. Were not worldly ſtandards those that had proved themselves moſt hollow and moſt inadequate? God was no respeĉter of persons; He spoke through those whom the world eſteemed foolish and despicable. Cowper should humble himself before any soul whom God had thought worthy to illuſtrate with the faith refused to him. And if Teedon claimed that he had special communication with Heaven, who was Cowper to deny it? Should he not rather take advantage of it, and through his mediation learn what the Divine Will had in ſtore for himself, induce even a ray of the Divine Grace to fall on him? As the princesses of ancient Russia proſtrated themselves before idiots as the bleſt of God, so Cowper humbly sought the spiritual direĉtion of Teedon. He asked him for his prayers, took no decision of any moment without asking Teedon to find out what was Heaven's will in the matter. He did his beſt to make some return for his kindness by giving him countless meals and an allowance of £30 a year. For his part, Teedon took Cowper's interest as a great honour, prayed for him by the hour, and was never too tired to toil over to Weston to retail any spiritual message he might have received. It was not long before he had to deliver one of importance.

In October 1791, Johnson, Cowper's publisher, wrote to him saying he was contemplating a new and sumptuous edition of Milton to be illustrated by famous artists; and he asked Cowper to edit it. He was not attracted by the proposal, which sounded laborious without being interesting; but still the offer might be providential. He himself had no means by which to penetrate the wishes of Providence; so he asked Teedon if he would make intercession to discover it. Teedon announced that God had directly called him to the work, which He would make a blessed one for him. Cowper still felt an aversion from it; but of course there was now no possibility of hesitation. With the solemnity and deliberation befitting the execution of a divinely-appointed mission, he set to work. But before he had got further than the preliminary preparations a sensational event took place, which rent the whole texture of his life from top to bottom. One afternoon towards the end of December, as he was sitting working with Mary in the parlour, he suddenly heard her cry, " Oh, Mr. Cowper, don't let me fall ! " He jumped up just in time to save her from falling to the ground unconscious. A doctor was summoned, who attempted to reassure Cowper's white face and agitated question by telling him she had only had a nervous seizure of an insignificant kind. But when she recovered consciousness she saw everything upside down, and walked and spoke with the greatest difficulty. And Cowper knew perfectly well she had had a stroke.

In face of such a catastrophe, all other plans and considerations vanished from Cowper's mind. It had always been agony to him to watch anyone suffer, but how much more when the sufferer was Mary— Mary, his oldest, nearest, dearest friend, with whom he had lived for twenty-six years, to whom he owed health, sanity, even life itself. Most likely, he felt, with a fearful qualm of conscience, she had made herself ill by working for him. He felt he could never rest, or read, or think on any other subject till she was well again. And he had a more personal reason for wishing her recovery: as he looked at her prostrate form, the thought came unbidden to his head, "Perhaps she is going to die"; perhaps he would have to finish the last steps of his bleak journey alone. The prospect was too terrible to contemplate, even for a moment. He brushed it aside, but he could not wholly forget it; and it gave an added desperation to his struggle. At whatever cost, with whatever difficulty, she must be saved. He gave up his whole life to the task. The order of his existence was turned upside down. The calls of his own health, his own spirits, were disregarded: Milton itself, the task set him by God, was put aside—not finally, of course, but until a more convenient moment. Such work as he did, such letters as he wrote, were done at odd times when he was not wanted by Mary. He nursed her, he read to her, he helped her in her first feeble attempts to walk. As the weeks passed, it seemed he was to be repaid for his efforts. A first stroke is often not a severe one. By March, Mary, though still weak, was able to walk and work and talk almost as well as before. It seemed likely she would get perfectly well. Cowper's fears began to wane, and his spirits rose. They were further heightened by the entry of a new friend into his life.

In March 1792 Cowper received a letter from a Mr. William Hayley; who said he was writing the life of Milton, and he thought it would be of advantage to both of them to work together. The letter was written in a rhapsodical style, flowery with compliments, and it concluded with a sonnet of admiration. Cowper, however, felt far too glad of any help with Milton to be critical. A correspondence was opened; and in May Hayley came to Weston for a visit Before the stranger's arrival, Cowper was, as usual, overcome by nerves. Perhaps he might not like Hayley: supposing he should be put off by his appearance—he judged a great deal by appearance—he would never be able to conceal his feelings for several weeks. However, Hayley's tall military figure, his eyes bright beneath their bushy brows, did not displease him; and after a few days of his company he had admitted him into the small circle of his great friends.

He was very different from his other friends. Like Newton, indeed, he wrote his Memoirs; but there the likeness ends. Hayley's book was a magnificent affair: two stately quarto volumes with a steel-engraved frontispiece, an elaborate dedication to Lord Holland and two thousand or so leisurely spaced, elegantly printed pages. But the magnificence of its dress, and still more the unfaltering grandiloquence of the style in which it was written, only served to throw out in more startling relief the pathetic absurdity of the story it told. This incongruity was the central feature of Hayley's existence. With the loftiest aspirations, and talents above the ordinary, it was his sad fate to be generally unsuccessful and always ridiculous. It was not the fault of his character, which was an excellent one: warm-hearted, disinterested and industrious. But he had a romantic.

temperament, no sense of humour and, like Marianne Dashwood, he had learnt his view of life from the literature of sensibility.

Of all dead-and-gone habits of mind, that expressed in the eighteenth-century novel of sensibility is the hardest to enter into. How could people, even in imagination, take a view of life so flagrantly false to every fact of their experience and observation ? It is even more incredible that anyone should have looked at their own life in such a way. But Hayley did. In the clear-sighted, plain-spoken world of Smollett and Dr. Johnson he managed to be, and to remain, the complete "Man of Feeling," who shed the tear of sensibility at a beautiful prospect, who could not without emotion so violent that it made him ill revisit the scene of a former happiness, who would rather die than offend in the smallest degree the delicacy of an elegant female, who would starve sooner than stain his honour by receiving a gift, whose heart was ready to thrill at any moment with filial affection, love of solitude, and the "passion for freedom." His mother —he had lost his father young—had intended him to be a lawyer. But to such a temperament the idea of a regular profession seemed intolerably philistine, and when he was twenty-one he announced that he intended to devote his life to benefiting mankind by any means in his power, but chiefly by composing literary works of an improving character. It was very high-minded of him, because he had no money, and philanthropy has never been remunerative. But Hayley was optimistic, and had, as he characteristically put it, a contempt for money "romantic and imprudent." Nor was he without grounds for confidence in his literary powers. Had he not written an ode on the birth of the Prince of Wales which had won the commendation of Dr. Roberts of Eton College ? He started off, therefore, with high hopes. Unfortunately Fate had endowed him with bad luck as sensational as his aspirations. He worked like a trooper, he laughed at failure, he was always ready with a new idea, he was delighted to modify what he had done in the light of any criticism. But somehow he never could make a success.

His first efforts were a tragedy, which he sent to Garrick, and an epistle of compliment, which he sent to the King of Poland. Garrick refused the tragedy, and the epistle was lost before it ever got to Poland at all. By 1771 Hayley ran short of money. Undiscouraged, he retired to Eartham, in Surrey, where, amid the shades of rural retirement, notoriously inspiring to poets, he began to compose an epic about Stephen Langton; a subject which, he felt, would both give scope to his own passion for freedom and stimulate it in others. However, he had hardly written a canto before he contracted an illness in his eyes and was forced to stop. A period of idleness in the company of his wife and mother seems to have persuaded him that there were other benefits of which mankind stood in even more pressing need than of the passion for freedom; for when he began work again in 1781 it was at a poem entitled "The Triumphs of Temper," expressly designed to exhibit "the effects of spleen in the female character" and to induce "his fair readers to cultivate a constant flow of good humour." For once he made a success. The poem went into several editions: it gained him a place among the leading poets of the day; and he had the gratification to learn from the "good and sensible mother of a large family" that it had entirely reformed the temper of her eldest daughter. Alas! this success was not to last. His romantic and imprudent contempt for money soon made away with

any that he had earned; and when he tried to make
some more, bad luck once again began to dog his
footsteps. He wrote a tragedy about a mad Javanese
Sultan, but on the very eve of its production George III
went mad, and the delicacy of a loyal subject compelled Hayley to withdraw it. Then he wrote a
novel designed to promote the interests of religion,
and dealing with the striking subject of " an elegant
young widow struggling between her maternal affections and an attachment of the heart to an engaging
young infidel." It was dedicated to the Archbishop
of Canterbury; but there is no record that he read
it nor any one else either. An opera adapted from
the German fared no better, though Hayley had
embellished it by a transformation scene in which
" magical personages " congratulated the British de-
fenders of the Rock of Gibraltar. Finally, despairing
of success on the English stage, he wrote a play in
French, and somehow managed to get it produced in
Paris. Paris must have been a very different place
from what it is now. The play failed because it
contained among its *dramatis personæ* a courtesan, and
the public representation of such a character proved
insupportable to the modesty of a French audience.
Even Hayley's hopes were checked by this rebuff, and
he stopped writing for the stage.

His private life had not proved more successful
than his public. With his mother—" a lady," he
tells us, " noted chiefly for her majesty "—he got on
well enough; but before he was twenty he had fallen
in love, and, true to the tradition of the sentimental
novel, corresponded with the object of his affection,
a Miss Fanny Page, clandestinely, with the help of
a friend of hers—Miss Eliza Ball. But other
friends made trouble, and Miss Page broke the
connection off. Hayley was, however, as ready to

cut his losses in love as in art, and without more ado
transferred his attentions to Miss Ball. Her mother
was mad, and Mrs. Hayley sought to discourage her
son from his new love affair; saying, no doubt with
her usual majesty, that such afflictions were hereditary,
and Miss Ball might go mad too. "In that case,"
replied Hayley magnificently, "I should bless my
God for having given me courage sufficient to make
myself the lawful guardian of the most amiable and
pitiable woman on earth." And he married her.
He lived to regret it. For the first few years, indeed,
Eliza was a charming wife, as full of sensibility as
himself, and so liberal in her views that she agreed
to adopt and bring up as her own a child of his
by a woman of Eartham village. But by 1781 she
began to change; by 1783 she was in a confirmed
state of nervous collapse. Poor Hayley was very far
from thanking God he was her guardian. Indeed
she was intolerable—sometimes silent and moodily
suspicious, sometimes in violent fits of hysteria. Her
sensibility became so acute that she would not come
near him when he was ill, for fear of ruining her eye-
sight by the amount of tears the sight of his sufferings would cause her to shed. And when she did
feel equal to seeing him, she did not make herself
pleasant. "You were the most agreeable man in
the world," she remarked one day, with an innocent
sincerity which must have made the remark doubly
mortifying, "but you seem to have lost all your
talents."

He became unable to stand life with her for long
at a time, and sent her, "with affectionate solicitude,"
on visits to Bath. But this was very expensive;
besides, she came back between whiles. And even
a day of her grew more than he could bear. There
was no doubt they must live apart. Mrs. Hayley,

now always alluded to as " my pitiable Eliza," was quite willing to go : she found Hayley as trying as he found her. But it was not so easy to arrange. Where was she to go to ? She liked Bath ; but Bath, as he knew to his cost, encouraged her to be extravagant. At last he made arrangements with an old friend of his, Dr. Berridge, to take her in as a paying guest. Just when he thought he had got her settled there Dr. Berridge died, and she came back. It was not till 1789 that he had her safely established with " a respectable circle of friends " at Derby. Even after this, there came an awful moment when she heard he was ill and she wrote to say that she felt it her duty to come back and nurse him. He rushed to his writing-table and with a desperate eloquence besought her not to come. His only wish was for her happiness ; and it might make her ill : let them rather communicate " by the frequent intercourse of affectionate letters." Their language to each other had, indeed, grown more high-flown as their feelings cooled ; and by the time they were living apart it was of a rhapsodical silliness that must be seen to be believed. They vied with each other in declarations of devotion in order to keep each other away. Eliza achieved the masterpiece in this kind when she implored Hayley to write less often, as the excitement of reading his letters was so great, that it prevented her from sleeping.

Repeated setbacks had not quenched the fire of Hayley's spirit. There was something heroic in his incapacity to profit by experience. Plays might be damned, books fail to sell ; after each successive blow he reappeared with eyes still bright and bearing still erect, undismayed and enthusiastic, ready with a new scheme for the benefit of mankind, confident that this time it would succeed. The world he looked on was still the world of sentimental literature : he himself was still the " Man of Feeling."

Even the ironical comedy of his own career he managed to re-stage in the theatre of his memory as a drama of sentiment : its hero " The Hermit of Eartham," a man of genius who retires undefeated by the blows of an unworthy world to a life of contemplation ; its heroine, his wife, brilliant and elegant, but too exquisitely sensitive to stand the rough friction of common life. In this guise his past could be contemplated without dissatisfaction, even with complacency.

In plain fact his life at this time did have its compensations, apart from the fact that he had got rid of Eliza. There were other ways of benefiting mankind than writing tragedies. All his life Hayley had promoted schemes—a new and nobler edition of Shakespeare, or the erection of a statue to Howard the philanthropist—and he continued to do so now. Nor had he stopped writing poetry. It was mostly occasional verse, but still designed to further some good object. Epitaphs, for instance—he was always ready to write an epitaph, whether he knew the man it was about or whether he did not, in order to soothe the sufferings of the bereaved by publishing the virtues of the deceased. And almost every day saw the composition of a lyric designed to reconcile an unhappily married couple of his acquaintance, or to promote charity to decayed musicians, or to encourage Mr. Wright the painter to disregard malicious criticism. One day Hayley read some of his poetry aloud to Gibbon. At the end Gibbon remarked with great animation, " When you began to read I was suffering from gout, but you have charmed away my sense of pain." Such is the only recorded occasion when Hayley's poetry did succeed in benefiting mankind :

it was unlucky that it was also the only recorded occasion when it was not intended to.

The mention of Gibbon brings one to Hayley's main source of happiness at this time. His longing to be an ornament to the race inspired in him a hero-worship of anyone who was; and he had always sought to get to know such men. With such effect that he became the intimate friend of Romney, Flaxman, Blake, Gibbon and Howard. The strange thing is that they should have liked him. But his admiration, though, like everything else about him, rather silly, was, also like everything else about him, sincere. And no one dislikes sincere admiration. Besides, all his virtues, his enthusiasm and generosity and disinterestedness, went to make him a good friend : he was always ready to listen, to appreciate, even to give practical help. As a result Eartham became a minor centre of the world of art and letters. He had spent a large part of his meagre earnings in building himself a library, adorned with portraits of geniuses whom he knew, and presided over, appropriately enough, by a large picture of Sensibility watering the sensitive plant, by Romney. There of an evening would the great men sit and take their ease; and sometimes one of the painters made a sketch, and sometimes one of the writers read his latest work, and all the time Hayley hovered round and rhapsodised and admired.

It was this enthusiasm for genius that made him scrape acquaintance with Cowper. And he had no difficulty in making Cowper like him. After a year's anxiety, sharpened by self-distrust, shadowed by a conviction of impending damnation, it was wonderfully soothing to spend the day with someone who thought all one's work of the first value and who was convinced it was only a prelude to greater things. Hayley had

s

too, in supreme degree, that quality of vitality which Cowper had always looked for in his friends, which had drawn him to people as different from each other as Newton and Lady Austen and Mary. Since Mary's illness he had been without such support, and now he reposed on Hayley as a tired swimmer on a buoyant wave. In addition to this, Hayley was the first professional literary man Cowper had met since he became a poet, the first friend he could talk to about his work on equal terms. And talk they did; and read each other's works and criticized and admired. It was no wonder that within a few weeks Cowper's liking had warmed to strong affection. Hayley, for his part, had even less difficulty in feeling enthusiastic about Cowper than about other things. Never, among all the geniuses of his acquaintance, had he met one so courteous, so modest, so gentle. Cowper's love for Mary and his intense desire that the visitor should appreciate her, especially moved him. "It seems hardly possible to survey human nature in a more touching and satisfactory point of view," he remarked.

The growing friendship was soon strengthened by a tenser bond. One morning, as Hayley and Cowper were coming back from a walk, they were met by a messenger who told them Mary had been taken by another attack. Cowper rushed home to find her speechless, helpless and almost blind. It was a second stroke—far worse than the first. In a moment of terrible illumination he realized that his darkest fear was now a practical possibility, that his hopes had been delusive, and she might be going to die. At once all his most sombre convictions crowded back into his mind, and he saw this new disaster as the last inevitable act in the course of his tragedy. How could he have expected anything different? Was he not the cursed of God? Surely therefore the most disastrous event was always the most likely. Beside himself with anguish, his face working, his eyes wild with sorrow, he tottered from the room. Hayley met him outside. " There is a wall of separation," cried Cowper, " between me and my God." " So there is," replied Hayley instantly, " but I can inform you that I am the most remarkable mortal on earth at pulling down old walls, and by the living God I will not leave a stone standing of the wall you speak of." He spoke without thought, from a mere impulse to say something that would comfort Cowper. His words had an immediate and formidable effect. Eagerly Cowper scanned his face for a moment: then a serene calm overspread his features, and taking Hayley by the hand, he said, " I believe you." Hayley's words of comfort, striking his ear as they did at such a crucial moment, had inspired him with the conviction that he was a heavenly messenger sent to help him. And from that moment he submitted himself to Hayley's direction with the unquestioning trust due to an angel of God. Hayley assumed his new responsibilities with his usual sanguine energy, recommended electric treatment for Mary, showed how to administer it, wrote for further advice from a doctor in London. By the end of May she was a little better, and he went away. Cowper felt his strength was leaving him. " Farewell," he said, pressing Hayley's hand with passionate tenderness, " farewell, I ne'er shall look upon thy like again." Actually he was to see him again very soon. Hayley had urged him to bring Mary to Eartham if she was strong enough for the journey, as he was sure the air there would do her good. By August she was well enough, and they started. Cowper could have shown no greater proof of the ascendancy Hayley had acquired over him. He had never gone back on that decision to retire from the world made at St. Alban's thirty years before. Indeed, except for his visit to Cambridge when John was dying, he had only travelled twice, and neither time back into the world. He had moved from one sequestered sanctuary at Huntingdon to another at Olney, and once again to Weston, and each time he had intended the move to be a final one. Now, at the age of sixty-two, when his health was failing, he took a three days' journey to stay for a short time with a man he had only seen for the first time three months before, whose house was a stirring intellectual centre of the day. Nor was re-entering the world a more drastic change in his life than leaving Weston. Long associations and love of Nature had combined to weave his surroundings into the texture of his life in such a way that without them he felt as awkward as without his skin. To take him from them was like rooting up a tree from its soil. If at any time he was asked to stay away, he had replied, with the brief finality of one declaring a law of nature, that it was impossible. Now, however, the object of his whole life was to cure Mary, and Hayley, the messenger of God, had said that such a change might aid her cure. There was no question that he must go. Indeed, her relapse had so deranged the whole order of his existence that nothing seemed impossible any more. Actually, as the time drew near he experienced qualms. In order to confirm him in his decision he asked Teedon to inquire the divine will in the matter. Teedon duly reported that he had received a message: " Go, and I will be with him. . . . And he went to Bethel to inquire of the Lord, who said, I will go down with thee into Egypt and will bring thee up again." This, if uncomplimentary to Hayley, was favourable to visiting him.

Trembling with agitation, therefore, Cowper steeled himself to go. The journey went more easily than he could have expected. They had Johnny and three servants to look after them, and Mary felt little fatigue. Cowper was only once disturbed: when they crossed the Surrey hills at night. To his untravelled eye they seemed as tremendous as the Himalayas, and as they loomed up bare in the baleful moonlight, a thrill of elemental terror ran through him. All was forgotten, however, in the excitement of arriving at Eartham. It must have been an extraordinary moment for him. Thirty years before he had fled from the world, wretched, broken, obscure; now, in his old age, he returned famous, to receive the homage of his distinguished contemporaries. Hayley had only asked a few people to meet him, but they were all distinguished—Romney, Mrs. Charlotte Smith the novelist, and later Hurdis the poet. They were struck not unfavourably by Cowper's modesty, his awkward and punctilious courtesy, as of some Rip van Winkle survived from a former age. Shy and awkward, Cowper stood blinking his eyes in the unaccustomed sunlight of their attention. He soon became happy enough in their company as long as he was not expected to talk too much. All the same, he was really happiest, because most at his ease, in the mornings when he and Hayley worked together at Milton. He had translated some of Milton's Latin poems, and Hayley suggested corrections. The loyal heart of Johnson was outraged by such impertinence. It is to be feared neither he nor Lady Hesketh altogether approved of Hayley. Who was this stranger who had assumed so sudden and so complete a sway over their " bard " ? A professional literary man, a friend of Gibbon—Lady Hesketh had heard rumours that he was an infidel. These proved untrue; but

Johnson was disquieted to notice that he never went to church, and he wondered whether such a friend would promote Cowper's happiness. Anyway, it was intolerable that he should presume to correct his poems. Cowper did not mind himself. No amount of admiration could make him vain; he even welcomed the criticism of Hayley's son Tom, a boy of twelve. He was a pompous child, already the true son of his father in the way he expressed himself. "Be assured that among all my young and sprightly associates you are not forgotten," he wrote to his father from school. But Cowper was disposed to feel more at ease with a child than with the other people at Eartham, and Thomas Hayley finally won his heart by the kind way in which he wheeled Mrs. Unwin out in a chair. When Cowper parted from him they both shed tears.

But he had not come to Eartham just to make friends, and they occupied a small part of his time. Except for the early part of the morning, he was with Mary; and at bottom his mind was concentrated on the state of her health. At first the change seemed to do her good: her voice grew stronger, her step firmer. But a delicate woman of seventy is not likely to recover from a second stroke. And as the days went by Cowper gradually became convinced the change was doing her no good and that the journey had failed in its object. With the realization, the gust of preternatural energy that for the last three months had supported him, subsided. It had been called out, it could only have been called out, to help Mary. When it failed to help Mary it collapsed: and his old inhibitions and prejudices reappeared, all the stronger for their brief eclipse. Talking to strangers seemed an intolerable strain, the unfamiliar landscape intolerably alien; he became consumed with a desire to go home. Early in September they went.

This return to Weston is momentous in Cowper's life ; for with it the curtain rises on the laſt act in its weary tragedy. Alas! it was to end on no classic note, " in calm of mind all passion spent," soothing and reconciling even while it saddens. No, in the Elizabethan manner, amid shriek and blood-boltered spectre and wild infernal darkness, was the scene to close. For the laſt time the forces of madness were to rise and overwhelm him.

The events of the laſt year had rendered them irresiſtible. Ever since 1787 he had, as we have seen, only kept them at bay with the utmoſt difficulty, and already, a year ago, they had begun to gain ground on him. Anything like a severe blow, and the battle would be irretrievably loſt. Actually the blow he did receive would have been fatal to him had he never begun to weaken at all. Mary's collapse was far and away the greateſt disaſter Cowper could have suſtained at any time in the laſt thirty years. For it meant the collapse of the foundation on which during that thirty years the whole order of his life had been erected. Always dependent on someone, on no one had he ever depended as on her. The illness of 1773 had irremediably bent the ſtem of his exiſtence ; but by clinging to her he had managed to train it to an upright position again. Afterwards, it is true, he had erected an elaborate ſtructure of occupation and habit on which to maintain his mental health. But he could never have got well enough to begin to put it together without her. Finally under the ſtrain of his third madness it had fallen to bits ; and he was left clinging to her once more. For she remained. Alone in all his experience, she ſtayed with him in light and darkness ; and though all his faith in God had vanished, he kept a sort of blind, instinctive faith in her. Now at a time when his health was beginning to fail, she was suddenly stricken with a mortal illness, and soon she needed support as much as he did. His only defence was gone; though he might still struggle, the battle was decided.

Of course if he had left her and made his home with other people in another place who knows that he might not have managed to stave off the evil day indefinitely? But even had such a course of action entered his head, his whole nature would have risen up to repudiate it. How often had she stood by him during his illnesses; and how patiently, how self-sacrificingly had she done it! Was it not her care for him, indeed, that had brought her to her present case? Now it was his turn to help her. And if to do so were to risk his life, it would only be a small recompense for what he owed her. But it needed no obligation of gratitude or loyalty to keep him at her side. Every other consideration was swallowed up in the great tide of compassion which welled up in him at the sight of her affliction. Mary, his Mary was suffering: his only thought was to relieve her. And recklessly, unhesitatingly he poured out any drop of vitality that remained to him in order to do it. By the inscrutable decrees that govern mortal destiny, his devotion was his destruction. There can be no doubt that it was the strain of nursing her that finally confirmed his doom.

It was no longer possible even for a moment to preserve that precarious balance which by desperate efforts Cowper had managed for the last three years to maintain between sense and madness. His incongruous double life was at an end. From now on, inexorably, unfalteringly, night began to gain on day, the world of sense to be obscured by the world of vision. Already

in the early summer, the time of year when he was
usually safe from worry, his sleep had been disturbed
by nightmares, fearful phantoms of death, carcases and
churchyards; and, more dangerous, he had once
more begun to hear spirit voices. While at Eartham
he had experienced those fits of depression when he
woke in the morning, that had tormented him in
1763. These, however, were only intermittent mutterings of the oncoming storm. When he got back to
Weston it broke in good earnest. The particular
circumstances of his life there were, indeed, the very
worst for him in every possible way. For one thing,
he was so much alone. Now that Mary could not
be a companion to him he was in double need of
visitors. And no one came to stay in the house for
months; so that there were hours in the day when
he had nothing to take his mind off its own thoughts.
Then again it was autumn, and to anyone with Cowper's
sensibility to environment every shortening day, every
sallowing leaf, spoke ominously of mortality. He
was conscious, too, that after autumn would come
winter, fatal period; and his spirits grew heavy with
melancholy anticipation.

Nor could he, as in earlier years, stave off his
depression by working. In the middle of the morning he was always with Mary; and as she was not
able to use her hands, he did not like to use his in
front of her, for fear of making her more painfully
conscious of her infirmity. So that he had only time
to write if he began by candlelight, at six or seven in
the morning. Besides, the work he had on hand
happened, most unluckily, to be a commentary on
the first books of " Paradise Lost." And as these
were all about hell and its fires, they tended rather
to deepen than to dissipate his depression.

But, anyway, even if he had enjoyed his work, and

even if he had been able to give more time to it, it would have made no difference. For he was too tired to do it. Time and again he would get out pen and paper and sit down at his table, and then an hour later get up without having written a word. The exertion of the earlier part of the year, the strain of nursing, the violent alteration in his ordinary routine and the constant anxiety, had been too much for his already failing constitution. And now he simply had not got the physical strength to make the effort of concentration needed for his work. On his general morale his exertions had not proved less disastrous. He had tried so hard and with so little effect that now he felt helpless and without hope. The visit to Eartham had given him especial cause for dejection. He had hoped so much from it: and not only for Mary. Buoyed up by the excitement of the struggle, half-formed hopes regarding his own disorders had begun to stir within him. If Heaven were intervening through the means of Hayley to save Mary, might it not also save him? Besides, supposing there was something in what people had always said to him, and that his own sufferings were, in part at least, the result of physical causes. Then the change might alleviate them. It was a faint hope, and he hardly admitted its existence even to himself: but he could not banish it from his mind. It proved as vain as his hopes for Mary. And the fact that he had hoped now added all the pangs of disappointment to his usual depression. Here was only another proof, so he told himself, that his troubles were incurable and he must carry them to the end.

Solitude, idleness, exhaustion, disappointment, and the time of year—all the circumstances of his situation had combined against him. It was no wonder that he took a rapid turn for the worse. A persistent depression took possession of his spirits, a depression which gradually identified itself with two subjects. One was, of course, his old fear of Mary's death. Now that he had acknowledged to himself that she would not get well, he felt she might die at any moment. And he was proportionately agitated. His other fear came from his inability to finish Milton. The task had been commanded by God; and now God had rendered him incapable of carrying it out. What could this portend? Was God once more forcing him to commit a sin in order to damn him for it? Convinced as he was of his damnation, this new proof of it sent a thrill of horror through him. Again and again in desperation he nerved himself to make another attempt to get it done. And with each successive failure suspense gnawed more cruelly at his heart. They were terrible days. Hour after hour he would sit silent, with Mary silent on the other side of the fireplace, brooding on his fears till they obscured his whole horizon. And the nights were worse than the days. No longer did nights of terror come spasmodically and far between, infrequent black patches on the pleasant-coloured surface of his existence. There was hardly an evening now when his candle did not light him up that quiet staircase into hell, hardly a night when he did not close his eyes to be haunted by horrible visions. In fitful, incoherent parable, they mocked the fears that tormented his waking hours. That destroying fire which is the symbol of damnation flared luridly through his dreams. "Friday, Nov. 16th. . . . Dreamt that in a state of the most insupportable misery, I looked through the window of a strange room, being all alone, and saw preparations being made for my execution. That it was about four days distant and that then I was destined to suffer everlasting martyrdom in the fire, my body being prepared for the purpose and my dissolution made a thing impossible. Rose overwhelmed with infinite despair, and came down into the study, execrating the day I was born with inexpressible bitterness." Another time he dreamt that he was in his own room waiting to be led out and burnt alive. Seized with a desire to carry some remembrance with him, he picked up a piece of the door plate. A strange and horrible thought struck him. The fragment he held was of metal and, growing red hot in the fire, would only exacerbate his agony. Once again, cold with horror, he awoke. But waking was as bad as sleeping. For then the voices would begin. He heard them almost every night now. Generally their purport was hostile, to warn him of Mary's death or his own damnation. But they clothed themselves in some short sentence, often a saying he had heard or a quotation. Once, for instance, he heard the words: "The wonted roar is up among the woods." It was a line from *Comus*, and no doubt it stuck in his head when he was working on Milton. But it was fraught with a new significance. The picture it conjured up before his inward eye was of no florid Comus rout, but of wrath and supernatural danger, a demon-hunt rather, of German legend, Walpurgis rider and baying hell-hound afoot after his soul. It was as if his obsessed mind involuntarily twisted any bit of experience present or remembered into a reference to the subject of his obsession. After the voices came a fit of dejection which lasted all the morning. Only in the afternoon did the peaceful daily life round him penetrate his spirit sufficiently to lift it to a listless torpor. And soon night would come; and with night the fearful cycle began again.

The strain of such an existence was more than

Cowper could bear. And, in a paroxysm of misery, he would at times curse the God that had made him. But a moment later he would realize that by the curse he had added one more to the tale of sins that were leading him to damnation. Beside himself with misery, once more he cursed God, to be stricken once more with an intolerable remorse. Caught in a vicious circle, his horror of damnation seemed only to make that damnation more certain.

But though the battle was irretrievably lost, he could not even now give up the fight. In the recesses of his being a last spark of his marvellous vitality still flickered. And with the desperate energy of a man snatching at his only remaining chance of life, he rallied in a final superhuman effort to achieve that faith which alone, in his view, could save him. He knew, none better, what it felt like to have it. To revive this palest glow of that feeling—this, and this alone, was the object of his every thought. He knew of only one man who could help him to it. With abject, hungry hope, he turned anew to Teedon. To Cowper's yearning eyes he shone out—poor, fussy, seedy Teedon—aureoled in all the glory of an angel of salvation. He was pleased to find himself in this splendid and unaccustomed rôle, as who would not be ? And he threw himself into it with a will. He prayed for Cowper assiduously, and generally with most favourable results. A comforting message would be revealed to him ; at once he would come hurrying over to Weston to deliver it. He also gave Cowper advice as to how to stimulate his faith. Let him say one collect over and over again ; if that had no effect, let him paraphrase it and say it once more. He, Teedon, had often tried both methods, and found them most helpful in inducing spiritual emotions. With a pathetic docility, Cowper accepted the messages and set himself to follow the advice. At first both did him good. He slept more calmly; and at moments, notably when he was walking in the fading autumnal garden, he was visited by a faint gleam of religious emotion. But these hopeful signs were not fulfilled. The gleams vanished, not to return, and his sleep began to be disturbed once more. Nor did Teedon's subsequent messages and advice repeat the good effect of his initial ones. How, indeed, should they? Teedon had not the slightest understanding of the nature of Cowper's malady, and so could not attempt to cure it. His methods and messages by their novelty had managed to revive the feeble remaining glimmer of Cowper's capacity for religious feeling. When, however, he grew accustomed to them, they produced as little effect on him as reading the Bible or going to church. And the consequent disappointment after hope now added to his dejection, just as his disappointment after his visit to Eartham had. A revulsion against Teedon and his advice took possession of him, which grew until, as usual, it found expression in his dreams. In February 1793 he dreamt God had declared to him that all the encouragement He had given him through Teedon had been meant in mockery. It was the end of Cowper's connection with Teedon. He continued his pension: and if Teedon wrote to him, answered politely in order not to hurt his feelings. But he looked for help to him no longer.

His last hope had failed him. And now at length he resigned himself to disaster. Disappointment had quenched that last spark of vitality: he could fight no more. He grew worse rapidly. As his despair grew wilder, his anxiety about Mary and Milton gave place to more immediate and sensational terrors. He became convinced that some fearful disaster was going to overtake him at once. It was not hard to fancy what form it might take. He dreamt one night that he asked a doctor for a remedy against madness. The doctor replied he knew a sure one, death. Death or madness—these were the two alternatives that faced Cowper; and daily he waited for one to strike him down. Spring was coming on, and in the ordinary way he would have felt safe till the following winter. But it is the measure of his decline that spring no longer stirred any response in him. The trees might grow green in Weston Park, the birds twitter along the alleys of the Wilderness; he heeded them as little as the drizzling rains of November. The darkness that swallowed in turn his hope and his resistance had now come between him and the visible world he had loved so long.

Meanwhile he had more mundane troubles to contend with. Mary was growing steadily worse. When they had got back from Eartham she had still been able, after a fashion, to walk and talk and take an interest in what was happening round her. Now she could hardly see; her conversation was an incoherent mumble; and it was with infinite difficulty, at a snail's pace, that she could drag herself round the garden with two people supporting her. The change in her spirits was even more marked. Nine months ago, hopeless though she must have known her case to be, she had still managed to keep up a gallant pretence that she was getting better. " She always tells me so," said Cowper tenderly, " and will probably die with the words on her lips." And when he had come into her room, wild-eyed, from some awful nightmare, she would notice and strive to stammer out some sentences of comfort. Pathetically, indeed, the two old friends had sought to bear one another's burdens, he to ease her body, she to soothe his mind.

Now all that was over. She was far too infirm to notice much about Cowper or anyone else; while under the pressure of disease and of the enforced idleness, so intolerable to one whose life had been exclusively devoted to practical things, even her iron self-control had begun to give way. She rose, hardly knowing how she would drag through the day, sat sunk in a gloomy lethargy longing for it to end, and from time to time broke out in vain lament.

Living with her must have been a terrible strain, especially to one in Cowper's condition. But he allowed no sign that he was conscious of this to escape him. Deathly ill, his every night an ordeal of unspeakable horror, expectant every moment of final catastrophe, he continued to nurse her, to feed her, to read to her, to comfort her. Nor did he for an instant relax his care, lose patience, utter a word of complaint. Even a thought of it, indeed, he would have suppressed as a disloyalty. If her illness had changed her, that only added fuel to the flame of pity which consumed him. What must she have gone through that she should succumb! His consciousness of the change showed, if at all, in an added assiduity of tenderness. Only once, as he looked back down the years of their friendship and thought of what had been and what now was, his full heart overflowed in a strain of mournful pathos.

> " The twentieth year is well-nigh past
> Since first our sky was overcast;
> Ah, would that this might be the last,
>   My Mary !

> Thy spirits have a fainter flow,
> I see thee daily weaker grow—
> 'Twas my distress that brought thee low,
>   My Mary !

Thy needles, once a shining store,
For my sake restless heretofore,
Now rust disus'd and shine no more,
        My Mary!

For though thou gladly wouldst fulfil
The same kind office for me still,
Thy sight now seconds not thy will,
        My Mary!

But well thou play'd'st the housewife's part,
And all thy threads with magic art
Have wound themselves about this heart,
        My Mary!

Thy indistinct expressions seem
Like language uttered in a dream;
Yet me they charm, whate'er the theme,
        My Mary!

Thy silver locks, once auburn bright,
Are still more lovely in my sight
Than golden beams of glorious light,
        My Mary!

For could I view nor them nor thee,
What sight worth seeing could I see?
The sun would rise in vain for me,
        My Mary!

Partakers of thy sad decline,
Thy hands their little force resign;
Yet, gently prest, press gently mine,
        My Mary!

And then I feel that still I hold
A richer store ten thousandfold
Than misers fancy in their gold,
        My Mary!

Such feebleness of limb thou prov'st,
That now at every step thou mov'st,
Upheld by two; yet still thou lov'st,
        My Mary!

T

And ſtill to love, though preſt with ill,
In wintry age to feel no chill,
With me is to be lovely ſtill,
    My Mary !

But ah ! by conſtant heed I know,
How oft the sadness that I show
Transforms thy smiles to looks of woe,
   My Mary !

And should my future lot be caſt
With much resemblance of the paſt,
Thy worn-out heart will break at laſt,
    My Mary ! "

Once Cowper was ſtrong and happy and brilliant :
now he was sick and miserable and crazy. But his
devotion to Mary makes it perhaps the crowning
moment of his life.

Mary's decline could not fail to haſten Cowper's.
Throughout the summer and early autumn of 1793,
helped by a visit from Hayley, he managed to maintain his exiſting condition. But with November
events began to rush headlong to the final cataſtrophe.
Swiftly the darkness began to eat up such shreds as
remained of the world of daylight. The nights
became even more terrible than those of laſt year.
Higher blazed the phantom fires of torment, fiercer
and more insiſtent clamoured the ghoſtly voices.
And now their activities were not confined to the
night. Out of the solitary bedchamber where they
had lurked so long the demons of his terror began
to creep : ſtealthily they descended the ſtairs, and
took possession of the world of day below. And
soon there was no place, no time of day when he was
safe from their attack. At meals, on walks, working
in his room, he heard their voices ; sitting with Mary
by the fireside, suddenly they would ſteal into his
thoughts and clutch with icy hand at his heart. And,

as the world of spirit grew more present, so the world of matter grew more insubstantial.   He could scarcely see his ordinary surroundings in the infernal light which now quivered round his every step : the sounds of daily life grew thin and inaudible beside the super-natural wailings that dinned incessantly in his ears. As for the world outside his immediate experience, it had lost all significance for him whatever.   It was 1793 : and every day the newspaper was full of the terrific events of the Terror in France.   But though Cowper read of them he could not muster up the slightest feeling of revulsion or pity.   Indeed, all the bloodshed of the guillotine might well seem trivial to him beside the nameless and stupendous spiritual horrors which were now the habitual element of his thoughts.

In January 1794—once more January—his suffer-ings came to their crisis.   He had never lost his sense that a catastrophe was impending over him.   But as the world of flesh gave place to the world of spirit, once again the object of his terror changed.   Madness and death were earthly ills, and as such the prospect of them no longer alarmed him.   In their stead a new and appalling idea presented itself to his imagina-tion.   He began to wonder if death, so far from being a disaster, was not to be the last mercy denied him by a wrathful God.   Could it be that the super-natural visitations which had pursued him during the last month were only the precursors of a more formid-able attack, and that the demons of hell were going to carry him off like Faustus, while he was yet alive ? In his shattered nervous state, the sheer horror of the idea was enough to make it irresistibly convincing to him.   With the conviction his remaining vestiges of sanity forsook him.   His dual existence was finally at an end.   The last streaks of normal daylight had vanished from his mental horizon; and nightmare darkness held dominion over all.

It was never to lift again. For the laſt time his lifelong enemies had gathered to the attack; for the laſt time they had overwhelmed him. His body lived on for six years more, but his spirit inhabited another world. Weſton, familiar Weſton, was become to him only a fragment of space beleaguered amid the waſtes of primal darkness, where the fiends howled and beat their wings and gnashed their teeth, greedy to snatch their prey. If his old friends came to see him, he shrank from them. What were they doing far away from the old homely earth? Moſt likely it was not them at all, but devils again, cunningly disguised in the shape of those he loved, to entrap him. The devils were coming to seize him: amid the confused cloud of fear and misery in which his brain now reeled that was the one faƈt that ſtood out with a dreadful, persiſtent clarity. Not for a day, nor for an hour, not for a minute during six long years did he forget it! Not a day, not an hour, not a minute passed which he did not confidently believe to be his laſt in the world. Sometimes he would make wild attempts to circumvent his enemies; refuse to leave his room leſt they should take possession of it, and he should find them there, ready to leap on him at his return. At other times, in a desperate effort to obtain redemption, he would impose ſtrange penances on himself: sit for long periods without moving, refuse to eat for days together. But generally he juſt waited. Rigid with fear, his breath coming in short gasps, his eyes keen to discern any oncoming shadow, ears agog to hear any approaching ruſtle, he would ſtand for hours; then, unable to contain himself, he would pace the room like a caged tiger; then sink into a chair inarticulately moaning, or perhaps rush to the writing-table and unburden himself in a torrent of words. " I cannot bear the least part of what is coming upon me," he scrawls in 1794, " yet am forced to meet it with eyes open wide, to see it approach and destitute of all means to escape it." Passionately he protests against the cruelty of his destiny, rehearses the long tale of Heaven's injustice to him, and at length relapses into a fatalistic dejection. " I was a poor fly entangled in a thousand webs from the beginning. . . . My despair is infinite, my entanglements infinite, my doom is sure." And finally, his feeling once more rising, in a strain of tragic eloquence he bids a last farewell to the God who has so strangely recompensed his devotion. " Farewell to the remembrance of Thee forever—I must now suffer Thy wrath, but forget that I ever heard Thy name. Oh, horrible! and still more horrible that I write these last lines with a hand that is not permitted to tremble."

One would have thought that Cowper's sufferings had reached their zenith. What, indeed, was there left for human being to suffer more? But a final horror was yet to be added to his existence. In April of 1794 Mary had another stroke. Once again she rallied from it; but this time it had touched her brain, and when she rose from her bed it was perceived that her personality had undergone a terrible change. The old Mary, stoical and selfless, with her calm eyes and quiet ways, was gone, and instead, hideously travestied in her shape, though with face distorted by disease, stood another woman: selfish, querulous, suspicious and exacting. To that same Cowper to whom she had dedicated her whole life she was now a peevish tyrant; never let him leave her for a moment, forced him, weak as he was, to drag her for hours round the garden. The little

house, which she had managed to invest with an
atmosphere that, even at its saddest, was sober and
dignified, now echoed with sordid scenes of her own
making. Losing all control, in mowing imbecile
fury she would scream out that Cowper's relations
and friends were plotting against her, that they were
taking him away, that they had designs on her property,
even that she had caught them trying to get possession
of her silver. It was the last drop in the cup of
Cowper's anguish. To lose the support of his good
angel had been sorrowful indeed; but to see her
degraded into something physically and mentally
repulsive was ten thousand times more painful.
Even now he was always gentle to her, submissively
obeyed her most unreasonable demand. Sometimes he
thought that she, like his visitors, was really a demon
in disguise. For once this delusion may have been
less unbearable than the truth.

Indeed, the change in Mary makes life at Weston
during these years too painful to contemplate. No
story, however tragic, is wholly depressing in which
the virtue of the characters is untouched by what
happens to them. There is even something exalting
and consoling in the spectacle of human integrity
triumphing over adverse circumstances. But that
this integrity can fail, and through no act of conscious
human will, but irresistibly impelled by physical
causes, strikes at the root of any confidence one may
hold in existence.

But even this, the blackest period as it was of all
Cowper's story, is relieved by a ray of light, the
devotion of his friends. Round the sombre pyre of
his supreme agony hover the figures of Hayley,
John Johnson, and Lady Hesketh. There is something comic about them. They are so wonderfully
unsuited to understand, let alone alleviate the psycho-

logical intricacies of Cowper's disease : their busy, mundane silhouettes stand out in such incongruous contrast to the apocalyptic flame and dark of their background. But there is nothing comic about their love. During one time or another of the next seven years each shows himself prepared to subvert the whole order of his life in order to relieve Cowper's affliction. It was a credit to them ; but it was also a credit to him. That a normal, conventional, prosperous Georgian lady like Harriet Hesketh, and a normal, conventional, prosperous Georgian divine like John Johnson should have been willing to give up a considerable part of their lives to him is the most striking testimony possible to the extraordinary beauty and charm of Cowper's character.

It is not so odd that Hayley should, for he was prone to fits of unbalanced enthusiasm. Nor, as it turned out, was he called upon to sacrifice so much as the other two. But the circumstances of his life at this time made it extremely good of him to exert himself on Cowper's behalf as much as he did. For his domestic difficulties had begun again. The Pitiable Eliza had deserted her respectable friends in Derby and established herself in London, where she filled the ears of all and sundry with complaints of the inadequate financial provision which, she asserted, Hayley made for her. Such accusations were peculiarly distressing to a man of his sensibility, especially as he was now, as ever, very hard up. However, when in the spring of 1794 he heard of Cowper's collapse, all his personal worries were forgotten, and travelling, with characteristic disregard of convention, alone with his housemaid, he hurried over to Weston to see if he could be of any help. With admirable ardour and patience, he sought to comfort Cowper and to reawaken his interest in Milton. His efforts were vain. But in administering to Cowper's material wants he met with more success.

Two years before Hayley had been profoundly shocked to find that Cowper was in financial straits. Surely, he thought, a man of genius who had benefited mankind ought to be supported by a grateful country. With him to think was to act; and early in 1792 he had immediately set to work to procure Cowper a pension. At first it seemed likely that his attempt would share the fate of most of his other schemes. For, as usual, the almost supernatural indefatigability with which he pursued his end was only equalled by the eccentricity of the means by which he sought to achieve it. At a critical period of English history he thrust himself upon eminent statesmen whom he hardly knew, harangued them for hours in a high-flown style, and when he could not see them bombarded them with letters both in prose and verse. The first man he applied to was Cowper's old friend, Thurlow. He listened to Hayley in silence, then ushered him out, earnestly assuring him he would do everything he could. Two years passed, and nothing happened; though Hayley had reminded Thurlow in a series of lyrics increasingly severe in tone. He therefore turned to Pitt himself, and set out Cowper's situation to him in a long and eloquent letter, culminating in a sonnet. What was his horror to receive the letter back unopened. With great difficulty he procured an interview with him, and one morning, in June 1793, fortified by port wine, he arrived at Downing Street and poured out his story in a speech even longer and more eloquent than usual. The effect was the same as it had been on Thurlow. Hastily and earnestly Pitt ushered him out, assuring him that he would do what he could. " In a tumult of sensibility " Hayley kissed his hand and burst into tears.

The game seemed won. But once again the months passed and nothing further happened. Hayley was dismayed but he was undefeated. He managed to enlist a new and powerful advocate, Lord Spencer, to assist him, and himself mustering all his literary powers, composed a letter to Pitt which should compel him for very shame to recollect his obligations.

" It is not often," it began, " that a Hermit can be deceived by a Prime Minister; yet I am an example that such an extraordinary incident may happen." Vigorously it rehearsed the details of Pitt's perfidy: and then, " I write in the frank and proud sorrow of a wounded spirit," it concluded, " with a cordial and affectionate wish that Heaven may bless you with unthwarted power to do good and with virtue sufficient to exert it. I retain a lasting sense of the very engaging kindness with which you allowed me to pour forth my heart to you on this interesting subject, and I am most sincerely, my dear sir, your grateful though afflicted servant, W. Hayley." Alas! the hearts of Prime Ministers grow hard to resist even darts such as these: yet once more Pitt did not reply. Hayley's hopes at last began to flag. But meanwhile Lord Spencer had been busy, and in March 1794, news came to Weston that his good offices had procured Cowper a pension of £300 a year. By Hayley's efforts Cowper was relieved from material difficulties for the rest of his life.

Lady Hesketh's was a harder task. She was at Weston at the time of Cowper's final collapse. Overcome with anxiety, she suggested he should go to a home kept by Dr. Willis, the most famous mental doctor of the day. Surely the man who had cured " the dear excellent King " was likely to benefit her poor cousin. If there was a difficulty about the expense, she would make that all right. But Mary in her present state of mind would not hear of Cowper going away. The "enchantress," as Lady Hesketh now bitterly called her, said that if the Archangel Gabriel were to persuade her to let him leave her, she would not comply. Clearly, however, it was impossible to leave him without care. So, without hesitation, at the age of sixty, Lady Hesketh left her comfortable, cheerful home in London and settled in the depths of the country to take the solitary charge of two lunatics. It was not an easy life for her. She tried to occupy Cowper by teaching him netting and mat-making, and she read aloud to him. But he was liable to think anything done for him was meant as an injury, and any kind word concealed an insult: suddenly when she was reading aloud he would leap up in a fit of passion and rush from the room. She had never been one to conceal her feelings, nor did she now. The post brought John Johnson page after page of lamentations over "the poor dear soul, my cousin," intermingled with denunciations of the "enchantress." But her old vigour of spirit never deserted her, and though she complained, she never gave in. With the consequence that at the end of two years her health was seriously impaired.

This presented a problem. Bereft of Lady Hesketh and unable to go to Dr. Willis, what was to happen to Cowper? At this juncture it was the turn of John Johnson to throw himself into the breach as unhesitatingly as Lady Hesketh had done. Of course, Cowper must come and live with him. He could imagine no greater pleasure and privilege than to look after his dear bard, and Mary too. It was true that his house was small, but he was sure he could manage to get them in.

" As for ourselves, my love," he wrote to the

unfortunate sister who kept house for him, " I know you will have no objection to the garrets."

We do not know how she received this proposal; but his other relations protested with a growing acrimony against the burden he had so quixotically shouldered. However, he paid no attention, and in July 1795 he took Cowper and Mary to Norfolk. Nor were they parted from him till death. He looked after Cowper with unremitting, solicitous affection, gave up his curacy at East Dereham, and moved his house from place to place in the neighbourhood, from village to open country, from open country to the seaside, trying to find somewhere that seemed likely to help his recovery.

But Cowper, far sequestered in his nightmare world, was impervious to his surroundings. How could any variation in that infinitesimal piece of matter called the earth make any difference to one who expected to be flung at any moment into bottomless abysses of perdition ? As a matter of fact, a few days before he left Weston, when he was taking a last look from the window of his room at his beloved garden, he was visited by a moment of emotion. His departure from the home of so many memories seemed the symbol and confirmation of that more irrevocable departure from the world of ordinary human hopes and fears. As with a gesture of valediction he wrote on the window shutter :

" Farewell, dear scenes forever closed to me,
   Oh, for what sorrows must I now exchange thee !
   Me miserable ! How should I escape
   Infinite wrath and infinite despair,
   Whom death, earth, heaven and hell consigned to ruin
   Whose friend was God, but God swore not to aid me ? "

But this impulse of feeling soon passed. Throughout the long journey to Norfolk and those shorter journeys

that succeeded it, Cowper followed Johnson as docile
and oblivious to all around him as a blind, deaf mute.
The sudden change from sheltered Buckinghamshire
to the skiey levels of Norfolk, the return to a district
poignant with memories of childhood, into what a
tumult of feeling would two such events have cast him
in the days of his sanity! But now he could only be
roused by some fact relating to his present condition.
In his aunt Bodham's house at Mattishall he caught
sight of a portrait of himself painted in former days.
The contrast between the mood in which he remembered to have sat for the picture and that which now
possessed him sent a twinge of horror through him.

" Oh," he broke out, clasping his hands in hopeless yearning, " if I could be as I was then."

As for the scenery, it did not stir the slightest
response in him any more. Only the sea had not
lost all its power. As he wandered on the stretching
sands, his ears filled by the monotonous thunder of
the breakers, his anguish was lulled as it had been
at Brighton and Southampton years ago. But even
this solace was reft from him. Brooding incessantly,
as he did, on the subject of his torments, one day the
idea flashed into his mind that Providence had brought
him there in order the better to fulfil its awful purpose;
and that over the limitless ocean, sailing from no one
knew where, a phantom ship manned with demons
might bear down on him as he was pacing the sands
and carry him off. From that moment with staring
eyes and trembling limbs he scanned the horizon for
a sail.

For his fears dominated him, if possible, even
more than at Weston. Sometimes he would welcome
Johnson in the morning with a loving look; but as
often with gloomy, terrified eyes, for he thought him
an evil apparition. And every brief note he scribbled

at this time contained a sentence to say that these were the laſt words fate was ever going to let him write. The feeling of foreboding about his journey which he had experienced that morning in his bed-room at Weſton turned out to be in a sense juſtified. His spirit had long ago taken leave of its surround-ings. But with his departure from his old home the laſt worn threads that had bound him even in memory or by association to the world of his sanity snapped; and the unfamiliar background known only in madness tended to confirm his confused mind in the impression that his old life was completely vanished. He fclt Heaven had transferred him to a ſtrange and remote place, there to infliĉt on him his supreme ordeal; and such shreds of his old self that might ſtill adhere to him slipped off. Even to look at, lean, livid and diſtraught, he was hardly recognizable as the plump, placid Cowper of a few years back. And the few letters he wrote after he got to Norfolk read like the letters of another man. For one thing, the handwriting, small, deliberate and shaky, is different; but more ſtartlingly different is the ſtyle. It is not imbecile or degraded: not at the height of his delusions were the processes of Cowper's brain impaired. But he writes no longer in the easy, flexible prose of his prime, or even in the Hebraic phraseology of his Evangelical phase, but in a new ſtyle, naked, throbbing, orcheſtral, falling in lamenting cadence like the cry of the gulls that swooped round the Norfolk cliffs.

" Adieu," he concludes a letter to Lady Hesketh, " I shall write to you no more. I am promised months of continuance here, and should be some-what less of a wretch in my present feeling could I credit the promise. But effeĉtive care is taken that I should not. The night contradiĉts the day, and I go down the torrent of time into the gulf that I have expected to plunge into so long. A few hours remain, but among them not one that I should ever occupy in writing to you again. Once more, therefore, adieu—and adieu to the pen forever. I suppress ten thousand agonies to add only William Cowper."

Yet changed though he was, he was not yet wholly unrecognizable. All the madness in the world could not root out the love and constancy which were the strongest qualities in his nature. Sunk in despair, he could never forget where he had once loved; cut off as he felt himself by an immeasurable gulf from his old life, still at times memories would stir in his breast and he would cast a longing, lingering look behind to Weston and all he had loved there.

" I shall never see Weston more," he wrote; " there indeed I lived a life of infinite despair . . . but to have passed there the little time that remained to me was the desire of my heart."

In a pathetic letter he besought the clergyman for news. " Gratify me with news of Weston," it begins, and finally, after many inquiries, " tell me if my poor birds are still living. I never see the herbs I used to give them without a recollection of them; and sometimes I am ready to gather them, forgetting I am not at home." Nor, confident though he was that his time on earth was short, did he cease from attaching himself to those around him. He grew very fond of a Miss Perowne, whom Johnny got to take care of him, while to Johnny himself he clung with a wild intensity of devotion. He would be ill with agitation for a whole day before Johnny went on a journey; and if he went away on Sundays, as he sometimes did, to take the service somewhere in the neighbourhood, Cowper used to stand in the evening, a bent, wistful figure at the garden gate, striving to catch the barking of a dog at a cottage further along the road which he knew betokened his return.

So passed a year and a half; and in 1796, since change of scene seemed to do Cowper no good, Johnny settled permanently at East Dereham in a house overlooking the market place. Not that he had given up hope concerning Cowper's recovery, nor had Hayley or Lady Hesketh. Absent from Cowper, they continued to think of him much as ever; were always writing letters, in Hayley's case varied by sonnets, demanding news and expressing hope. The trio of Cowper's active friends was now become a quartette by the addition of the conscientious Rose; he was found useful since he lived in London for the purpose of extracting Cowper's pension from a dilatory exchequer. Shy and awkward, he was not naturally fitted for such a task.

"With all the little Rose's *Sense*, *Genius* and *Learning*," declared Lady Hesketh on one occasion, " he was quite at a *standstill* in a very plain, simple affair and had not that *bold*, *courageous animal*, Lady Hesketh, made a *Row* about the matter . . . we might all have gone a-begging together."

Her activities on Cowper's behalf were not confined to harrying Rose. She also recommended remedies. They were of a simple kind. Restored as she now was to a normal life, she had returned to her normal frame of mind; which was not one appreciative of the mysteries of lunatic psychology. And she tended to think Cowper's a physical disorder arising, she ingeniously suggested, from checked perspiration. Let him, therefore, try warm bathing, or, if that was not possible, eat peaches, figs, sago and large quantities of ass's milk. In the flood tide of her reaction from the gloom of Weston, she began to think that such a diet, consistently adhered to, might very likely cure him completely. Indeed, her chief anxiety on his behalf did not relate to his illness. The French war was at this time raging, and Lady Hesketh wondered if Norfolk was safe. It was so near to France that it might well prove to be the landing-place of an invading army; could not Johnny move Cowper inland? At any rate let him collect as much gold as possible. She did not trust this new-fangled paper money: one could not be sure that the French, so diabolically cunning to ruin honest English people, might not by some despicable trick render it valueless at any moment. In 1798 news that the French army was safely involved in the Egyptian campaign raised her spirits. "Don't you long to be *certain* that the dear Arabs have swallowed Bonaparte and made mincemeat of his army?" she exclaimed in an ecstasy of patriotic fervour.

Hayley was also optimistic about Cowper's illness, and he also had his remedies. But they, as might have been expected, were of a more sensational kind. Indeed, a scheme he originated in 1797 provides the one melancholy gleam of comedy that lightens the blackness of Cowper's last years. On June 20th he received a letter from Cowper, the first he had written to him since he had left Weston. It was in his customary strain, and the benevolent Hayley, horrified by the condition it betrayed, set to work with even more than his usual ardour to devise some method of relieving it. The result of his frenzied cogitations expressed itself in a letter to Cowper, the most extraordinary composition that even Hayley ever made accessible to an astonished world.

"My very dear dejected friend," it began, "the few lines in your hand, so often welcome to me and now so long wished for, affected me through my heart and soul both with joy and grief, joy that you are again able to write to me, and grief that you write under the oppression of melancholy.

" My keen sensations in perusing these heart-piercing lines have been a painful prelude to the following ecstatic vision : I beheld the throne of God, whose splendour, though in excess, did not strike me blind, but left me power to discern on the steps of it two kneeling, angelic forms. A kind seraph seemed to whisper to me that these heavenly petitioners were your lovely mother and my own. . . . I sprang eagerly forward to enquire your destiny of your mother. Turning towards me with a look of seraphic benignity, she smiled upon me and said : ' Warmest of earthly friends ! Moderate the anxiety of thy zeal, lest it distract thy declining faculties, and know that as a reward for thy kindness my son shall be restored to himself and to friendship. But the All-merciful and Almighty ordains that his restoration shall be gradual, and that his peace with Heaven shall be preceded by the following extraordinary circum-stances of signal honour on earth. He shall receive letters from members of parliament, from judges and from bishops to thank him for the service he has rendered to the Christian world by his devotional poetry. These shall be followed by a letter from the Prime Minister to the same effect ; and this by thanks expressed to him on the same account in the hand of the King himself. . . . Hasten to impart these blessed tidings to your favourite friend,' said the Maternal Spirit, ' and let your thanksgiving to God be an in-crease of reciprocal kindness to each other.

" I obey the vision, my dear Cowper, with a degree of trembling fear that it may be only the fruitless offspring of my agitated fancy. But if any part of the prophecy shall soon be accomplished, a faint ray of hope will then be turned into strong, luminous

U

and delightful conviction in my heart, and I trust in yours, my dear delivered sufferer, as completely as in that of your most anxious and affectionate friend, W. H.

" P.S.—If any of the incidents speedily take place which your angelic mother announced to me in this vision, I conjure you in her name, my dear Cowper, to communicate them to me with all the kind despatch that is due to the tender anxiety of sympathetic affection ! "

The rest of Hayley's plan is sufficiently apparent from the letter. It is a curious fact that his plans always did seem to involve entering into communication with eminent men ; and he proposed, without of course saying anything about the vision, to ask the leaders of English public life referred to in it to write letters of sympathy to Cowper, who, convinced by this fulfilment of the Maternal Spirit's prophecy of the certainty of his salvation, would be immediately restored to health and sanity. It was an ingenious plan ; but it was marred by one important defect. Hayley did not know any of the public men ; it was unlikely that he ever would ; and even if he did manage to scrape acquaintance with some of them, there seemed not the smallest reason to suppose they would agree to write an uninvited letter to a total stranger on a delicate personal question just because Hayley asked them to. However, his optimistic spirit, intoxicated by the fertility of its own invention, brushed all this aside. He was sure all that would come right in the end : Providence could not fail to assist any scheme for the cure of a man of genius. Accordingly he sent the letter off to Cowper, and communicated the plan to Johnny. Poor Johnny, rendered desperate by two uninterrupted years of Cowper's society, welcomed the idea enthusiastically.

But Lady Hesketh, to whom he explained it, was more doubtful. Of the general scheme of "the charming vision" she approved; but its details shocked her moral susceptibilities. These were peculiar. She did not mind the whole thing being a lie, but she did disapprove of Hayley saying he had seen the throne of God, when he had not. And the fact that he could do so reawakened her old suspicion of his orthodoxy. "I fear he is a stranger to the Great Truths of Christianity," she said. In addition to this, her practical mind saw very clearly the difficulty of procuring the required letters. However, she too was glad of any scheme which might help Cowper, and she volunteered to get into communication with some of the public men.

It was thought unwise to attack the most exalted straight away. So, as a preliminary attempt, overtures were made to Mr. Wilberforce, a Member of Parliament, Lord Kenyon, a Judge, and three bishops, Dr. Beadon of Gloucester, Dr. Watson of Llandaff and Dr. Beilby Porteus of London. Their responses were only partially satisfactory. Lord Kenyon, who was approached through Rose, did not answer at all, and Dr. Beadon wrote angrily, by the hand of a third person, to say that he could not think of granting such an extraordinary request. On the other hand, Mr. Wilberforce, Dr. Watson and Dr. Beilby Porteus all wrote off admirable letters to Cowper immediately, and Mr. Wilberforce even sent him a book he had written. Fortified by this support, Hayley made one more attempt on Lord Kenyon. This time, again saying nothing of the vision, he persuaded Thurlow to speak for him. But Thurlow's pleadings had no more effect on Lord Kenyon than Rose's had done. They were not, indeed, ardent. "I have been pressed," began his letter, "by one mad poet to ask of you for another a favour which savours of the malady of both."

Meanwhile the unhappy object of their schemes had not reacted satisfactorily to them. To Hayley's original letter and to that of Mr. Wilberforce Cowper had listened in gloomy apathy. And when that of Dr. Porteus was read to him he had interrupted in a tone of anguish: "It was written in derision—I am sure of it." "Oh, no, no, no, my cousin," protested Johnson, in shocked tones. "Say not so of the good Beilby, Bishop of London." Cowper's feelings were made yet more explicit after Watson's letter arrived. Johnson and Miss Perowne, anxious to see what effect it had had on him, carefully steered the conversation at dinner round to the subject of Hayley's vision, and Johnson said, as if by chance, that in this last letter there seemed to be signs that its prophecies were being fulfilled. "Well," said Cowper, "be it so. I know there is and I knew there would be, and," he added significantly, "I knew what it meant." If Hayley and Johnson had listened more carefully to Cowper's ravings, they would have known too. Was it not one of his chief causes of misery that he had been explicitly told by God that any promise of hope he might receive was given in mockery? So that even if he believed Hayley's vision to be genuine, it would be no comfort to him. But whatever their diagnosis of his despair, it was clear to his friends that the letters had done him no good; and the scheme dropped. To the end of his days, however, Hayley would never admit that it had failed. Cowper, he insisted, would have been worse without it.

But the time for remedies, good or bad, was past. Cowper's sufferings were nearly at their period. Mary was already dead. In the winter of 1796 she had begun to sink rapidly, and on the evening of

December 17th it was realized that she could only live a few hours. " Is there life above stairs, Sally ? " Cowper asked the maid who came to call him in the morning. She said yes. He dressed, came down and quietly asked Johnson to go on with the book he had been reading to him. A few minutes later Johnson was beckoned from the room to be told Mary was dead. He came back, resumed reading, and after a few pages stopped and broke the news. At first Cowper remained calm ; but a few hours later he was seized with a violent agitation. Wildly he protested that he was sure Mary was not really dead, that she would be buried alive and then wake in her grave, and that if she did it would be his fault, as he had been created to cause her every imaginable suffering ; and he demanded to see her. Johnson took him up to her bedside. For a moment he continued to protest that he could see her stir, then, as he looked more closely, he grew still. The distortions with which disease had disfigured her countenance were smoothed away, and she lay there, calm, strong and benignant as in former days. At length she had been given back to him, by the hand of death. For a long moment he gazed at her, a supreme, unwavering look. Then, for the first time since he had left Weston, his self-control completely forsook him, and he flung himself down in a torrent of sobbing. It did not last: after a few minutes he asked for a glass of water, and recovered his composure. Nor did anyone in the four years that remained to him of life ever hear him mention her name again. He was not told about her funeral, for fear of reviving his agitation. A few nights later her body was secretly hurried down the hill and buried in Dereham church by torchlight.

It is not likely that Cowper would have broken

down again even if he had known. For under the continued pressure of misery the excitement which had characterized his state of mind at Weston had now given place to a dull apathy. It is beyond the capacity of human nerves to continue in a state of violent agitation for several years, even if faced by the prospect of damnation. Cowper was acquainted with sad misery as the tanned galley slave is with his oar; and if custom had not made his suffering easier, it had at least made him numb. As a consequence, he began to appear more like his former self, tidier, fatter, rosier; he had taken up some of his old occupations, revising Homer, translating, and he asked to be read aloud to. Johnson proposed reading his own poems to him. Cowper refused to hear John Gilpin : the contrast between his present condition and the care-free mood in which he had composed it was too painful. But to the rest he listened calmly enough. More striking, during the last months of Mary's life he had volunteered to read the Bible to her if she wanted. And when the servants trooped in for family prayers he no longer left the room.

But of course none of this meant that he felt any happier. Now his nerves were quieter he needed distraction to make the day pass. But none of the distractions gave him any satisfaction. " My thoughts," he writes, " are like loose and dry sand, which the closer it is grasped slips the sooner away. Mr. Johnson reads to me, but I lose every sentence through the inevitable wandering of my mind." And " Wretch that I am," his servant would hear him mutter to himself, " thus to wander in quest of false delight." As for his attending prayers and reading the Bible, far from being signs of religious hope, they only meant that he was now so hardened to the thought of God's wrath that references to it no longer accentuated his suffering.

Nor had his visionary torments abated. He told Johnny how his bedroom was every night the battleground of a struggle between good and evil spirits, and how in the end the evil always vanquished the good, and then "Bring him out!" they would cry, "bring him out!" And even in the day when he was sitting alone he would often look up and see a spectral figure advancing on him, who, with menacing gestures, announced some fearful and immediate doom. His disordered fancy played round his woes in whimsical flourishes. One morning he told Johnson that a spiritual voice had spoken this message to him:

> "Sadwin, I leave you with regret,
> But you must go to gaol for debt."

"Do you know the meaning of Sadwin, my cousin?" said Johnson.

"Yes," replied Cowper, "the winner of sorrow."

Thus for four years longer dragged on the days.

From them one extraordinary incident stands out. Long ago at Olney Cowper had read a story in *Anson's Voyages*. It told how a sailor had fallen overboard in the Atlantic; how his companions had vainly attempted to save him; and how, after a long struggle, he had succumbed. Now one day in March 1799, as he was sitting lost as usual in aimless brooding, the story strayed by chance into his mind, and immediately arrested his attention by the analogy it presented to his own life. Had he not fallen early in life from the ship which carried normal mankind from the cradle to the grave? Had not his friends tried to save him in vain? And now, after a lifetime of struggling, was he not sinking exhausted to death?

He, too, was a castaway, the castaway of humanity. The story lit up his past like a sudden flash of lightning : stimulated by it his old powers of mind reasserted themselves, the incoherent, lethargic muddle that was his thoughts fell once more into order ; and he turned to survey, as from a high mountain, the whole rugged path over which his steps had wandered since they left the Berkhamsted vicarage sixty-nine years before. As he looked, the accumulated anguish and despair of his life of unparalleled disaster caught fire and blazed up in a last towering flame of poetry.

" Obscurest night involv'd the sky,
    Th' Atlantic billows roar'd,
When such a destin'd wretch as I,
    Wash'd headlong from on board,
Of friends, of hope, of all bereft,
His floating home for ever left.

No braver chief could Albion boast
    Than he with whom he went,
Nor ever ship left Albion's coast
    With warmer wishes sent.
He lov'd them both, but both in vain,
Nor him beheld, nor her again.

Not long beneath the whelming brine,
    Expert to swim, he lay ;
Nor soon he felt his strength decline,
    Or courage die away ;
But wag'd with death a lasting strife,
Supported by despair of life.

He shouted ; nor his friends had fail'd
    To check the vessel's course,
But so the furious blast prevail'd,
    That, pitiless perforce,
They left their outcast mate behind,
And scudded still before the wind.

Some succour yet they could afford ;
　　And, such as ſtorms allow,
The cask, the coop, the floated cord,
　　Delay'd not to beſtow.
But he (they knew) nor ship, nor shore,
Whate'er they gave, should visit more.

Nor, cruel as it seem'd, could he
　　Their haſte himself condemn,
Aware that flight, in such a sea,
　　Alone could reſcue them ;
Yet bitter felt it ſtill to die
Deserted, and his friends so nigh.

He long survives, who lives an hour
　　In ocean, self-upheld ;
And so long he, with unspent pow'r,
　　His deſtiny repell'd ;
And ever, as the minutes flew,
Entreated help, or cried—Adieu !

At length, his transient respite paſt,
　　His comrades, who before
Had heard his voice in ev'ry blaſt,
　　Could catch the sound no more.
For then, by toil subdued, he drank
The ſtifling wave, and then he sank.

No poet wept him : but the page
　　Of narrative sincere,
That tells his name, his worth, his age,
　　Is wet with Anson's tear.
And tears by bards or heroes shed
Alike immortalize the dead.

I therefore purpose not, or dream,
　　Descanting on his fate,
To give the melancholy theme
　　A more enduring date :
But misery ſtill delights to trace
Its semblance in another's case.

> No voice divine the storm allay'd,
>   No light propitious shone;
> When, snatch'd from all effectual aid,
>   We perish'd, each alone :
> But I beneath a rougher sea,
> And whelm'd in deeper gulphs than he."

The verses are written in his characteristic, simple measures, in his characteristic, formal language; but the passion which informs their every line raises and sustains them at a height he never touched before. It is Cowper's final considered and terrible judgment on his own life: it is also the unique occasion on which he enters the realm of great poetry. By the last and most baffling caprice of that destiny whose plaything he was, those afflictions against which he had exhausted his life in struggling, now, in the very moment of his defeat, revealed themselves as the instrument of his greatest achievement. If Cowper had been victorious in his struggle, if he had vanquished his deformity and his delusions he might never have been quickened to that intensity of feeling in which alone the greatest art is born. Experience taught him to repudiate life: but in that repudiation his own life found at last its highest fulfilment.

He only lived for a year more. In January 1800 his health began to exhibit alarming symptoms; by March he was confined to bed. He lingered another month, watching the daylight wax and dwindle along the dark-wainscoted walls of his bedroom, the brass sphinx heads on its door. In a final dedication of his affection Johnny threw himself into the task of nursing him; and, with a passionate desire that Cowper should once more see light before he died, and at least leave the world in hope, he sought with ardent words to convince him of his salvation. But the evil fate which so early had sworn itself Cowper's comrade kept faith with him to the end. He was to look his last on a world on which no thinnest ray of hope had penetrated the pervading shadow. He listened with his usual apathy when Johnson spoke of the general truths of Christianity; but when he mentioned God's love for Cowper himself, the certain happiness that was preparing for him in the next world, he interrupted and besought him to speak no more. One day the doctor asked him how he felt. " Feel," he replied, " I feel unutterable despair." On the 19th of November he was observed to be weakening. Throughout the following night he lay, conscious and still. Once Miss Perowne asked him if he wished for a drink, but he refused. " What does it signify? " he said, wearily. They were his last words. At five in the morning he became unconscious; twelve hours later he ceased to breathe. Then, and then only, was Johnny's wish granted. As he took a last look at the still face, he noticed with awe and amazement that on Cowper, as on Mary, the healing hand of death had wrought a change. The strain and the apathy which so long had marked his wasted features were gone, and instead they lit up with a rapt, unearthly wonder, " a holy surprise." Was it a mere chance effect of dissolution? or could it be that during those hours of unconsciousness a momentous event had taken place in the unseen territories of Cowper's spirit: that on the very threshold of the grave it was vouchsafed to him, for the second time, to behold the supreme vision of St. Alban's; and gazing with unveiled eye at the Beatific Glory, he learnt that, after all, his despair had been founded on delusion? We shall never know.

He was buried in Dereham Church by the side of Mary. And it was universally agreed among his friends that his grave should be marked by a memorial.

Memorials, however, are notoriously the subject of controversy; nor was Cowper's an exception. Lady Hesketh wanted a plain slab of marble; anything ornate, she said, " tho' quite in character for a *grocer* or a *soap boiler* who had acquired Immense Wealth, would be degrading to the Memory of Our Cousin." Hayley, on the other hand, anxious, no doubt, to do honour to two geniuses at once, was in favour of a more elaborate monument to be designed by Flaxman. His proposal carried the day: and though in general he cannot be looked on as a trustworthy arbiter in matters of taste, we cannot regret his success. For the memorial is so characteristic of the period in general, and in particular of the little group of people who erected it. There in a transept of the well-kept, unfrequented church, with the sunlight shining mildly down on it through the painted windows, and decently protected by a neat railing, it still stands, a block of dark marble. On the top, carved in pure white, are disposed two volumes, the Bible and "The Task," across them a classical palm branch : below is Cowper's name, and yet below that, on two medallions, are those of Mary and Miss Perowne. Underneath each is engraved an epitaph in blank verse by Hayley.

It is the light of Cowper's fame which has irradiated the little circle of people round him, and so rescued them from that darkness of forgotten time, in which most of their contemporaries lie buried. When he dies, it is withdrawn. But we have travelled so far in their company that it may be permitted us, before we say farewell, to watch the figures of his friends as they grow dim and are lost in the encroaching shadows of oblivion. Little Rose is the first to disappear. He had never swerved from the road of conscientious self-improvement which he had

marked out for himself so early in life. He had
worked conscientiously, and not unsuccessfully, at
the Bar, conscientiously married, and was, by the
time Cowper died, already the conscientious father of
several children. But in 1804 he contracted consumption; and early in December of that year he
learnt from his doctor that he had only a few weeks
to live. In these tragic circumstances his con-
scientiousness assumed heroic proportions. He was
already supported by a lively religious faith; but he
had always doubted whether it rested on a sufficiently
strong intellectual foundation. The last days of his
life, therefore, he dedicated to reading Paley's *Evidences*
and the works of Loudon. He was gratified to find
their arguments completely convincing. After this he
took a suitable farewell of his family; and, composed
to the last, died on the 20th September.

Three years later he was followed by Lady Hesketh.
Hers was a happy nature, and in spite of Cowper her
last years were very happy ones. She divided her
time between Bath, Clifton and Weymouth, had a
great many friends, wrote a great many letters, held
a great many strong opinions and took an interest in
everything. Two events in particular gave her satisfaction. For one thing she actually got to know the
King and Queen. One would have thought that to
meet George III and Queen Charlotte in their unlovely
old age must have damped any loyalty, however
ardent. But Lady Hesketh's was of a kind that burnt
all the higher for the intractability of the fuel which
it was forced to consume. The Queen's face, she
said, was "full and convincing proof of the triumph
of *Countenance* over *features*"; and as for the King,
he was "so good, so pious, so kind and benevolent
to everybody that one cannot look at him without
wishing he might live forever!" Her other source

of especial pleasure was Hayley's *Life of Cowper*, which came out in 1802. There were two points in it, indeed, to which she took exception. It emphasized Cowper's Whig views in a manner which she felt would put the King against him, and the fact that she herself was mentioned in it by name offended her sense of the decorous privacy which should shroud an English lady. Surely, she said, Hayley could have called her Lady Dash. But these small defects were overwhelmed in the flood of delighted enthusiasm into which she was thrown by the rest of the book.

"Oh, my dear good Johnny! how can I ever express or *describe* to you what I think of *Cowper's Life!*—You, indeed, do right to call it The Life—it is indeed The Life, and I hope there never will be another of anybody—no one, indeed, should attempt writing one who has not all the happy Talents and all the Sensibility of our friend Hayley." In 1807 her end came peacefully from mere old age.

Hayley's was a stormier voyage. Poor Hermit; fate had treated him with an unmerited severity during the last few years. Such fame as he had possessed was diminishing; he was still in want of money! and he, whose happiness depended so much on those he loved, had lost Gibbon, Blake, Cowper and his adored little son. For such disasters, the departure of Eliza in 1797 from a world for which she was unfitted was not a sufficient compensation. Still, he had a gallant spirit; within a short time he had pulled himself together; and a little battered, but still undisillusioned, was soon hard at work, as we have seen, celebrating the virtues of those whose loss he deplored by composing their epitaphs, writing their lives, and promoting the erection of their monuments. In 1809 he had so far recovered his optimism as to marry

again, a girl years younger than himself, but " willing
to enliven with the songs of tenderness the solitude
of a poetical hermit." Alas, his luck in domestic
matters had not turned; within four years his wife
had parted from him. He survived to write his
memoirs and die in 1820.

There remains Johnny. And of him there is little
to be said. When he saw Cowper laid in his grave,
the work which had made his life memorable was
done; and he retired to the peaceful, uneventful,
useful life of the prosperous country clergyman he
was. He married, had five children and lived till
1833. Before he died Cowper's popularity had
already begun to wane. In the thirty years that had
elapsed since his death a revolution had taken place
in English letters: the monarchs of Augustan
tradition had been cast from their thrones. And in
their stead a new race of poets—youthful, lawless, hag-
ridden with genius, catastrophic—commanded the
homage of the inconstant hearts of men.

Printed in Great Britain by
Lowe and Brydone Printers Limited, London, N.W.10